Gouger of The Bulletin

PART II

Tpr 358 5th L.H.R.

Gouger

of

The Bulletin

2: More Paragraphs & Short Stories by

Ion (Jack) Idriess

Compiled by Jim Bradly

ETT IMPRINT
Exile Bay

Published in Imprint Classics by ETT Imprint, Exile Bay 2026

This book is copyright. Apart from any fair dealing for the purposes of private study, research, criticism or review, as permitted under the Copyright Act, no part may be reproduced by any process without written permission. Inquiries should be addressed to the publishers by email on ettimprint@hotmail.com or at this address:

ETT IMPRINT
PO Box R1906
Royal Exchange NSW 1225
Australia

First published by Idriess Enterprises 2013
First electronic edition ETT Imprint 2020
First published by ETT Imprint in 2021

Copyright © Idriess Enterprises Pty Ltd, 2020
Selection and introduction © Jim Bradly 2013, 2020

ISBN   978-1-923527-14-0   (paper)
ISBN   978-1-922473-21-9   (ebook)

Cover design by Tom Thompson

Cover image: Jim Pryke's group prospecting in New Guinea 1910, by Charles Kerry

FOREWORD

MY GRANDFATHER was about to hit 70, and living in Sydney, by the time I was born in central NSW. We only had occasional visits to the city during my childhood, and he made one visit to us on the farm (our Shetland pony attempted to eat his hat!), as he was by then very frail due to the regular revisitations of malaria that he contracted in WWI. I treasured the tales he told, and the advice he wrote in wonderful letters, but it was mainly through reading his books that I got to know him and the marvels of his life and the world he inhabited and explored with such gusto.

Jim Bradly has done an incredible job in tracking down my grandfather's earlier writings and helping us to learn more about his wanderings. I have enjoyed dipping into the first *"Gouger of The Bulletin"* discovering new gems and uncovering the seeds of later stories, and I am eager to explore the contents of *this* diligently researched volume.

Wendell Peacock
Singleton NSW
October 2012

For Amanda and Carmen – my two shining lights.

To 'Cyclone Jack' whose books remain the most collected and collectable in Australia today, and whose stories stirred my imagination and set me on my own path of discovery.

And, of course – to 'The Bushman's Bible'
'The Bulletin'

Cyclone Jack

PREFACE

FOR THOSE not familiar with the first *"Gouger of the Bulletin"*, a word of introduction. Ion Idriess wrote a large number of articles and short stories in the now defunct Bulletin magazine, mainly between 1911 and 1932 (minus his war years). The articles were submitted to the 'Aboriginalities' column, a generalised name for the pages containing written comments about virtually anything and everything that the contributors wished to discuss or make known. The articles mainly came from within Australia or its close island neighbours, but sometimes from Great Britain, USA, Europe etc.

The contributors in nearly all cases used pseudonyms either selected randomly, a deliberate jumbling of a person's own name or else chosen for reasons known only to themselves. Some wrote often, some only once. Many wrote over a number of years but not necessarily using the same pseudonym each time. This is where the 'detective work' and acquired knowledge comes in to help weed out just "who" wrote "what". That was the basis for, and resulted in, the eventual publication of the original *"Gouger of the Bulletin"* in 2008.

In the first 'Gouger', I made the comment that I believed I had collected most of the articles if not all of them. I could not have been more wrong! In the course of pursuing new pseudonyms which you will find in this second book, I made the monumental discovery (as far as admirers of Idriess are concerned) that his numerous articles "overflowed" into two other columns in the Bulletin. Firstly, in the "Society" column I discovered many small stories and comments about his time at Gallipoli and in the desert campaigns, usually (but not always), written by "Gouger" and secondly, under 'Business, Robbery etc', I found more comments by him concerning Australia and the surrounding Pacific islands. To my knowledge no one (living) knew of this "overflow" or if they did, it was never mentioned by anyone, anywhere.

He also travelled much more widely than previously reported and I have traced him to Tonga, the Solomons, the Dutch East Indies, The Trobriand Islands etc. I knew that while in New Guinea, he had visited the islands further out such as Gilbert and Ellice among others etc., as a former (much younger) work colleague of his had informed me thus. But – even he did not know of the two additional columns reported above, or the extent of his (Idriess) island hopping. The *"Sea Nomad"* articles refer to much of this. There are whole slices of time (for which I cannot account) between the dates of some of his paragraphs, so who knows where he was or what he was doing. I do not have one single item written by him in 1923 (for example). Also, there are stories by him about opium smuggling and shipboard incidents which lead me to believe he may have travelled much more widely than even I suspected.

One item of particular interest I came across was an entry by "Lone Pine 358" (Idriess) to a short story competition (worth £500) run by *"The Bulletin"* in 1928 The entry was titled *"Drums of Mer"*. The competition was won (from hundreds of others) by Katharine Susannah Prichard with her powerful novel 'Coonardoo' which was shortly afterwards serialized in the *"The Bulletin"*.

When I originally started out on this (self-imposed) project my main purpose was to "bring-to-light" some of the early writings of this (I believe) truly remarkable Australian. Little did I realise the treasure trove into which I was about to tap. It has been an intriguing task "tracking" Ion from his early days outback and at the "Ridge", through the turbulent times of W.W.I and finally, back home again to the land he loved so intensely.

It has been a long and winding journey with my old friend *"The Bulletin"*, but an extremely interesting and rewarding one, as we got to know each other better and its secrets were slowly revealed. There well may be still more Idriess articles scattered throughout later editions of *"The Bulletin"*, but, that is for others to discover. One has to start and finish somewhere, else the searching might never end, (or at least that is how it sometimes feels).

My special thanks to Rob and Matilda King who worked tirelessly (and patiently) to help produce the finished work you now see before you.

Once again, I hope you enjoy reading these articles as much as I did collecting them and I'd like to think that maybe, even Ion would "give me the nod" and agree that my "digging" had turned up "lots of colour".

As always (to quote Ion),

"Good health and happiness to you!"

Jim Bradly
Bolton Point
2012
jgbradly@optusnet.com.au

Gouger
of
The Bulletin

Newly
Discovered
Pseudonymns

THIS first section of the book includes the newly discovered pseudonyms with their comments from the various columns showing once again Ion's incredible power of observation, relentless quest for knowledge, eye for detail and ability and desire to record it all. There are other pseudonyms which may well be his but as I am unable to substantiate them they are not included in this collection, except for the ones indicated in the "special note" at the end of the book.

23 January 1919

"Gouger": A quaint wedding took place on the Daintree River lately. The bride had been a widow for 20-odd years, living by herself in one of the loneliest parts of N.Q., her nearest neighbors a couple of white men across the river, half a dozen aged kanakas, a turbulent tribe of blacks and the alligators which bathe in the river and devour the lady's goats. The parson was transported all the way from Cooktown in a ketch, which also carried the bridal gown. Owing to no measurements being given, or the fashions or the lady's waistline changing in the last quarter-century, the frock wouldn't fit at all. The bridegroom had to be hulloed for across the river and he finally put in an appearance in his working flannel, cossack boots and Sunday whiskers. When the parson mildly suggested that he should wear a coat, it was discovered that he didn't own one. "Anyhow," he said, "she don't want to marry the coat".

16 October 1919

"Gouger": During five weeks of the seamen's strike my mates and I, in Far North Queensland, had to live on wild pig, fish and yams. Often we went close to starvation. The position set us thinking that we would have been in exactly the same position if an enemy squadron had been blockading our coast. In that case, the women and children of the little northern towns would be deprived of ordinary food, and would be compelled to rely on the bush --- which would mean death. Northern Queensland is not connected to the South by railways. Between almost all the northern towns on the coast are practically impassable mountain ranges. To get from say, Townsville to Cairns, or Cairns to Cooktown overland, the traveller has to go hundreds of miles inland to dodge the coastal ranges. The track overland to Cooktown, after leaving Mt Carbine, is a faint, seldom used pack-horse trail of 130 miles. So the idea of a transport column hurrying up from the railway terminus (Gladstone) to the inhabitants of Cape York Peninsula in the event of an enemy cutting off communication by sea is ridiculous. A fleet transport of aeroplanes would be the only possible means of doing the trick. I hope the Defence authorities have got them. What is going to happen if a strong enemy force lands anywhere on the unpeopled shores of the vast Northern Territory? A fairly strong naval Power would easily checkmate our fleet before Great Britain could arrive. It would be a matter of months before Australia could move an army across the hundreds of miles of railless and inhospitable country that lies between North and South, and it would arrive to find the enemy in possession of all the great

cattle-stations. That would mean sufficient meat supplies to last the invading army for years. It's about time that big overland line was built.

1 January 1920
"Gouger":   A word with Randolph Bedford over his "Journey by Angles" (B. 17/11/19). He says he came up during the strike to find the "starving North" and couldn't find it. I found it. So did the people on the Bloomfield River. They lived for months on sweet spuds and maniocs. My mates and I, a little further out, had to knock off work and go into the scrub, chasing wild pigs and digging for native edible roots, just to keep ourselves alive. There was no tobacco procurable and as for beer --- well, shortly after the strike started Cooktown ran dry, and it didn't get wet again until long after the strike ended.

6 May 1920
"Gouger":   The greatly-increased price of shellfish of every class has made business boom at Thursday Island. In one shed alone £5000 worth of shell was recently stacked. Under a new agreement all pearls are now the property of the fishermen, and this has brought Japanese pearl-buyers to Thursday, as their countrymen are the fishermen .The brown men are thriving. Their merchants and shipbuilders already cater for the fishing fleet's necessities; and in a very short time the Jap will absolutely own the Barrier fishing-grounds.

10 June 1920
"Gouger":   Cockies in the Cooktown district (N.Q.) are doing well out of peanuts. The soil is particularly suited to the vegetable and as the price now is a little over £100 per ton, the cultivation and harvesting not over-costly, and the demand for many purposes very large, growers are beginning to see a rosy time ahead. Most of the crops up here average from three-quarters to a ton per acre. The good rainfall and the fact that plenty of shelter is available favor the crop. It was wind, curiously enough, that spoiled the chances of the biggest peanut-growing enterprise in the South. This was undertaken by Metters, the stove-man, when he retired from the firm that still carries his name. The land was a sandy area alongside the Murray; but it was too loose, and the strong winds of those parts didn't give the plucky cultivator a chance. But he's doing all right with vines.

8 July 1920

"Gouger": Southerners can say what they like about North Bananaland being no white man's country; but it starts the springs of life anew. It has been closely noted that married people of advanced age, after settling in the Cooktown district, have invariably been startled by a visit from the Stork years after that dignified bird had ceased calling down south. I know one delighted couple who, after such an unexpected and thrilling experience, wrote to two friends who had long courted the solemn-visaged bird in vain. The experiment was made, and after 18 months of Cooktown the bird arrived with a fine baby boy in his old carpet-bag.

15 July 1920

"Gouger": The Cooktown Planting Pty. Co., of Melbourne has taken up 6000 acres outside Cooktown (Q.) for an experiment in peanut-growing. Fifty to 100 acres are to be under cultivation by the end of the year, and big things are expected to follow. There is a vast supply of rich, cheap, well-watered land available in the district; and if the co., working with modern tools, makes a success of the venture it will have performed a national service.

9 September 1920

"Gouger": Such shocks as finding his tin concentrates mixed with metallic iron, black sand or tourmaline, not to mention worn-out sledge-hammers carefully concealed in the bottom of the bag, have all contributed to make the ore-buyer a suspicious man. Some of the wolfram buyers at Bamford (N.Q.) lost heavily a few years back through buying roasted iron pyrites for wolfram. The roasted rubbish has exactly the same appearance and cleavage. Some of the buyers also bought tons of their own wolfram. The stuff was lying in stacks awaiting transport. The bags of concentrate were simply borrowed through the night, sold in daytime to the buyer, who obligingly made a new stack of them ready for the next night's raid.

27 April 1922

"Gouger": has an idea: – My mate and I have found by hard experience, that surface alluvial gold and the old alluvial beds down to the bedrock slate or granite are played out. But surely this does not mean that all the alluvial gold of Australia is exhausted. If so, this continent must have been well behind the door when the yellow stuff was issued. I prefer to believe that most of the gold with which Australia was endowed in the beginning of things has never been struck. Well

then, where is it? We are told that originally the gold came up from the bowels of the earth, through volcanic crevices, in the form of vapor, or else in the pure molten state where it united with quartz and formed the gold-bearing reefs which are so damned hard to find today. In the course of ages rivers broke up these reefs and washed the gold into the river-beds where we find it – sometimes.

Now as to coal. We all know that coal is the wood, etc., of bygone forests converted by the pressure of layers of rock. Besides huge trees, the coal seams show the remains of shrubs and fresh-water plants of dense tropical growth, also innumerable fossils of shells, fish and land animals. This argues clearly the one-time presence of great rivers. Now, where are the washstones of these rivers? I've never heard of a river-bed yet without its washstones. It's among the washstones of the tropical rivers of N.Q. and New Guinea that we get the gold to-day. If we can find the missing washstones of these old coal-seam rivers we may open up exhaustless fields of new alluvial wealth. The washstones can't be up above the coal-seam because the coal-miners would have worked through them when sinking their shafts. Clearly the wash must be lower down beneath the coal-seams. At least that's my idea.

25 May 1922

"Gouger": A Chinese packman showed a Queensland policeman a neat opium-smuggling trick on the old Cooktown-Palmer-road. The policeman stopped him in the bush about 40 miles from Cooktown and thoroughly searched his outfit. Every case, every bag of flour and sugar was opened and overhauled. The lining of the pack-saddles was prospected for signs of the drug, and so even were two large jars of rum. J. Hop gave it best at last, and accepted a courteous invitation to sample the rum. There was a false bottom in each of those jars, and that's where the opium was. But the policeman did not know it. Not until months afterwards.

17 August 1922

"Gouger": The old Cooktown Plantations, Ltd., is now the N.Q. Products, Ltd., re-capitalising for £200,000. The idea is to start a big settlement scheme and grow rice, ginger, peanuts and a score of other tropical and semi-tropical crops for which this part of N.Q. has long been proved suitable. Later on it is proposed to build an oil-treatment mill to exploit the peanuts. The idea is to work the ground on the share system, so the men on the subdivided farms will in course of time own them.

21 September 1922

"Atherton:" A timber that deserves more attention than it gets from cabinet-makers and house-furnishers is the Atherton (or Queensland) red oak. It has a texture very similar to Queensland maple, but when polished up looks twice as well. The difficulty is, however, that it grows only in Northern Queensland, whence it is difficult to obtain small supplies. Some beautiful samples were exhibited in Sydney last year by the Queensland Government Tourist Agency, but when I inquired after some to make a few contraptions at home I couldn't find any in Sydney. The Agency would supply a ship-load but no less, and that at about six months' notice. Meanwhile, huge quantities of this magnificent timber are being destroyed by settlers, who must remove it from their holdings but are unable to sell it.

2 November 1922

"Gouger's" Tribute: The Bowen (N.Q.) Red Cross is the dinkum article. It is carrying on today just as it did when red-crossing was a fashionable sport; and in these late hard years many is the footsore ex-Digger who, passing through the little coastal town, has been handed an issue of much-needed clothes and given the helping fin generally. The local climate may be injurious to humans, as Southerners like Barwell claim, but it's a great place for humanity.

17 April 1924

"Gouger" goes paspalum-picking: -
Now is the hurry-up season (four or five weeks) for picking paspalum seed. There's money in the game while it lasts, given favourable conditions. You may pick for the cocky either on the halves, or for so much per pound. If the former, you either sell your take to the dealers straight out or hold it for a rise. The price of picking per lb. Is generally 3d.; a good man going to work on a good crop will pick 100lb. A day; "ringers" have been known to do 130. A few days later, a second picking is ready, but this time 80lb. Will be good work, and for the third and last pricing 40lb. The holding of the seed for a rise is the attractive part of the business. At present seed is 6d. per lb. In November, when the new ground is cleared and ready for planting, it may be from 1s. 6d. per lb. to 2s. 3d. Often there is a catch in it for the buyer. In many parts paspalum grass is reaped for conversion into fodder when the seed is only half ripe. Some cockies mix three bags of this reaped seed with one bag of the hand-picked stuff, the result being that only about a quarter of the seed comes up. The purchaser may pay anything from 6d. to 1s. per lb. for finding this out.

19 June 1924

"Gouger": Are garnets in large quantities of any commercial value? I know of a mountain between the Musgrave and Coen, Cape York Peninsula, which practically consists of garnets. The red stones are set in the Mountain rock very much like pebbles in cement. I once met a couple of men who were coming back from this country in a state of great excitement. They had their pack-horses loaded with bags of garnets, and reckoned they had found the greatest ruby mine in the world, or out of it. All the same, I suppose it would be possible for a few rubies to be mixed up in that gigantic heap.

7 August 1924

"Gouger": Lots of shellfish besides the oyster have the power of producing pearls. I have seen the niggers get an occasional one from the fresh-water mussel. Most of the bivalves of the Barrier Seas strive to produce the delight of Cleopatra, but their products are seldom of much value. Even the big clam occasionally brings forth a pearl, though his is mostly a gradual accretion of irregular layers of shell over any foreign substance that may have found its way in. The best haul I ever made with pearls was when raiding a coastal niggers' camp in search of a runaway "boy". A piccaninny was playing in the sand with a mutilated goanna in one hand and a pearl in the other. I killed the goanna and make a present of it to the kid. The pearl they didn't value and had no use for. It realised £213.

14 August 1924

"Gouger": Is it any wonder we're asking for a new State up north in N. S. Wales? An inspector was required to furnish a report, through a country Lands Office, on the number of stock on a returned soldier's holding. The inspector enumerated in his report so many forward springing heifers, so many backward springing heifers. The document duly came back with this indignant commentary across it: "The inspector should refrain from making facetious remarks". Evidently the idea of a heifer springing backwards had been too much for the Sydney office to swallow.

14 August 1924

"Gouger": "Moe" (B. 10/7/1924) need not go to America to find snakes living in harmony with Brer Rabbit. Almost every Australian burrow shelters its creeping boarders; also boarders that are far more dangerous to bunny than the

snake, viz., domesticated cats. Some burrows also keep the damp off porcupines, lizards, giant spiders, centipedes, and several species of birds with dark habits. The cats and reptiles apparently live on friendly terms with their landlords and pay their rent on the entente system, the understanding being that they must dine only on the baby rabbits of other burrows. It is the principle on which more than one nation has been compelled to buy dear peace and uneasy security.

13 November 1924
"Gouger":   Though I had just blown in from our farthest north, this shingled hair didn't seem strange. All the little black girls of Cape York Peninsula have their wool cut once a year. The subject sits on a rock, while the barber places a flat stone underneath the tangled locks and bangs at them with another stone. The operation causes the ends to look a bit frayed, but that does not matter. Sometimes the shearing instrument is a jagged piece of quartz or glass. For some inscrutable reason the females always prefer the barber to be a man. The discarded hair is woven into wigs; and, ornamented with scarlet berries and colored feathers, they are reckoned to have a very fetching effect at corroborees and dances.

18 December 1924
"Gouger":   The warden in the old Palmer (Q.) days had a strenuous time rounding up the elusive Chinese diggers for their miners' rights. Officialdom soon tired of the monotonous "Whaffor." And one night a mob of contumacious pagans found themselves hand-cuffed to a chain stretched among the trees surrounding the lock-up. John's swag was collared, and no more notice was taken of him until the ten bob for the right was forthcoming, which happened very quickly. At Maytown and Byrestown 150 Chows came to understand whaffor in a single night. On the Byrestown portion of the Palmer alone £4000 was obtained from Ah Sin in 12 months for his right to disturb Australian soil. As the Palmer was nearly a hundred miles in length, the number of yellow aliens can be guessed at. An enterprising Caucasian, scenting easy money, slipped into a police uniform and waited on the main road for the incoming mobs of Chow diggers, collecting ten bob in exchange for every slip of paper purporting to be a miner's right. He made a great haul, but his luck was right out: a genuine constable nabbed him as he was stepping on the Cooktown boat for Brisbane.

8 January 1925
"Up Top": "Mary Scott" (B. 18/12/1924) need not fear that her mango-trees when in fruit will bring fleas about; having lived the last 10 years in luxuriant mango country I am convinced there is nothing in the superstition. Incidentally, does "Mary Scott" know that if she peels her mangoes, cuts the flesh into thin strips, and sun-dries for a few days, the fruit will last in the same way as dried apples and apricots? The housewives of Cooktown fatten their husbands on mango pie long after the tree is bare. It is unnecessary, no doubt, to remind a girl of the North that mango chutney puts "pep" into a man, as also does pie, and far more so does mango wine.

8 January 1925
"Up Top": During a recent heat wave in North Queensland a girl friend of mine got either sunstroke or heatstroke in a queer way. After a long drive she was violently sick. Next morning on endeavouring to walk to the door she found she was walking away from it. All her efforts of will were of no avail; her legs absolutely persisted in taking her in the opposite direction to that which she wanted to go, and for a month it was the same. A mate of mine possessed hair of which he was very proud: a thick, crinkly, curly brown mop. A morning came when as he was sluicing his head the hair came away like a wig, and he was down with heatstroke. Four months later his hair re-grew, in dirty-looking patches. A bad sunstroke generally comes suddenly, and with paralysis invariably. The temperature rises and a man is either dead or better within a few days. In heatstroke the attack may come gradually, and rarely with any marked rise in temperature, but is always accompanied by headache and giddiness and with pains and cramp in the body. If a man gets violently delirious and then becomes unconscious, he may be dead in a few days if his luck is out. First-aid is to loosen all clothes immediately and remove the patient to the coolest place possible with the head low; then douche the head, neck and face with cold water. In cases of severe collapse, artificial respiration is necessary. Put the patient to bed in a dark room, and then, if the doctor can't fix him, the undertaker will.

22 January 1925
"Up Top": On Cape York Peninsula the milk tree, at the period when its new twigs are forming, exudes a substance which the sandalwood-getters swear by as a sure cure for corns, and it is with this tree that Professor Campbell has been experimenting to obtain material for the chewing-gum people. The Professor

told me the gum was equal to the best from South America, and wanted me to undertake its collection. The trunks were to be tapped like the rubber-tree. But although Campbell is known the world over as a scientist, his financial theories do not appear to be worked out with the same precision. And I, not being a scientist, would not take on the job. But the tree is there, and may be a sleeping Australian industry.

22 January 1925
"Up Top": What curious sense is it that makes men when perishing of thirst dispense with all clothing? In a wandering bush life I've been present at the finding of 18 men who had died of thirst. In every case their poor torn bodies were stripped of clothes. It almost seems as if the mind reverts to its first state. Why lost men should invariably travel in a circle is another hard thing to understand; there are very few men who, if without bushmanship enough to pick out landmarks, will not travel in the unavailing circle. Most people lose their heads completely when "bushed", but this does not explain the fatal circling.

19 February 1925
"Up Top": When a little abo. Is coming a reincarnated soul has entered into the mother. In North Australia, anyway. To have acquired this spirit she must have walked close by a sacred spirit-ground. Here the souls of the departed collect, strictly in their totemic groups, and await the passing-by of a likely-looking earth-mother. If a girl does not want to do her duty, she camouflages herself as a doubled-up old woman. When a spirit-child enters a woman to be re-born it drops its sacred stick, without which no abo. can come back into the world. When the child is born the mother tells the father where she thinks the youngster entered into her, and dad and the old men search the spot for the sacred stick. If it has vanished the bucks cut one from the nearest tree, and this becomes the sacred stick of the youngster. The tree is generally called the nanja-tree, and a strong relationship thereafter exists between the buck and this tree. Many regard their nanja-tree as so sacred that any bird which alights upon it is also sacred to them. Which is why white men have at times been earnestly entreated by a nigger not to cut down his nanja-tree.

5 March 1925
"Up Top": I think pretty well all over Northern Australia there breed caterpillars that make enormous parchment-like nests in the branches of tree.

"Boree-moth" I've heard the things called. A man who knows will never camp under one of these caterpillar-community trees. Should the wind blow a nest down and its beastly contents burst on the sleeper's face, he stands a very good chance of going blind. The bags are full of yellow powdery stuff and very fine hairs. I know a new-chum who chopped one of the trees down and broke open the nests out of curiosity. A week after, his arms were covered with a horrible itching rash that necessitated hospital treatment. A bush mate, who should have had better sense, lashed a nest open with his stockwhip. He didn't take much notice of part of the stuff falling on the horse's neck near the saddle. But very shortly after he did, because the horse went mad and smashed its rider's knee against a tree.

19 March 1925

"Up Top":   A wonderful sight is the evening flight of the glossy starlings to their island camping-grounds, off the N.Q. coast. Far up over the mainland they arise in small flocks, which unite until they form huge, dense clouds. As the stragglers come in the main clouds fly in great circles, which suddenly drop low, to rise again in a long, spiral column, looking like an upward winding cloud of black smoke. Re-forming into one cloud they rise higher and higher, circling and sweeping, sometimes almost invisible in the sky; then they move for the island in one enormous black flight as the last sunrays shine on their massed backs. When they near the land they swoop low, skimming the water with wonderful speed and roar of wings, to crash in a shrieking mass into the mangroves.

9 April 1925

"Up Top":   Some N.Q. tribes are certain that ghosts cannot cross water. So when a member passes west they shift camp across a river, immediately after having disposed of the body in such a way as will be pleasing to its ghost. Several tribes go to extremes to prevent the spirit's unwelcome attentions. After planting the body they blaze the trees in a circle around it. When the ghost hops out of the graves and chases his retiring friends he'll follow the tree-marks and never reach anywhere at all. To be dead-certain they jamb coals in the dead man's ears before planting him, which keeps the ghost encased for a considerable time. They also light fires around the spot, preferably in trees, because the ghost will surely delay his pursuit to warm himself. Then to make a racecourse certainty of it the whole tribe go for the lick of their lives for the nearest river. Some tribes spike the ghost's wheel in this way: they cut off the corpse's head, roast it and smash

the skull to bits, leaving the remnants in the fire. When the ghost hops from the grave he misses his head and gropes blindly about until he burns his fingers in the coal, and is then jolly glad to duck back into his six-by-two. Yet other tribes smash the bones of a dead man's body, and weigh it down with heavy stones before finally covering it. This all helps to keep the ghost underground as long as possible. But the nigs always take care to leave plenty of tucker close by the grave for the ghost's breakfast. Otherwise he'd get into a fury and break things. Although the burial customs differ much, the reincarnation belief is universal. The ghost wanders for a time upon the tribal hunting-grounds, then, becoming lonely, hops off to the spirits' waiting-room, and in such congenial company "walks about" until his time comes to be born on earth again. All niggers that are "civilised" explain the dying-out of their race by the fact that "black man he die. Jump up quick-fella white fella".

23 April 1925
"Gouger":   Have you ever seen buleroi? Though almost worthless as timber, it has the exact appearance of camphorwood, bar the scent. In Hong Kong planks of it are soaked in long troughs containing wet camphorwood chips. The buleroi absorbs the scent from the shavings and is eventually sold in the much-prized form of camphorwood chests. Sandalwood, with its powerful perfume, is imitated in the same way. So when your bride complains that all the nice perfume has left the once fragrant "toiley" box, you'll know where to fix the blame.

14 May 1925
"Up Top":   Every 12 months or so a pearling lugger needs a spring cleaning, and that's the time to get cheap fish. The boat is weighted down on the beach so that the incoming tides will swamp her decks. The year's crop of cockcroaches hop from their hiding-places and come up for a breather. That's when the fish get busy. The boys, with brooms sweeping the 'roaches from the masts, and the white men, using dynamite, collect a great haul of fish. The 'roaches originally come aboard attracted by the fragments of meat adhering to the oyster shell, breed quickly, and then raid the crew's provisions. This, of course, means retaliation. And so life laughs on, everything eating everything else.

28 May 1925
"Gouger": The hair of animals sports three colors. The tip is called the "over-hair", while the fluffy woolly stuff hidden from sight below is the "under fur". Over coat and singlet vary in growth and density according to whether the animal has to be protected from rain, cold winds or sun heat. Under strong sun heat alone there is generally no under-fur. In rigorous climates both over-hair and under-fur are abundant. In the tropics a light under-fur alone is often found. In heavy-rain countries the dense under-fur is the animal's raincoat. As the seasons change so do the fashions in animal land. The red 'roos discard their reds for a light grey suit in the male; this is easily done, as the under-fur is grey and the over-hair red. The female, true to her sex, does exactly the opposite. Her shimmy is bright red, while her shoulder-straps and stockings are grey. Towards winter the over-hair of her dainty "fur" grows longer. Similarly you'll notice an improvement for the better in the hair of the human species as cold weather draws near.

28 May 1925
"Atherton": Can any bush timber-man tell me a way of getting good big logs down from a 2000-feet scrub-mountain without smashing them to splinters? There's a fortune in some beauties I know if they could only be brought to the low country. The ordinary chute method is no good. We tried three logs that way and never found their splinters. I saw close on a quarter-million feet crumble into matchwood when chuting them below the Bloomfield Falls (N.Q.). It was a good straight chute, yet many of the logs jambed, and others coming behind tore the lot into driftwood. When a few did finally land in the water, their speed and weight sent them end on to the rocky bottom and they split straight up. From the top of the chute to the water was barely 1000 feet. The logs were mostly cedar. Burns, Philp and Co. lost an enormous amount of timber when they tried to float it over the Barron Falls years ago. The Bloomfield idea was to drop the logs in the water below the falls. But it didn't act.

11 June 1925
"Up Top": In a North Queensland scrub I saw a defunct carpet-snake that had come a great thud. Its coils were round a porcupine whose tough quills had pierced the snake in many parts. It had evidently tightened around old Porc., who had then got the spike. The ant-eater wasn't inconvenienced more than to appear a bit tight-laced, and I suppose he'd carry on that way until decomposition caused the corset to drop off.

11 June 1925
"Atherton":   On my first visit to Darnley Island the niggers were savage, but this did not prevent me poking my nose inside one of their beehive-like huts. As I became used to its hazy darkness I found the smoked mummy of the hut owner's late missus standing lashed to the centre pole, a spear propping up her chin. Hubby had gouged her eyes out and in their place set pieces of mother-o'-pearl, with a rough imitation of the pupil painted on them. The naked mummy was blacky-brown, shrivelled, hideous and skeleton-like. Later I learned that the islanders used to take away the interior organs and, stretching the body upon a wooden frame, lash it upright to a post. As the houses are grass or palm-thatched to the ground, with only a small opening for entrance and exit, the departed soon became thoroughly smoke-dried, and the several I've seen would undoubtedly keep for years. In those great days the dead person's tongue would be eaten by the nearest relative and the liver and kidneys by the male relations, with the universal nigger idea of "making 'em brave". Of course when white Gub'ment came along, these customs were stopped, but the niggers slyly say it hasn't yet stamped them all out.

18 June 1925
"Atherton":   "There's more in it than the eye can see" applies to the white-ants' nest. Birds, snakes, lizards, centipedes and beetles bore into it as if it were a residential flat rent free. Many small bush-things get their first glimmer of light within its mud walls. McLarren, the Cape York Peninsula birdman, some three years ago found in a nest a hitherto unknown species of parrot, some of whose offspring are, I'm told, doing well at Taronga Park, the Sydney Zoo. Sometimes a colony of rats will bore into a large anthill until it becomes a sieve that collapses. At other times the ants are eaten out by thousands of beetles, who, I suppose, live on the baby residents. An anthill is of occasional value to the prospector as well as to the naturalist. I saw one nest at Roseville (N.Q.) broken down with the pick and put through the sluice box. It yielded 1¼ cwt. of stream tin. The ants had built the little black and grey grains into their nest. On Ebagoolah goldfield one nest was dished for 2½ oz. of alluvial gold. But such cases are very rare. It is only when the ants are building their nests near a dry watercourse with a big "bar" running across it on which the alluvial specks lie bare that the ants pick up the gold. Still I know prospectors who try an antbed just on the off chance. One such forlorn hope had a rich reward. The dish showed rough colors of reef gold. As, there was no creek near, and as the men guessed the termites had most likely got their building

material from close handy, the party trenched on all sides of the nest. They struck a rich trail of flour gold, and on deepening one of the trenches came on a rich floater. It was the cap of a leader just covered by the soil. Inside seven months it brought them £2800 a man before pinching out.

2 July 1925

"Up Top": A superstition which has caused thousands of deaths among North Australian Abos is connected with the pointing of the death-bone. No white man has the slightest chance of shaking their faith in the power of the bone to produce a corpse. The instrument itself is sacrosanct. For a woman to even look at it means death. It is of three parts. The actual pointer, about 5in long is a piece of bone taken from the human fore-arm and ground down to taper at the point. Affixed by bush gum to the blunt end of the pointer is the "string", made of human hair and in some cases, 20ft long. The other end of the "string" is attached to the bottom of the "case", which holds the pointer and the string when not in action. This case is a cylinder of shin-bone, and when dirty work is done, holds the victim's blood.

The witch-doctor who points the bone, does so at night only, and is very secret about it, as the prospective victim might employ other doctors to retaliate on him. If within a few miles of his enemy, he does the job alone. The cylinder is placed upright on the ground with the pointer between the operator's toes and adjusted in the direction of his victim. He holds the string with his hands, and never on any account lets it touch the ground. At times, however, the victim is a long way off, and for reasons of native etiquette, it may become imperative to call in other doctors. The receptacle is then lashed to a tree, the string tautened and the bone-pointer placed within a forked stick pointing in the direction of the doomed man's camp. There may be at the one time, four doctors kneeling and holding up the connecting string. The chief of them mumbles snatches of corroboree song, alternately making passes with his hand towards the enemy's camp, each sweep ending up at the sharp end of the pointer. This is supposed to make the blood flow freely through the intervening space on to the pointer, then along the string, and into the open cylinder.

But perhaps the "patient" has a friend among the operating doctors. In that case the connecting string suddenly breaks. It is solemnly bound up again and the ceremony proceeds; but if the string breaks again the whole business is declared off and the apparatus wound up. The doctors may have a very fair idea of the one of their number who cut the string, but say nothing. One doctor can

point the bone at another, so they never know whose turn it may be next. The curious fact is that once they fully carry out the rite the man nearly always dies. If however, he is a very self-willed abo, and doesn't in the least wish to die, he may possibly find some extra-strong witch-doctor who will ferret out the man who has pointed the bone, and in turn, point it at him. In that case, the witch-doctor himself, dies.

9 July 1925

"UP TOP": A few of the bucks on the finger point of Cape York Peninsular, use a spring line for catching fish. As some of the "boys" have been on bêche-de-mer luggers, I've a suspicion they pinched the idea from New Guinea. A long elastic sapling is chosen as a fishing rod, and its butt end rammed firmly into the river bank, or between rocks on a coastal pool. To the tapering end of this rod a fishing line is secured. A straight sapling is then driven in close by. About a foot below the top of the latter is tied a string about 2ft. Long. To the end of this string a peg 6in. Long is affixed. The rod with the fishing-line is then bent over the water so that the baited hook is a few inches off the bottom, and the peg line stretched across and over the bent rod. An adjustment is then made which constitutes the peg the spring of a trigger. The trigger itself is the hook, and the fish the trigger finger, the line pulls the peg, and, the "bolt" being released, up flies the rod, with the fish dangling a good 2ft. above water, so that no other fish may scoff him during the night. My mate and I used the idea, and often found it an easy way of obtaining breakfast.

30 July 1925

"UP TOP": "Nomads" (B.18-6-25) ball of dazzling light which entered a Victorian schoolroom during a thunderstorm was almost certainly the curious electrical display known to sailormen as St Elmo's Light. These uncanny fireballs play on the mast-tips and run along the yardarms during a storm when the air is charged with electricity. The cause is not yet thoroughly understood by science. In appearance they usually take the form of a moving ball of greenish-blue light. Cases have been recorded in Australia where the balls have run along the roofs of houses and the branches of dead trees during a bad storm. I saw only one display personally, and that was during a sudden tropical storm on the N.Q. coast. My mate and I were sheltering under an overhanging granite boulder jutting from the mountain crest. Close by were some very wide ironstone reefs, but whether they were in anyway responsible for the display we saw I don't know.

In the height of the storm, three vigorous fireballs came bouncing along the crest. Backwards, forwards and across they moved in a sort of hopping roll. Never stationary, they distinctly hissed at times, and repeatedly shot out brilliant tongues of white-and-blue light. My mate and I weren't at all sorry when they disappeared as suddenly as they had come.

6 August 1925

"Up Top":   Niggers' legends are mostly poor things, but occasionally there is a classic among them. One such is the story of the giant KA-KAN, a N.Q. abo who brought fire to the earth. KA-KAN and another were fighting beneath the wonder tree. This tree, men used to climb to their paradise. The grass around the base of the tree was very dry, and the struggling feet of the giant KA-KAN and his enemy finally set it afire. Unfortunately, the blazing grasses burnt the tree down, and the abos on top had to stay there.

3 September 1925

"Atherton":   A dog that stowed aboard our lugger during a cruise among the Torres islands earned his keep as a look-out man. He literally smelt a reef, even when the coral was not showing above water. If we were approaching one at night he'd run up in the bows and whine plaintively. In the day he'd bark even though we couldn't see a warning curl of foam. He was never mistaken, though at times we were. As we had a lot of night cruising in dangerous waters, he was far and away the most valuable member of the crew. It was the first cruise he'd signed on for, and the skipper wouldn't let him sign off at the finish.

10 September 1925

"Up Top":   I saw a nigger "go west" in a startling fashion. The lugger was cruising off Cape Melville (N.Q.) in dirty weather, and aboard was a Melville "boy" pining to visit his sweetheart. In an unguarded moment he slipped the dinghy over the side and was away down the wave crests laughing delightedly as the wind blew away the skipper's furious curses. He got through the surf right enough, and we saw his nigger cobbers running down to meet him. Then the dinghy was completely blotted out by a sheet of fire, and the welcoming niggers streaked for the bush like black bandicoots. Later we learned the lightning had shattered the dinghy into matchwood and settled Romeo. It was a bit of a shame too, for Juliet, inconsolable, jumped over the Melville cliffs. There was no disobedience on our lugger after that. The *mana* of a skipper who could kill

a disobedient boy by throwing a great and invisible fire-stick at him quickly spread all along the coast.

17 September 1925
"Gouger":   From time immemorial man has been loath to part with his most cherished possession. The Egyptians took their scarabs with them, the Viking his drinking cup; and many a savage man took his wives in the form of cinders, it is true. At the present day the practice may be more common than might be supposed. An Adelaide publican asked that a favourite cockatoo should be buried with him; and I've known several where the hooves of favourite horses have been buried with their masters. A pearler, after years of heart-breaking search, found the three pearls that meant a fortune to him – and then was carried off the cutter a dying man. He swallowed the pearls and begged to be buried at sea. A bushman in Cape York Peninsula built a funeral pyre, shot his favourite dog and placed it on top, set fire to the pyre, climbed up and then blew his own lights out. He scratched a note on the bottom of his pannikin explaining things. I know an opal miner who asked that his favourite gouging–pick might be buried with him; and a sea-captain friend went west with his favourite telescope. Perhaps he thought it would be of value in locating reefs and shoals. Fairly numerous bushmen have been buried with their stockwhips. But the silent emblem that touched me most was a pair of brightly –worn stirrup-irons lashed around a rude coffin in the sympathetic bush.

21 September 1925
"Atherton":   Cudgerie is a tall smooth-barked Queensland tree which may be found useful for medicinal purposes. The flowers are very fragrant, often bunching in threes, the centre one being female. The fruit is a black nut. Its shell contains a dye which is soluble in soda, but not in ether, alcohol or water. The kernel contains 65 p.c. of oil, similar to laurel oil, and has a narcotic smell. The wood is dark grey in color, its grain close. It is light and soft, and has been successfully used for carriage and furniture-building and lining-boards. The Queensland red-ironbark is a great tree of which unknown millions of feet have been sent up in smoke. It is one of the best all-round engineering timbers the Commonwealth grows, and has been used for almost every purpose where tough, durable wood is required. The strongest gun-carriage wheels known are made with spokes of this timber. A little-known Queensland tree is the apunyah, growing freely in the inland North. It is accustomed to a hot climate

and seldom grows over 30ft. high. The wood is tough and has answered well to the hard work put upon it by the outbacker. A wonderful tree is the N.Q. walnut, absolutely equal, if not superior, to the American. It grows well over 100 feet high. The wood is chocolate colored, similar to the English timber, is of first-class grain, and dresses well. Also it takes a good polish, figures excellently, and seasons very rapidly. It possesses great strength. Queensland grows some 600 distinct kinds of timber, many of them equalling the best in the world. There are vast areas of virgin scrubs and forests in the tropical North. Some day they will be active with the life of big lumber camps.

15 October 1925

"Gouger": A wedding ring that promises to age into an heirloom was lately slipped on the finger of a bonny northern bush bride. The gold was panned off in a Queensland creek over 30 years ago, and an Australian jeweller moulded it into a ring for the miner's wife. On the day the couple bought their farm the ring disappeared. The young wife had been cleaning it, and being hurriedly called away left it on the sewing-machine at the open window. Search was unavailing. Sixteen years later the eldest boy found a dirt-coated metal ring in a bower-bird's nest in a dark patch of scrub a mile from the house. When her boy went off to the war the mother sewed the ring in a tiny bag and tied it round his neck. The boy went through four years of war unscathed. Through them and the years that since have passed the ring never left him until a month ago. Now he smilingly says it only left his neck to rest against his heart.

22 October 1925

"Atherton": Are these facts links in a chain which in past centuries bound the tribes of men together. Berosus, a high-priest of Baal, was a Babylonian historian and is supposed to have lived in the time of Alexander the Great. He has left us an account of the Deluge, also of Oannes and his disciples, or tribesmen, the Annedotus, beings who were half human and half fish, tree or animal. They appeared to the ancient Babylonian and instructed them in the arts and sciences. The Aussie abo. is far removed geographically from these vanished civilisations and far inferior to them mentally. Yet a belief is held by Northern tribes akin to that of ancient Babylon. He believes that the Great Spirit sent down to the earth beings in the form of half-man and half-fish, tree or animal. These creatures originally spread over the land, making the earth habitable for the coming of men.

22 October 1925

"Up Top":   What elixir does nature put into the abo.'s blood that heals dreadful wounds so quickly? I've seen niggers recover from spear wounds though the long barbed spearhead's protruded a foot through the body. A big black foot was pressed against the wounded man, and the swaying haft was twisted and pulled out by main strength, its barbs bringing with them flesh etc. After that a handful of roots and herbs was boiled down and placed over the wound, and a plaster of feathers and mud applied. In 3 weeks the patient was sneaking through the bush trailing the man that spiked him. Yet an abo. will lie down and die without a murmur when the witch-doctor points the "bone" at him. A white man nearly always collapses under a spear wound through the body, and if he does not die within a few hours, he generally has a lingering death extending over weeks. Yet under certain conditions, what would kill a nigger with fright and shock, wouldn't so much as shake the ash from the white man's cigarette. It's the grim old war I'm thinking of now.

12 November 1925

"Atherton":   The tern season is one of plenty for the nomads of the Barrier islands on which the birds lay their eggs among the broken corals. They build no nests nor make the slightest attempt to hide their masterpieces. The shell is grey and brown with a camouflage of colors and queer patterns. The eggs thus merge into the grey-white flakes of broken coral, shells, driftwood, leaves and tide-stranded seaweed. A man could look on a thousand eggs and not see one. The young birds also are quite invisible. I've stared at a clump of the fluffy little balls and failed to see a bird in it until a dislodged lump of coral made one move. They're dressed in a comical down-suit which blends perfectly with the coral fragments. The little beggars will not move even when a man picks them up. They are utterly helpless and unprotected against the ravaging hawk, but nature has camouflaged them so well that as long as they don't move they are safe.

10 November 1925

"Up Top":   In the days of my innocent youth I matched my guile against the cunning of the crow. The prize was 6d per knob, offered by the local Pastures Protection Board. With a great display of camp-fire smoke I breakfasted in an open space among the bloodwood trees. A crow flopped along and settled in a tall tree overhead, apparently taking not the slightest interest in my business. He shrank himself to half his size and remained as immobile as the dead branch

on which he nested. Between bites of damper and cold mutton I ostentatiously threw lumps of gristle and fat around the camp-fire. Then unconcernedly I threw away some poisoned meat scraps, and picking up my rifle walked off among the trees. A few minutes later from my hiding-place I watched the crows congregate around the sentinel. He answered their verbal inquiries with a few bored quawks.

The flock at once volplaned to the camp-fire, and I counted my prospective sixpences. The black scavengers strolled leisurely among the scraps, cursorily inspected the baits, passed on and contemptuously scoffed all the damper crusts. After which, they flew leisurely away, having given me my first lesson in the cunning of the wild.

19 November 1925
"Atherton": North Queensland abo. tribes have certain foods tabooed them during certain periods of life. Thus before initiation into warrior-hood the youngsters are allowed foods which are strictly barred them during the following 20 years. In some tribes certain foods are held sacred to the greyheads. Penalties for eating tabooed foods are based mainly on super-natural fear. The wounds of any lad or girl disobedient during initiation ceremonies will inflame and become poisoned. Quite possibly the spirits will caused portion of his or her body to drop off. During pregnancy both wife and husband have certain foods denied them. Indulgence in them means possibly the death of the woman and a weakening of the man's spear-arm. Relatives of the newly-dead are denied certain foods for three months. Failure to conform means that the spirit of the dead will haunt them. A widow is placed under a ban of silence for, in some cases, 12 months. She sits in camp with all her clay, ashes and ochre daubs of mourning upon her. Only certain foods may she collect herself, the other necessary eatables being placed silently before her. She is expected to wound herself with the sharp-pointed yam-stick and the glowing firestick. When her ban of silence ends there is a tribal ceremony at the gathering of the grass-seed, and the woman once more takes her place as a normal female.

26 November 1925
"Up Top": In the days of the Palmer rush (N.Q.), loading from Cooktown to Byerstown soared to £100 per ton. One day a packer found a horse useless over the stony ground, he having cast a shoe. Nowhere could the man find horseshoe-nails. Another carrier, Billy Yates, offered him five nails for their

weight in gold, and the offer was immediately accepted. The nails were weighed out and balanced by gold. That afternoon the horse packed 150 lb. 11 miles and 1s. per lb., so earning £7 10s.

17 December 1925
"Up North":   There are a few sunken treasure-ships off the Australian coast (B. 19/11/25), but, as far as is known, their cargoes are not worth any fabulous sums. When the Gothenberg foundered on the way from Port Darwin she had £3000 of gold abroad, apart from what passengers carried in their belts. Several ships loaded with diggers, who in turn were loaded with gold, have gone to Davy Jones's locker. A perfectly authentic story is that of Jardine's find off Cape York Peninsula. Glancing over the bows of his cutter at very low tide he saw the mud-covered ribs of some queer craft. He sent his diving-boys down, and from beside an almost-vanished anchor they brought up heavy lumps of metal. The lumps proved to be Spanish and Mexican dollars in good preservation, roughly cemented together by the action of sea-water. Jardine sold his trove for more than £3000. It is a pity he hadn't divers properly equipped. Who knows what that old Spanish wreck and, and how much specie may still be lying there feet deep in the mangrove mud! Happy-go-lucky native diving-boys would never have brought up the lot.

17 December 1925
"Up Top":   The N.Q. abo. loses no chances where his tucker is concerned. Any hollow log lying by a likely-looking waterhole he slings into it, for fish have a habit of nosing into hollow logs in search of tucker. Passing that way later he dives in, blocks the hollow with his hands, and brings the log to the surface. There's always the off-chance of an inquisitive fish being inside. In the river-ways eels have a liking for submerged tree-trunks as residential chambers. Lying on the banks above Binghi patiently probes the log with a long, pliable strand of lawyer-cane, the probing end of which has been chewed. On withdrawal, should the end be touched with a film of slime, he knows the cane has grazed an eel. Then follows a game of skill and patience. With persuasive prods Binghi gently lures the eel from its inaccessible cranny into the main hole of the log. Then he can dive into the water and thrust straight down with his long-pronged fish-spear. Most sea-eels are very vicious, strong, and quick as greased lightning, their hideous heads being armed with a formidable array of needle-sharp teeth.

14 January 1926
"Up Top": Queer how native legends that tally closely with Bible accounts keep cropping up. The aboriginals have a "Flood" legend, and the islands also have theirs.

In the Banks group a hero of many legends is the spirit QAT. On Gaua is a lake and lower down a big waterfall, but where the lake now is were once hills and forest country. QAT made a giant canoe from a great tree. The tribesmen scoffed at him for building such a craft on high land, and jeeringly asked how he proposed to drag it down to the sea. He replied "Wait and see!" The vessel finished, he compelled his wife and brothers to embark, together with two of every kind of living thing on the island, down to the tiniest ant. He next wove a cover over the boat, enclosing all. Then it rained and rained and rained. Gradually the valleys filled until the flood burst through the hills and foamed down to the sea. That is where the great waterfall now tumbles. The canoe ploughed through the water to the sea, where it vanished.

The people say that with QAT went the best of everything on the island, and someday he will surely return. When Bishop Patteson first visited the island he was taken for QAT come back. All over the island are traces of a vanished people in the form of stone foundations and walls, pointing to the former existence of a large and advanced population.

28 January 1926
"Atherton": The padymelons were dining. From cover I waited my chance of a shot. Up a gully crept a red dingo, so evidently on special business that I lowered my rifle out of curiosity. His prickears peeped above the gully-bank; then his body rose. Instantly the padymelons sat back, alarmed, and several thud-thud-thuds told of the hasty retreat of some to the scrub. The dingo lifted a forepaw to the sky and yapped complainingly. He rolled over and over, his tail thrashing the grass, his tongue licking his paw. It was so evident he was thinking of nothing but the splinter in his poor foot, I noticed that each roll carried him a little closer to the padymelons. They gazed with perked ears, curiosity overcoming caution. The dingo ignored them entirely. He drooped on his scraggy haunches, dolefully shaking his paw like a school-kid after tasting the master's cane. Then with low, exasperated yaps he rolled over again, his claws scratching gravel, his nose buried in the ground, and so he gained another few yards. Once more he arose, and on three legs chased his tail in circles. Each concluded circle took him just a little nearer the padymelons. Then again he

rolled – accidentally – towards the 'melons. Several of them became uneasy, and, hopping to the sheltering scrub-edge, sat back with curious brown eyes watching this most unusual dingo. Presently but one incautious 'melon remained in the open. The dingo's rolls became faster. As the 'melon drooped his body to hop the dingo was up in a flash, and his galloping rush caught the 'melon even before it had attained full speed. I was left reflecting that brains had secured an evening meal where civilised man with a rifle went without.

11 February 1926
"Up Top": Binghi believes love-charms to be invincible. They vary according to the witch-doctor who compounds them. His charms are, of course, far more potent than those of an ordinary individual. The philtre has to be swallowed by the object of the lover's attentions. It is a power whose ingredients are a secret, but here are some of the ordinary components. The ashes of a full-grown (male) lizard of a dwarf variety, the ashes of a few hairs from Romeo's armpit, a tiny pinch of pituri ash, water-lilly seeds powdered and a seed of wongai. These are mixed and "sung" over for hours. It is the doctor's "singing" which gives a "kick" to the mixture. He it is, too who places the love potion in her kaikai. A more universal charm is a small wood carving attached to a string which Othello whizzes round his head when some distance from the camp in the dead of night. As the charm vibrates he sings of his overpowering love. This song is supposed to be taken up by the charm, whose insinuating "whir-rr-rrr" carries it to the ears of the sleeping beauty.

11 February 1926
"Up Top": In the N.Q. "season" the gins have a busy time collecting grass seed. The dilly-bags being full, a hole about 18 in. in diameter and 6 ft. deep is dug, handy to the low leaning branch of a tree. The seed is then poured into the hole and a gin steps in and treads the mass down with her feet. Seed is continually poured in while the gin's tramping feet and screwing toes separate the seed from the husk. The seeds keep sinking to the bottom of the hole, leaving on top the husks, leaves and small twigs. The seed is transferred to bark coolamons and thrown in the air to be winnowed by the breeze. It is then ready for grinding into flour between stones. Water is gradually added, and the resultant paste is scraped into a bark trough. It is then cooked as damper in the ashes, unless it be a kind which must first go through many water washings to dissolve away any vegetable poison.

11 February 1926

"Atherton": Environment plays queer pranks. A white resident in China for 50 years assures me that the growing slant in his eyes is purely a matter of environment. He tells of cases where white mothers have given birth to children with slightly slanting eyes , the only explanation being that the mothers had for many years looked on slant-eyed children. I know of my own knowledge, that white men living among the niggers for years unconsciously take on many of the black man's characteristics.

25 February 1926

"Atherton": The China camp tin miners thought they'd solved the tucker problem when they saw the Bloomfield River niggers eating the clay of the antbeds, which are scattered in millions over that district. But only certain clay is eaten, and to the white man it is very unpalatable. The blacks scoff it plentifully and without preparation, when short of other tucker. Around Cooktown and the Bloomfield streaks of what seem to be white kaolin are found in the creek banks. The clay – if it is clay - is dug out, powdered, and sifted free of grit. It is then kneaded with water into a stiff paste, formed into cakes and allowed to sun-dry for a week. These cakes are afterwards wrapped in leaves and roasted. They are eaten when cool and considered a luxury.

4 March 1926

"Atherton": What are the cheapest, best and easiest hobble straps to make where a big string of packhorses is concerned? Greenhide fills the bill in the North. Long strips 1 ½ in. wide, cut circle-wise off a hide, will make many straps. It is an expensive mistake and a waste of time to rivet buckles to each strap. The Cape York Peninsula "nigger's head" knot is quickly made and fully answers the purpose of a buckle, besides doing away with the frequent curse of a jambed buckle tongue. Cut each strap at least 4 in. longer than the necessary length, roll one end up very tightly for 4 in., then push the knife blade right through the centre of the fold. Thin the strap end, shove the point through, and pull the strap completely through. This means the complete strap is passed through a slit far smaller than itself, which forces the knot into a compact knob. The tighter you pull, the more pronounced becomes the knob. To fasten it around the hoof, cut a small slit 1 in. distant from the strap end and then force the big knot through. It catches "automatically". Make all slits very small, as in long-grass country on dewy nights the hide straps become very wet and the holes enlarge

as the strap itself stretches, thus making the knot liable to be jerked away. That is the main fault with greenhide - stretching when wet. Make each hobble-strap of double length, then double it in the centre to make one strap, which of course, makes it doubly strong. Another method, but less quick and effective, is to cut one slit in a greenhide end and two slits in the other end. Pass the strap around Baldy's hoof, then run the double-slit end through the single-slit end and push a wooden peg into the two slits, thus clinching the strap. The peg must be nicked to prevent it falling out. But the pegs take time and patience to make, and fall out easily on a wet or dewy night. I saw very good and strong hobbles made from a used motor-tyre. But motor-tyre straps need buckles. And when a sandalwood-getter has 40 pairs of hobbles to fix each night, he wants his material handy and cheap, otherwise at the year's end leather, buckles, rivets, tools, time and labor are going to cost him a small fortune in repairs. If leather straps are used, a periodical greasing gives them double life.

15 April 1926

"Up Top": Gins and piccaninnies on the Cape York Peninsula collect the loquat-like nuts of the Zamia plant and roast them. The nuts are cracked, the shells thrown away, the kernels soaked in water for five days and then pounded into flour between stones and the grit sifted out. The flour is next put into a basin-shaped dilly-bag near a running stream. A palm-leaf trough lets a continuous stream of water fall on the flour within the bag, the flour being carefully regulated so that none escapes over the lip of the bag. The water continuously running over-night dissolves the vegetable poison held in the flour and carries it away. The residue is dried and can be kept for three days before being baked into johnny cakes.

13 May 1926

"Atherton": In the Daintree jungles (N.Q.) thrives the father of all worms. Sometimes he is 5 ft. long and has a chest measurement of 3 in. He burrows into decayed vegetation. For wear he has a bright purple robe or a dark green shirt, but on dark and drizzly days you can see him glowing amongst the blackened leaves in an overcoat of phosphorus. He has a comical method of progression. First he secures a rump holt, then shortens his body into a thousand stout rings; next his head reaches forward, then the wrinkles one by one unfold, and he becomes a tremendously long, narrow worm. When fully extended, he grips something ahead, puts his shoulders down and draws up his wrinkled body. His domicile

often spreads for yards underground, and he can travel there at surprising speed. I watched a wild pig rooting after a worm with grunts of anticipation. Suddenly he ceased work, sniffed in all directions above ground, grunted again, and some yards further on made the leaves fly once more. But he missed again and the sniff-locating was repeated. His anguish was heartbreaking when his snout told him that the underground dinner had got beneath a bank too deep down for snouts.

20 May 1926
"Atherton":   The silence made a bush mother I know cease work and listen. Childish laughter set her running down the hill. At the scrub-edge she stood aghast. Her two toddlers had discovered a playmate. Its new skin blazed gold and brown upon the blady grass. Both toddlers' chubby hands grasped the heavy tail and pulled it. One baby's fingers slipped on the scales, and she tumbled head-first upon the coils. The mother's heart leapt to her throat. The 13 ft. python lifted his head and stared at the children. Without hissing, his tongue shot out and caressed his blunt nose. Well fed and sleepy in the warn sunlight, he showed no anger. The mother thought only of the coils which might crush both children with ease. They lifted the tail again, down towards the end, where their fingers could nearly grip. They pulled 3 ft. of it out of the coils. Seemingly without the slightest effort, the tail drew back within the coils, and the curly heads bumped together as the youngster landed on the snake. The mother commenced singing. The youngsters redoubled their efforts to show off the playmate. The snake's tongue shot out a little faster. The mother as she sang walked slowly forward and, still singing, bent over the children and gently loosened their fingers. With the youngster under each arm, and without ceasing her song, she walked up the hill. The snake, motionless, watched her until the voice broke; then it uncoiled and made for the scrub.

20 May 1926
"Atherton":   With plenty of energy and 8s. in money my mate proceeded to put up a house four years ago. It has needed no repairs since. The job took him 10 days. The house was of two rooms, 24 x 12 feet, with pug chimney. These were the materials: broad-leafed ti-tree posts and rafters; river-oak wall plates; palm battens; blady-grass roof; wire and nails. In the thatching he exposed the grass roots instead of the blades, as the Malays generally do. With the roots to the weather, the thatch is apparently much stronger, has a longer life and does not harbor vermin as badly.

24 June 1926

"Up Top": What is the source of the premonition that warns man when on the brink of disaster? One night I paused with out-stretched hand, controlled by an impulse so strong that I lit a match to see if anything was there, and saw a black snake coiled around the kindling wood. A mate of mine on coming to a bush bridge was held back by a sense of danger he could not withstand. A light was made and showed that fire had smouldered through the bridge. Three mates of mine on different occasions were working in mining tunnels. A quite unaccountable feeling pulled them away from the face just in time to witness the roof cave in.

24 June 1926

"Up North": The northern abo. draws a well-defined color line against John Chinaman. In the Palmer days hundreds of yellow diggers simmered on Binghi's cooking-stones. The Palmer tribe thought the white man had brought these droves of Mongols into the country as a propitiation for his own people having driven away so much game. Black Brother is quick to reflect White Brother's attitude. At the Laura store a Binghi violently ejected a Chinese customer because the yellow man in his due turn was served first. A Chinaman who endeavoured to drive past a mob of Binghis travelling on the lonely Byerstown road had his cart overturned by way of putting him in his place. But wily John more than got even. For every hundred Chinamen eaten in the early days, a whole tribe of Binghis bit the dust through opium charcoal, and Binghi, once the lord, soon became an abject slave under tragic circumstances.

1 July 1926

"Up Top": What is the strength of a jet from a 2 in. nozzle under 200 ft. of water pressure? At the Annan River Workings (N.Q.) I saw an embryo Hercules stand beside the nozzle, and swinging an axe with all his strength, bring it down to cut the jet. Axe and man were hurled a distance of 20 yds. And the dangerous experiment was never tried again.

8 July 1926

"Gouger": With conditions favourable, Binghi can smell animals an extraordinary distance away. Different beasts emit different odors and I've known abos. who could name treed animals by the sense of smell alone. They can also differentiate between white men, black, yellow and brown. I remember

a case in Cape York Peninsula where one located a prospector friend of mine (dead) in a waterhole. "Me smell him white-man fat," he declared. Most abos. can smell smoke from afar, and recognize the different grass or timber being burned. Strangely enough, the older men have the acuter smell perception. I have known old gins to unerringly smell out birds and tree animals where there was not the slightest visible sign of them, and I knew one ancient gin who could distinguish unseen wild cattle from buffalo, and even correctly tell the sex of the animals.

22 July 1926

"Up Top":   Up near the Fingerpoint there thrives a weeping fig, one portion of its hollowed butt so trellised over with bark as to form almost a new covering. On peering through the interlaced bark, you are grinned at by a yellowish-brown skeleton. The bones are mildewed, though the natives swear that with the dying of the moon the spirit comes back to it and laughs aloud. The legend tells that he was the lover of the chief's wife. The pair eloped but were betrayed by a ray of moonlight as they lay in one another's arms. The warriors hollowed out one side of the fig, chiselling the wood in strips as a guide for the bark to grow over. Romeo was fastened within, and for a time was kept alive on wild figs.

22 July 1926

"Atherton":   In the Far North the jacket of the big paper-bark tree supplies an ideal mattress and blanket for the bushed wanderer. The bark, an inch thick, is composed of many soft layers and can be stripped quickly with the help of a stick. A sheet on the ground is comfortable and waterproof, while another sheet above supplies warmth and defies rain. Being very oily it blazes instantly when other wood is sopping. The natives use the bark extensively for waterproof gunyahs, and one particularly fastidious Gulf tribe make their gins adorn and wear an apron of it.

12 August 1926

"Ili":   Out on the Barwon (N.S.W.) 100 head of our ewes were missed. An abo. specked their tracks and we followed them into rough country. Dingo-pads mixed with the sheep-tracks showed that the dogs had cut out the jumbucks from the main mob, and worked them into the wild. Breaking through brushwood, we found the sheep huddled together at the base of a precipitous washaway. The survivors were stricken with terror. A score were dead, and as many dragged their entrails. Hemmed against the washaway with the pirates

snapping at their flanks, there had been no escape. Tracks showed that four dingoes only had engineered the massacre. It was a scene of ruthless carnage, since one sheep would have been sufficient to feed the marauders.

12 August 1926
"Atherton":   In North Queensland the abo. kids play for hours at "cats' cradle," and it is certain that no white man introduced the game to them. There are ball games, too – a hank of fibre and feathers sewn around with emu skin makes their ball. Also there is a sort of tipcat and rough spinning-tops, which suggest that the kids of the whole world are brothers and sisters under their skin. A picturesque pastime of the abos. is the spinning disc. About a foot in diameter, it is at times laboriously carved from a block of wood, sometimes modelled in stiff clay strengthened with grass and feathers. When in a good humor the tribal artist decorates it with circles of colored ochre so that, as it spins in the sunlight, it resembles a ball of rainbows. The bucks roll it from the top of a gently-sloping hill. Piccaninnies and older piccaninnies line the hillside. The disc quickly gathers momentum and runs the gauntlet of many spears. Loud is the shout and big the chest of the thrower whose weapon pierces the wheel.

12 August 1926
"Up Top":   The other day in Brisbane, to advertise a new picture, a down-and-out was hired to laugh all day through a megaphone while the auto drove through the streets. Ever and anon Queen-street would echo to a burst of mirth which made the populace gaze questioningly around. Sounds easy enough, laughing for a crust. But just try it for hours on end. And I suspect this performer was only laughing because his belly howled. The hideousness of it!

2 September 1926
"Gouger":   A prospector mate of mine in the Gulf Country had recently a narrow escape. He was stalking 'roos among clumps of buffalo grass. When he was almost within shot the animals became uneasy and he moved forward by crawling, taking advantage of all available cover. He was cautiously raising his rifle when a rustle in the grass behind made him wheel and fire simultaneously, the thought flashing through his mind that wild pig might be much better meat than kangaroo. As he jambed another cartridge home on the chance that the presumed pig might charge, a dozen painted myalls sprang up from the surrounding grass and, with a yell, disappeared. My mate ran to the grass knoll

they had left and examined his "pig". It was quite black in color, and one hand still clenched a long barbed spear.

28 October 1926

"Three E.'s": Here are some methods of opium-smuggling that have come under my personal notice. The traveller wearing the soldier's badge who left one of his legs somewhere in France finds the artificial limb an ideal receptacle for the contraband; he fact that he wears the thing so well that no one suspects his loss renders him free from any suspicion on the part of the Customs officers, to whom he is well known. I have seen a man cheerfully pay the demanded duty on 200 cigars, every one of which was merely an envelope for a tin cylinder containing something much more precious than tobacco. A passenger went ashore, unsuspected, with his camera and a dozen rolls of films, to secure some typical Australian snap-shots every one of those films, each bearing the maker's name on the colored wrapper, was a well-camouflaged tin of opium. I know of a gentleman wearing clerical attire who used what looked like a Bible and prayer-book for opium containers. A lady passenger came under my notice not so long ago. Several of her friends were waiting on the wharf to meet her when the vessel came in. One had an extra-nice bouquet of flowers for the traveller, and obtained permission to go on board with them. But what Customs officer would suspect a bunch of flowers that he had seen go on board? And so that game runs on.

25 November 1926

"Up Top": Scrubbers calved in tropical scrubs impenetrable to horsemen feed at the forest edges, can sniff a human a mile away and are gone with the wind. Their hides only are valuable. The hunter must know the scrubber's habits. He must understand their peculiarities of eyesight, of curiosity, of feeding hours and, above all, of smell. He must be a horseman unafraid of gullies, hills, forests and swamps – a genuine bushman and an unerring shot, built of grit and run on nerve juice. Otherwise he won't make salt, but may make a corpse. The scrubbers, when cornered or even merely taken by surprise at close quarters, have a habit of blindly rushing the first thing moving. If wounded, they invariably do the same. The experienced hand coolly dumdums the beast at close range.

This may sound easy, but a beserk bull takes stopping. Miss your beast and you yourself are missed. Run and you are lost. If others of the mob are handy, they will immediately wheel and make straight for the running thing. Though a sharp-pointed bullet may go straight through the brain the impetus of the

beast will nevertheless carry it many yards. Wound a beast, then follow him, but hasten slowly. If his blood drops upon the grass are frothy, then you will be able to locate the beef a few hours later. Or, if you find a blood patch you will know that he's been resting at the point of exhaustion. If he's only get a "blighty", don't waste time following him up. I've seen cattlemen gallop up to a steer and with one twist at the butt of his tail spin him to the ground. No man has ever done that to a Fingerpoint scrubber.

9 December 1926
"Up Top":   In parts of Cape York Peninsula death-adders are fairly numerous. They are found almost invariably in proximity to a wild-grape vine. To see the one usually means that the other is near at hand. The abos. swear by the root of this vine as a cure for adder-bite, and I know of no death amongst them when it has been applied. They crush the grape-vine root and chew it; also grip the bitten part and squeeze the juice into it. Possibly it may be an antidote for all snake bites. I do not know if it has been analysed.

30 December 1926
"Up Top":   'Ware riding or walking through scrub-country that has recently been burned. One danger lies in the butts of the trees. A horse stepping into a red-hot funnel of ashes is often crippled for life, and a man who does it has an agonizing time. Often thick roots smoulder for weeks underground. The burrows of animals are another trap.

6 January 1927
"Up Top":   The "Dooks" sheep with the gold ring embedded in its tongue (B. 21-10-26) has a parallel amongst Queensland cattle. A steer killed at the Biboora meatworks owned a tongue which resembled a football tightly belted in the middle. As a calf, when feeding, it had poked its tongue firmly through a loose hobble ring. In Syd Rammage's Townsville museum is, or was, a beast's leg-bone which had grown completely round a twist of fencing-wire. Apparently when the animal was a youngster the leg had been entangled in a wire fence, and in the breakaway a portion of the wire had remained twisted round the leg. The bone had grown inches high around the wire. A week ago we shot a wild boar of gigantic stature and violent temper. Embedded in his hide were three abo. spear-prongs, besides a spear-blade of chipped quartz and a hideous barb of chipped glass.

27 January 1927
"Up Top": "Old Harry" has lived the life of a hermit on Deliverance Island (Barrier Reef) since about '91. Occasionally a pearl-shell boat drops anchor and leaves the recluse tobacco, flour and tea, together with a memory of human companionship, to sweeten possibly a year's loneliness. Time flies in the tiny vegetable garden and among the fish-traps, and fairly buzzes during the turtle season. With luck, Harry catches a few tortoises and trades their shell to the occasional boats. About 1910 some soft-hearted T.I. people had him brought in, but the old fellow pined, and he implored to be allowed to go back, so they returned him to his island home. About 1921 Dick Roach, on his way from New Guinea, called in to see if the hermit was still alive. He was, and was taking a serious interest in the affairs of the world, his first remark being, "I heard there's a war on. Is it over yet?" Last year Frank Hurley dropped in on the old chap, and found him carrying a bingey like a football, due to many years' turtle-eating.

17 February 1927
"Gouger": Two white stowaways in a steamer bound north from Thursday Island had a short but hectic time aboard. They arranged with the Chow bos'n to hide and feed them for £4, that being their entire capital. The boat left at night, and they were easily smuggled into the forepeak, in a space in which they could not comfortably turn round. When well under way, the bos'n and his satellites crept down and demanded £10. It was not forthcoming, and the Chows promised unmentionable things to the "white mongrels." Matters looking nasty in the darkness, the stowaways made a rush. The Chows scattered like squealing rats. Then they put the show away. A white officer peered at the two cornered strays. Without a word the forepeak was battened up, and the stowaways had an inkling of what the Black Hole of Calcutta was like. The ship hove-to, and wirelessed for a launch from the island. Meantime the yellow crew had gathered around the forepeak and poured out on the stowaways their filthiest language. The whites at last retaliated, and the Chows emptied foul water and refuse upon them. Two very thankful lads were finally handed over to the police. The adventurers had a hazy notion of joining the Chinese Civil Service (whatever that may be), or of becoming officers in the disturbance over there. But they tell me they were so startled by their first-hand experience of yellow hatred for the white that they never want to meet the Chinaman in a place where he is the boss.

3 March 1927
"Up Top":   Three "scrubber" heifers grazed in an open pocket in a Cape York forest. From deep within the jungle floated the bellowing inquiry of a bull. A short silence, then in the opposite distance a prolonged bellow. The heifers raised their heads, standing motionless. A deep-throated roar boomed across the jungle. The challenge had been accepted.
The bellowing, followed by intervals of silence, came gradually nearer. A steady trampling of undergrowth heralded the approach of a thick-set red beast with wicked eyes wrinkled up. Vines swished noisily in the opposite direction, and from the scrub a black beast thrust out. He stretched his shaggy neck, and the hills reverberated to his bellow of defiance and challenge.
Slowly the bulls advanced towards one another, pawing the earth. Fifty yards apart they halted within lowered heads, then advanced at a swinging walk. Ten yards apart each rumbled deep down in his throat, then with toss of horns and tail they bounded forward. The impact was not a crash, but rather, a dull grinding. They thudded, forehead to forehead, horns to horns, their necks deep wrinkled under the tremendous strain. Thus they pushed, silently but for the grinding of horns and the gurgle of foam as their sobbing breaths wheezed in.
Each strove to force his antagonist down. For what must have been close on half an hour they strained thus, the heifers looking on, little concerned. The black bull gave first, his horns ground the gravel as the strove to hold the mighty strength against him. Frothy blood dripped down their muzzles, for the crunch of the horn-butts had ground away the forehead hide. Then for a hundred yards the black bull was pressed back. Behind him was a thread-like depression in the ground. On the brink of it his hooves slipped momentarily only, but the quiver was conveyed to the tautened neck. Instantly the red bull's horns flashed unlocked, and as the massive neck jerked sideways, then forwards, a shuddering bellow echoed through the trees, and his horns slipped in deep behind the black bull's shoulder. Then the red bull put all his weight into a goring, crushing pressure, utterly irresistible, and the black beast's haunches sank to the ground.

10 March 1927
"Sea Nomad":   The spectators in the Thursday Island picture-show present a study in color, from pure white through all its stages to the blackest ebony. And the darker shades predominate by ten to one. At present it is the Jap season, this being laying-up time in the shelling fleets. Cowboy pictures, with plenty of shooting, are favourite films, but the crowning joy is the sheik flick, in which

the dusky nomads give the whites the devil of a towelling. In a picture recently shown, as the whites were being slaughtered the applause became enthusiastic, and when the sheik carried off the struggling heroine, to be later on manhandled by dusky subordinates in the slave-market, the acclaim hit the skies. One particular scene, where a nigger concealed behind a curtain successfully shot a white man in the back, was received with frantic plaudits. In the final tableau, where love, beauty and white blood triumphed, the colored portion of the audience didn't appear to be interested. It shows the way the wind is blowing. The white nations are thoughtlessly inviting trouble by showing this class of picture – American of course, to colored audiences.

10 March 1927

"Up Top":   Once a flock of tiny sea-snipe guided me to a quick £50 on a stretch of the west coast of Cape York Peninsula. It was a dark night during the turtle season. On bare feet I patrolled the beach, listening for the gasping hiss of turtle when they rise upon the surface of the water, and for their subsequent energetic scratching on the sand. Suddenly a bevy of unseen snipe twittered antagonistically. I hurried to the sound, and there saw Mrs. Turtle busily digging her nest. I allowed her to deposit her eggs before turning her on her back, for on the performance of that duly depended at least 100 future little turtles. Along the beach the snipe twittered again. I marathoned into the darkness, and secured another prize. Altogether, the night brought me 14 first-class shells.

10 March 1927

"Sea Nomad":   Pearl trafficking is occasionally as thrilling as a gamble in opals, a pearl may be a good one, but blemished by a tiny spot. Perhaps it is worth £200 as it is. But its brilliant lustre suggests a gem beneath the enveloping layer if so, the pearl may be worth thousands. On the other hand the enclosed pearl may be a dud. Shall the owner remove the layer thus getting rid of the detrimental spot, and risk exposing a gem or a dud? A Jap diver recently brought to Thursday Island an exceptionally fine blister. He hawked it round town at £35, without success. It had a blackish scum on it, and the dissatisfied Jap decided to take a risk. He did so, and out rolled a pearl for which he is now asking £1300. A while back some local youngsters played with an apparently worthless blister. When shaking it their dad thought he heard something inside. He broke the blister and secured a pearl worth £400.

31 March 1927
"Sea Nomad":   Around the shore of Thursday Island (Q.) there are sometimes caught, especially off the hospital, a species of snapper which, after lying for 20 minutes in the dinghy pervades the atmosphere with a strong odor of iodoform. The hospital is built on the sea beach, and a far-fetched theory is that the fish feed on the drainage from it. The generally accepted explanation is that the fish live largely on a seaweed heavily impregnated with iodoform, and that on contact with the air a chemical reaction take place within the fish's internal organs, and liberates the iodoform. The belly of the sea chemist is invariably stained yellow. The same fish have been caught in the surrounding islands, but their capture has not been followed by the iodoform smell. They make capital eating.

14 April 1927
"Sea Nomad":   An experienced recruiter was recently nonplussed. Eleven "boys" had volunteered for service and sat down to the customary gorge. "I can't quite make it out," mused the recruiter. "Eleven boys came aboard and eleven are here, but one, a herring-gutted specimen is missing, and a pot-bellied pig has taken his place." It turned out that the herring and the pig were the Jekyll and Hyde of the same boy. The enormous meal of rice consumed by the herring had so altered his appearance as to make him unrecognizable. The native's power of extending his stomach is phenomenal. The pot-bellied youngsters train themselves on bananas. After hard times especially, the quantity of food a native can and does consume is unbelievable. Billy Turnbull, of Hicks Island, played the double cross on this fact when a swarm of drought-stricken abos. canoed across to him from the mainland cadging for tucker. He gave them a daily ration of rice uncooked, and advised them to eat it so, and when again hungry, to take a good drink of water. Black Brother complied, and when hunger pecked again the water swelled the rice and gave him the comfortably-full sensation he loves. The abos. put it down to the white man's magic, but it carried them through till the drought broke.

21 April 1927
"Up Top":   Of all kind of ill-temper, is there any more insane than that which leads a man to wreak his wrath on an inanimate object? I've seen a man stub his toe on the doorstep, then turn around and kick the obstruction until he howled with pain. Another temporary idiot, who had clumsily stumbled over my billycan, booted the dashed thing down the paddock until it was only

a shapeless mass of tin. A cobber of mine flew off the handle because he had leaned his axe against the wall and the blamed thing slid down. He bashed the offending implement against the wall until he'd smashed both. The same chap tripped over a broom. He promptly snapped it into matchwood and then chased an interfering dog with a crowbar. And I could tell of a hundred other similar instances. But did ever anyone see a woman do anything so silly, though woman is ordinarily the far more emotional sex?

12 May 1927
"Sea Nomad": West of Thursday Island lies treacherous Glamis Castle rock. A steamer of that name hit it in 1881. The vessel was of course named after the Duchess of York's home-place.

12 May 1927
"Sea Nomad": Recent mention of the Quetta recalls that a diver who later wandered over her declared that the engine-room dial still showed "Full Speed." Quite likely as she went down in three minutes. The pilot, who was saved, said he felt as though he was standing in a box which sank beneath his feet – a pinnacle of rock had ripped her open. The wreck was bought some time after and divers went down to secure the considerable amount of sovereigns in her safe; but when they got there the cupboard was bare – rather naturally so, human nature being what it is and the coral seas alive with pearling boats.

26 May 1927
"Up Top": Give plants their head and they become wild in a very short time. If edible, they lose their food-giving properties and run to leaves and stalks, or, if flower plants, the blooms quickly lose their size and beauty. In the early days the miners on the tropical Queensland fields planted orange, lemon, mandarin, banana and mango trees, also pineapples and maniocs, sweet potatoes and other vegetables. Most of the old fields are now abandoned. The banana-trees have gone completely wild, being now only shrubs with tiny fruit, all seeds. Many lemon-trees survive and still bear small, crude products. The orange-trees have died and no longer bear sweet fruit. On many old fields an odd mandarin-tree is still to be found, but its fruit is nearly always wooden. The mangoes have thriven best, but not so well as when near civilization. Pineapples are scattered in many places; the plants are smallish with very dwarfed, intensely red and sweet fruit. Odd maniocs have grown in clumps the size of saplings. Nearly all the "sweet-

buks" have disappeared, though I have occasionally met them grown into a sort of yam. All other vegetables have vanished, as also most of the flowers. Some of the latter, however, have adapted themselves to environment and thrive, though in color and form quite different from what they were 20 years ago.

26 May 1927
"Sea Nomad":   Many people dare not ascend to a great height because of the overmastering urge to jump off that they know will come upon them. I once had to fight the same impulse in different but perhaps parallel conditions. A line of men, on hands and knees, were chipping the rust-eaten deck of a dismantled gunboat in a northern port through which the tides rush at the rate of six miles an hour. The day was overcast and squally, with a strong sou'-east breeze. The gunboat was pitching heavily, the choppy waves occasionally spraying the deck. There was no railing, and the deck where we worked was barely two feet above water. My right eye being nearest the water was continually subconscious of the huge torrents capped with frothy foam and hissing bubbles that went whirling past. Again and again I found myself working towards the extreme edge of the unguarded deck, and checked myself with a shudder. Had a man fallen over he would have been gone like a chip, and yet the fascination persisted. At knock-off time one of the men confided to me that he had put in a hell of a day: it took all his will power a dozen times to hold him from lurching head first into the racing water.

26 May 1927
"Atherton":   Civilisation is fast robbing the native of his skill and knowledge of the wild. In all except the few tribes as yet untouched by the white man the young bucks, instead of becoming warriors, go working on the northern fishing-fleets and cattle-stations. They eat the white man's tucker, wear his clothes and assimilate a distorted conception of his habits and his commoner thought. There is no longer need of unceasing training in the habits of animals, birds, reptiles and fishes, the phases of the seasons and the laws governing edible plant growth. At least once a year the abo. returns to the tribe, but if the season is dry, and game consequently scarce, he can go back to the white man for easily-earned food. The younger generation has already lost a great stock of nature lore that took its forefathers centuries of striving and hunger to accumulate. Many of the young fellows cannot even spear a wallaby. And the fathers of the tribes, seeing their people dissolving into nothingness, and despairing of keeping their heritage intact, are carrying the deeper tribal secrets with then to the grave.

2 June 1927
"Sea Nomad":   Unlucky stones? Years ago, when the Yongala went down off the east coast of York Peninsula, Hughie Giblett was cutting sandalwood near Lloyd's Bay. The niggers brought him a wicker-work basket with some clothes in it, picked up on the beach. There was a shirt with a set of sleeve-links and studs of rolled gold, inset with a gem supposed to bring ill-luck. Later Giblett spent a holiday in Thursday Island and offered the trinkets to Serenalis, the jeweller. The latter was superstitious and at first refused to deal, but finally he bought the links and put them in his window on the off-chance of a buyer. Fate sent him an engineer from the Koombana. She sailed and was never heard of again, going down in a cyclone off the Westralian coast as suddenly as the Yongala had done.

9 June 1927
"Up Top":   While the Bishop of Carpentaria was on a trip to the new mission-station at Lloyd's Bay, a "boy" who had been sent out to work on a cattle station returned. "Hullo Billy," said the missionary. "Why have you come back?" "Oh" the abo. explained, "boss he growl all a time, he tellem me go to Hell outa this. So I come back longa mission".

9 June 1927
"Up Top":   A prick from a coral splinter is sometimes dangerous. I've known even niggers to get dreadful feet from its poison when working amongst the Barrier reefs. Some say that virus arises only when the coral is dead and mangrove mud gets into the wound. It was from such poisoning that one of the most loved men on Thursday Island met his death years ago – and he a doctor, too. He suffered for nearly a fortnight, in the meantime giving directions as to the treatment of the wound. While lancing it the attendant doctor pricked his finger. The matron immediately snatched his hand and sucked the wound. Hope was built on a serum which was wired for but never came to hand.

16 June 1927
"Atherton":   The shell-fishers of Torres Strait experienced a gusty beginning this season, half the fleets having been forced back to T.I. and other safe anchorages for shelter. From New Guinea, throughout the Strait, across to the Barrier and down the east coast as far as Cooktown the sea was "dirty". The water was impregnated with extremely fine silt. This prevented the divers from seeing shell and bêche-de-mer on the ocean floor. During eight months of the year the sea

is clear as crystal, except for occasional heavy storms. The treacherous nor'-west season of about three months is always laying-up time for the fleets, the water being "dirty" for practically the whole period. The flooded rivers of the mainland and New Guinea then wash their detritus into the ocean, the torrential rains eat a little more out of each of the thousands of islands, the sand-and mud-banks of the sea are stirred up by the storms, and the whole is scattered as sediment over a thousand miles of ocean by the tide. Shellers blame the recent prolonged vagary of the sea to some submarine upheaval. Divers operating around New guinea describe the water on the sea floor as being like a liquid mass of rust.

16 June 1927

"Up North": What about sponge-growing as a side-line to the shell and bêche-de-mer industries? Saville Kent says the sponges are already there and any variety can be propagated. In the West Indies where sponges grow readily, a valuable trade was built up by using imported cuttings. Our Barrier Reef is a vast marine mine full of riches. As yet we have barely begun to scratch the surface.

23 June 1927

"Sea Nomad": Bramble Cay upon which old Tasman ran aground in Torres Strait, has proved a veritable graveyard for ships. The names of some of them will never be known; all that is left are the coral-encrusted ribs occasionally found by the native divers. Recently a 45ft. concrete beacon-tower has been built upon the Cay, which should make navigation in these seas less perilous. But it will still be dangerous enough. Skippers making towards Darnley Island are apt to sheer off towards the east coast of Stephens Island and try for a passage between it and Nepean Island. Not long ago a big boat ran in on the wrong side, causing much excitement on shore. She continued on a course which meant inevitable disaster. She must have dropped the mud-hook when she found reefs everywhere; anyway, next morning she jazzed back past the island and picked up her right tracks. Later on a steamer bound south came bowling along, blissfully unaware that she, too, was heading straight for perdition. A warning flag was run up at Darnley Island just in time to enable her to side-track with swiftness and precision. Probably the only aggrieved people were the Stephen Islanders, who look on this sort of thing as an interference with their vested rights. In the old days they were as confirmed wreckers as the Cornishmen of a few centuries ago, and to put a ship on the right course seems to them like the refusal of a gift from the gods.

23 June 1927

"Up Top": Queer are the ways of N.Q.abos with snakes. Riding across country I spotted an ugly black head projected from a hole. "You killem snake Charlie?" I inquired. "More better no boss", Charlie said . "We gottem plenty tucker longa saddlebags. S'posem someday I walkabout longa this country hungry, me catchem this fella then!" On a scrubby bank of the Pascoe the niggers found a large but thin carpet snake. "Bye-em-bye he grow fat fella", they explained, "him fella good Kai Kai that time." Next day they treed a wriggler in size almost a python, his bulging coils around the great fig-tree branch merging their color into that of its bark. That snake had luscious rolls of fat lining, a rather uncommon occurrence with snakes. Squatting with a juicy blubber of fat in one fist and a hunk of roast snake in the other, the niggers made a picture of physical enjoyment.

30 June 1927

"Sea Nomad": Ships invariably carry stowaways. Snakes, lizards, mice, rats, centipedes, beetles and humans are the main varieties. The life found down the dark hold of a big ship is surprising. Boats seeking the treasures of the Indies, the Straits, Java and the tropic isles are favored havens of these voyagers. They come aboard mostly in crate and bale cargoes, many of them having already travelled over mountain, jungle and swamp. I remember the consternation caused down the hold of a South American tramp when a monkey leapt from the darkness and clung around the neck of the bos'n. The man screamed like a maniac and only the mate's tripping foot prevented him from leaping overboard. But it is generally smaller fry that are thus shanghaied. Aboard one of the big oil-tankers a lizard recently selected his quarters in the chart-room. He ventures into the light only occasionally, but is heard every night chasing cockroaches. The stowaways quickly make themselves at home in their new environment, where they live under ideal conditions of darkness and warmth and fascinating smells. For tucker they have the cargo and themselves.

7 July 1927

"Up Top": When Lord Apsley was on his tour through wild Australia he pulled into Berundie (N.Q.) for a breather. Larrikin, a young gin, was given the job of cleaning his tan boots and leggings. She had never seen tan boots before but was civilised enough to know that boots were cleaned with blacking. The startled owner complained next morning that his boots had changed color. "What did you do him boots that color for, Larrikin?" asked her distressed

mistress. "Yesterday him fella boots altogether same half-caste" explained Larrikin. "Him proper fella blackfella boot now".

14 June 1927

"Sea Nomad": Has any wanderer dropped across the Goldie Reefs? They are charted as just off the Portlocks on the Eastern Fields, roughly 120 miles west of Port Moresby, but I've never met a sailorman who's seen them, though many luggers have searched for them as a likely fishing ground for trochus. Murray Island is about 90 miles west; the Eastern Fields themselves lie roughly between the New Guinea coast and the mainland. All the waters in between have been cruised over for years by the shelling fleets. Yet I've never heard of the Goldie Reefs having actually been located.

21 July 1927

"Gouger": Traffic in human skulls (B 14/7/27) has gone on for centuries throughout the Torres Strait islands, right to New Guinea, though in the Torres Strait groups the interfering missionary has almost effected its disappearance. In the earlier pearling days the trade boomed, the mainland abo. supplying most of the raw material for the head-hunters from overseas. The white man's skull realised quite a fancy price because of its scarcity, which added to the tribulations of the shipwrecked mariners in these cruel coral seas. With the last of the sou'-east trade winds each year the great canoes travelled wonderful distances to dispose of the yearly catch, returning at the beginning of the nor'-west monsoons loaded with weapons, vegetables, shell money, pigs and new canoes, all grist in exchange for skulls. Even distant New Guinea tribes were traded with, European skulls especially being bartered from tribe to tribe until they finally disappeared in the gloomy mountains of the dread interior. Occasionally the acquisitive traders lost their own skulls in the business, but that was all in the game .

28 July 1927

"Up Top": The pig has an acute sense of smell and a dog-like capacity for using it. Overland and telegraph linesmen at their camp in the MacDonnell Ranges reared a number of piglets which became an encumbrance on account of the scarcity of tucker for them. The men took them a few miles into the bush and let them loose on a patch of country containing plenty of wild feed. Two days later, while at dinner, they heard a delighted squealing and saw a line of pigs hurrying

down the bridle track. They took the same pigs, trussed on packsaddles, still further into the bush and left them. In a few days the unwanted guests were back in camp, having smelt their way home along the packhorse trail. Yet again they were taken miles away, this time into a thick scrub through which ran a broad creek. They were carried a considerable distance down the bed of the stream before being let go and given a "hurry-up" scatter on the opposite bank. A week later two reported to camp, the water had beaten the others.

28 July 1927

"Sea Nomad": The gardens of the sea flaunt their nettles as well as their weirdly - beautiful flowers. A pest detested by the bêche-de-mer skin-divers is the porcupine nettle, found principally along the bottom of Queensland's N.E. coast sea. It grows in somewhat the shape of a porcupine and with prickles similar to its quills. The prickles are in color either black or black with a grey tip. A touch from them means a severe sting, followed by pain such as that inflicted by the giant nettle of the scrubs. Another pest is a greyish seaweed much resembling maidenhair fern. Its dainty leaves are armed with minute spikes which after stinging a man, can be seen through a magnifying-glass adhering to his body. Occasionally the cable connecting Thursday Island with Cape York has to be lifted for repairs and experience has taught the cable-men to be wary of all suspicious-looking seaweed twining around the news-transmitter.

4 August 1927

"Sea Nomad": The windows of the big lighthouses dotting the Queensland coast are regularly and scrupulously cleaned. If that were not done they would be blurred within a week by a film of fine dust from the contact of countless moths' wings. The automatic lights which flash at regular intervals are not so affected because the periodic spaces of darkness destroy the attractive effect a steady light has for insects and night birds. If the windows of a stationary light were left uncleaned, the continued accumulation of moth-dust would effectually dim the light. In another way, though fortunately it rarely occurs, the tiny moth is responsible for putting out completely the automatic light. Though the sensitive lighting mechanism is guarded by an ingenious contrivance, the moth occasionally gets inside and flutters out the minute pilot light, thus causing the gas-bursts to ignite and flash. In this way the automatic light on Clarke Island, where the Tasman recently grounded, went out. Some time back the same kind of insect stopped the light on Hammond Rock near Thusday Island. The going out of

the light on Clarke Island was reported on several occasions, and the lighthouse people rushed up a vessel, only to find that it had been sent on a wild-goose chase. On the third reporting they waited for confirmation – and the Tasman confirmed.

18 August 1927
"Sea Nomad": A wonderful sight in Torres Strait and thereabouts are the massed clouds of dewa, seabirds the size of pigeons and colored black with white top-knots. Recently I spied (as I thought) an island where no land should be, and on levelling my glasses distinguished what appeared to be the branches of many trees. The "boy" crew exclaimed "Dewa!" but not till sundown was I fully convinced that I had not discerned a new island . Then it was transmuted into heavy clouds visible till they melted into the dark, as they moved towards Halfway Island. Though I have been long at sea, the illusion was so complete that I have since wondered whether some of the mystery islands charted and never found again were not in reality clouds of these birds, hovering in the distance. On their favourite roosting islands the tree branches are weighed down by them, so numerous are they. They lay eggs spotted dark-green and the size of hens'. Sacks are filled with the eggs as fast as men can pick them up. When tired the birds float in great numbers on the water. The sunlight has a most peculiar effect on them when flying. They often manoeuvre in an endless line, then for some reason wheel and form two lines which pass one another. One line will appear snow-white, the other jet-black.

18 August 1927
"Sea Nomad": A wonderful thing is the egg of the bailor shell-fish. I never knew that shellfish were oviferous until I saw an egg attached to this big fellow. It resembled a mass of jelly in weight from one to two pounds and in form like a pine cone. It was perforated by many tiny holes in almost everyone of which was a minute black speck of matter. The egg eventually becomes detached and floats to ground on a reef suitable for its development. Each black speck is an embryo shell, and the islanders explained to me that as the egg matures the holes expand and a little shell drops out from each. I estimated that there were hundreds of such shells in this mass of jelly.

18 August 1927

"Sea Nomad": York Island is a strip of sand resting upon a huge coral reef. On it grow many cocoanut-trees, and it holds a grass-grown village of sturdy natives. It also harbors centipedes of large size and of great variety in color. A particularly nasty sort clings to the grass-blades by night and hitches to the natives' legs as they brush by. Its bite is exceedingly painful. An old lady there is known as the "centipede woman". She pins down a big crawler with a stick and (using her finger-nails, apparently) nicks something from its jaws, or possibly touches it with some stupefying juice. Then she lets the loathsome thing crawl all over her body, but never receives a bite. On a speck of pure sand just off Cocoanut Island, a swarm of centipedes will come from apparently nowhere to eat the crumbs from your meal. How they get into such inaccessible spots, far out to sea, is a mystery. The only place I have seen them in equal numbers is at Rum Creek in the Territory. One night after a thunderstorm they swarmed over the verandah of our house and in the moonlight we killed 30 within 10 minutes. Then they disappeared as suddenly as they had come.

25 August 1927

"Sea Nomad": In the old days pearl thieves had to be more expert in the business of larceny than even gold-pilferers. The shell was opened on deck before all eyes, and a sleight-of-hand had to be almost perfect before it could deceive the practiced watchers. On Aru Island, where pearl finds were extraordinarily plentiful, an occasional diver did the thieving under water. With wonderful quickness of hand and fingers he wrenched open the shell and felt for the pearl. If there, he slipped it into his mouth and threw the discard behind. Coming to the surface, he kept the treasure under his tongue, and if suspicious of being thoroughly searched swallowed it. Several world-famous pearls have been treated in this way. The suit diver used to slip the stolen treasure into the sleeve of his diving-dress or into the stocking. When concealed in the sleeve of the dress the tender above had necessarily to be in the know, otherwise the pearl would fall on the deck. Some divers on coming to the surface made the bottom of the lugger their hiding-place when apprehensive that the vessel and the crew would be searched on reaching port. Little bags containing pearls were sometimes attached to the keel of the boat. Pearl-thieving by opening the shell under water was practised only in localities where the percentage of pearl-bearing shell ran high. In almost all the Torres Strait waters where 200 shells might be opened without finding one pearl, it would be folly to try that form of pilfering.

1 September 1927

"SEA NOMAD":   Thursday Island is the place for electric torches. Only seven of the white inhabitants are without them; the majority sport two or three. The unlighted town and the dark hill paths by night, after a picture-show, seem to be dotted with giant fire-flies. Islanders and New Guinea boys employed on the shelling fleet greatly covet these torches and spend their salt-encrusted wealth in taking a flashing treasure home to their brethren; at many a village dance the star performer is now outlined by an electric flashlight, instead of by the time-honored pandanus torch. When the batteries run out loud is the moaning in the villages. One grizzled old cannibal complained to me: "This feller he no like sun, he go out altogether, Me fill imm longa kerosene, him no light. Dam sulky feller this one."

8 September 1927

"UP TOP":   That new curse the Singapore ant, about the size of a grain of sand, can raise a lump as big as a marble. These pests have a liking for the armpits and more tender portions of the body. From Port Darwin as far down as Pine Creek along the railway line they are to be found, having, it is supposed, been introduced by Asiatic laborers. A lad at the creek left his hat atop of the mosquito net overnight. Next morning he jambed it on his head and had to bolt to the shower to get rid of undesirable immigrants. When he came out his forehead was swollen to an enormous size and his face was red as a cooked lobster. The pests appear in most unexpected places without apparent cause and their minute size makes them difficult to avoid.

8 September 1927

"SEA NOMAD":   Natives of Torres Strait have a peculiar idea of "sympathetic pain". Thus, if the wife is soon to greet the stork and hubby gets a tummy-ache or toothache, he blows his chest out and reckons he is relieving his mate of her birth-pains. On the child's arrival the husband frequently dives into the sea, and sometimes stays in the water for hours, believing that the cooler he makes his body the cooler his wife becomes. I don't know how it would fare in the event of twins. Probably the husband would never know of the catastrophe, as it is considered a great disgrace among island women to bear two at birth. One is inevitably strangled, and it is always the girl if there is one of each.

22 September 1927
"Up Top": One of the Gulf island mission cutters brought to T.I. a lady teacher much troubled about cockroaches. She had left her teeth the night before on the cabin cupboard, and the 'roaches had wired into the vulcanite with distressing results. A dental misfortune upset also a teacher from Moa Island. She quitted St. Paul's with the natives' curiosity unsatisfied as to whether she was able to remove her teeth "alla same teacher before." The cutter Banzai misbehaved, and the lady was dreadfully sick on deck. She looked up in agony of mind to see a grinning "boy" holding out to her a set of grinders. I suppose both girls are now jazzing down south, where niggers, molars, sea-sickness and cockroaches trouble them not.

27 September 1927
"Sea Nomad": There must be huge profits in opium smuggling. A friend of mine a ship's officer, had an elaborate proposal put to him while he was staying a couple of days at a Hong Kong hotel. The "boy"-in-waiting was to introduce a suitcase into his room. A 'rickshaw would take the officer and suitcase (the boy would see to that) to the waterfront, where a sampan would bear them to the steamer. Arrived on board the officer was to hail the quartermaster: "Mr. Hardtack, please put my suitcase into my cabin. I'm spending the night ashore." He was to make sure that the suitcase went straight to the cabin; then he was to go to another part of the ship for 10 minutes . When he returned and opened the suitcase he would find 200 notes where a few minutes before were 200 tins of opium. Before declining without thanks he was told that European and Chinese spies were making the turning of a dishonest penny very risky for the opium gentry, and that it required deep thought to circumvent them. The suitcase of a responsible officer, it was explained, was unlikely to be suspected, especially when he was returning almost immediately to spend the night ashore.

29 September 1927
"Up Top: While walking through the gloom of the tropical scrubs one sees flower-petals upon the countless roots, and yet no sign of the flower that shed them. In the Daintree Ranges (N.Q.) some flowers grow far up amongst the impenetrable foliage. That is the place where the only chance of sunlight is found, so nature has evolved strange beauties that make a home upon the tops of trees. Again, there are vines and growths flowering up the tree trunks midway between earth and the trees' branches, seeking neither moist earth nor light, but only the free space between. It is rare indeed to find a flower growing upon the earth, for

in the dense jungle the soil is nowhere visible. It is covered by an inextricably entangled mat of roots and rotted vegetation upon which no unbroken ray of sunlight shines. Down some of the great gorges of the Daintree Valley I have seen an unusual sort of creeper carrying grape-like clusters of pure white flowers, with petals bearing the suggestion of having been moulded in wax. These flowers seem different from their brethren of the sun. Gazing at a cluster clinging far down the walls of a precipice, one gets an impression of utter stillness and ghostliness.

6 October 1927

"SEA NOMAD":   Rough weather on portions of the Barrier has been stirring up the sea-snakes. For some unknown reason they come up only on certain areas of the ocean, perhaps above a favourite feeding-ground whose weedy depths have been obscured by disturbed silt. In some parts the snakes can be counted from the masthead by the score. Their presence is, as a rule, a good indication of shell bottom, since their food lies upon these areas of ground where pearl shell generally thrives. Many of the Torres Islanders will not kill a sea-snake because it is one of their chief Totems. I've seen a wriggler hooked on the towline, and the boys go to much trouble to unhook the brute without hurting it – in a rough sea, too.

20 October 1927

"SEA NOMAD":   The Devil was recently let loose on Yam Island. Balsa and Miami were going to be married and Balsa had brought from Thursday Island a young bull calf. As the cutter crew slung the dinghy overboard and manhandled the calf into it, all the people flocked to the beach. They had never seen a "bull-cow" before. In his anxiety to reach dry land, the calf upset the dinghy and, with a bawl that shook the palm tops, made straight for the crowd. A particularly red lava-lava on a brown-limbed girl was his special objective. She leapt for a palm-tree, and, paralysed with fear, hung there a second until the calf's slobbering nose nuzzled her. With an awful cry she fairly flew up the tree. The calf then turned his attention to the astonished crowd. With tail and hooves in the air he passed strong men shinning up cocoanut-palms, confining his attentions to the women and children who made frantically for the nearest grass-thatched house. Bawling, he mixed himself into the jumble, and presently half the side of the house came down, pierced through with a score of kicking legs. Then the calf cleaned up the village of its terrified fowls, bucks in the palm-tops slinging cocoanuts at him as he cavorted underneath. The only valiant man in the village was the sorcerer who had to put up a show for his profession. The calf lowered his head for the

sorcerer's posterior but missed; he collected a polthogue on the side of the ear from a stone club in return. Bellowing in disapproval of this unsportsmanlike conduct, he charged some girls hiding in a banana garden. Finally the sorcerer, with dire threats, gathered the cutter's crew and all the village warriors about him and rushed the fearsome beast.

3 November 1927

"Sea Nomad": Quarantine and other regulations in northern waters sometimes carry a little tragedy with them. A lugger trading between Thursday Island and New Guinea recently anchored off Yam Island. Most of the crew were Yam Island boys who hadn't seen home for 12 months; and though their mothers, fathers and sweet-hearts shouted to them from the beach, the regulations would not allow them to land. A lugger enroute to Thursday Island, passed Darnley Island. One of her crew lay dying. He was a Darnley Island man and his little daughter waved from a grassy knoll to her father's ship. It was his return voyage, but first of all he had to be signed off at T.I. and then shipped back to his village. They buried him, however, on a sandbank before "Thirsty" could be reached.

3 November 1927

"Up Top": Just before the Nor'-west season Beidam, the shark, tilts his starry nose towards the sea. This is the signal to Torres Strait islanders that the turtles are mating. In the old days the Zogo-man anointed the Zogo-stone with human oil and supplicated the elements to bring good weather and turtle in plenty. He called upon the spirit an energy to imbue the eyes and arms of the harpooners with quickness, accuracy and strength. The canoes were garlanded with crotons and made flash with island flowers, a big bamboo filled with water was taken aboard, and the first cruise of the season commenced. By some crooning reef near whose grass-grown bottom the turtle fed, the canoes would halt and the witch-doctor would make charm again to attract the turtle from the sea. To the four winds he scattered gifts of bananas and yams for the good spirit which fills the bellies of men, and raised his arms and voice to attract the spirit from the skies. The feast commenced with the capturing of the first green-backed turtle. If the first catch happened to be a tortoise its mottled pleats were fashioned into lovely ornaments for girls and men, the meat being cast away.

10 November 1927
"Sea Nomad":   A most feared magic among the Torres Islanders is "Kamer". It has the appearance of a red powder, and is apparently the decayed remains of fungus that grows in driftwood from New Guinea. The stuff is carefully scraped by an arrow point into a bamboo stem, the sorcerer being masked with a banana-leaf so that he may not inhale any of the poison. To make it still more virulent, decomposed matter of red coral is mixed with it; the scraped kernel of a rotten goa-nut is added. The spiky rib of a cocoanut leaf is placed in the mixture and then poked into bananas or yams, which tainted food is presented to the unconscious victim. He does not die immediately, but a nasty disease burns out his throat. If a girl is jealous of a rival she touches this other huzzy's nostrils with the tip of a frigate bird's feather, previously dipped in kamer, when she sleeps. The nose is the first to go, then the throat, then the wench herself.

24 November 1927
"Sea Nomad":   The Manua recently came into Thursday Island with a catch of 11 tons of trochus-shell, fished in seven weeks. It realised £70 per ton – not a bad return for an island vessel, captained and manned by islanders, but exceptional, of course. Some of the "boys," by the way, have learned too much. On the strength of what certain grinning savages represented as a sample bag full of first-class shell, a Chinese buyer bought their whole catch. When he found that the other bags were filled with second- and third-class stuff, his wails nearly blew the guns off the fort on the hill.

1 December 1927
"Sea Nomad":   There exists keen rivalry among all the Torres Strait island boys in the handling of their up-to-date shelling fleet. The western islanders lose no chance of depreciating their cousins of the eastern group; Badu and Sibi boys are especially vituperative. But a long drawn-out spell of bad weather has hit the western islands in the eye and the average of the shell recovered is evening up. The islanders fish and man their own boats, cutters and luggers, and are very keen as to speed, seaworthiness and carrying capacity. They are splendid sailors, and know their intricately – reefed island waters in and out. Often they sail at night, navigating their boats by the stars and keep an accurate course over the most dangerous sea in the world. The islanders would be insulted if you did not class them as Australians. They dislike the Japs. Last season they put £22,000 into their savings account; this money won by their own shelling-boats in their

own waters, is helping trade in and around Thursday Islands. The £20,000 won by the Japs last year went straight to Nippon, hardly the price of a packet of fags having been spent in an Australian port.

8 December 1927
"Sea Nomad":   Torres Islanders place an incalculable value on their Totems, sacred masks and sacred drums. They will occasionally lend one, but never give or sell it. A lady teacher on one of the islands having for some years endeavoured vainly to buy a sacred drum, was readily granted the loan of it to show some visiting friends. Months afterwards the time for the ceremony in which the drum was used came round. They natives asked for their drum to be returned, then demanded it. It had, they were informed, gone to England with the visitors. This plunged the islands affected by the drum cult into such a fever of unrest that the authorities traced the instrument and had it restored. In New Guinea I have known a man lose his life through stealing a huge sacred mask which previously he had offered to buy at a price that meant wealth to every soul in the village. These "sacred" things represent to the islanders what our hope of a future life means to us. The drums and sacred masks do not really belong to the natives; they belong to supernatural deities who watch over the tribes and guard them from sickness and evil influences.

8 December 1927
"Sea Nomad":   The Torres Islanders credit furred, feathered and finny things with conforming to communal and domestic laws similar to their own. In their belief sharks, dugong and the like have their boss fishes, who make laws relative to hunting rights and so forth; while animals and birds have their council grounds, where laws are made, disputes settled and hunting areas prescribed. If a man disturbs these meeting places he is liable to incur a penalty. I once saw a burning-off-fire get out of the natives' control. To their consternation, the flames licked up the grass upon a little rocky knoll, and singed rats scurried in all directions. That mound was the rats' Zogo-ground, and as human being had violated it the rats would play havoc among their growing crops by way of revenge. As it happened, the rats did.

15 December 1927
"Gouger":   Queensland's biggest submarine cable job has been completed, in spite of continuous south-east blows. The cable connects the overland telegraph-

line at Cape York and runs to Horn, Thursday, Hammond and Goode islands; part of it has been down for 30 years. Vic. Doig, a young Townsvillain, did the job; the craft employed were a launch and a surf-boat.

22 December 1927
"Sea Nomad":   In the long ago, Stephens Island had no cocoanuts. One day a warrior, when spearing fish, saw a brown thing rolling in with the tide. It looked like the blunt snout of a sabay fish. He speared it and slung it ashore. "Its no fish" he said, "it's no good to kaikai – what is it good for?" In a spirit of spite he buried it so that it should no longer see the sun. Long afterwards a shoot sprung up and developed into a tall tree bearing green nuts. One sunshiny morning, while the warrior was snoring under the tree a nut "plopped" within an inch of his head. Jumping up, startled, he seized it and angrily dashed it against a rock. The nut cracked, and milky water oozed out. Curiously, the warrior opened the nut, and saw the white meat inside. Being distrustful, he scraped out some of it and gave it to the ants, which hurriedly ate it. He then offered some to the lizards, which gobbled it. So he tasted the milk, and then drank in freely. Quickly also he ate the white meat, and declared the nut "good feller kaikai." Everyone then planted a nut, and now Stephens Island grows many cocoanut trees.

29 December 1927
"Sea Nomad":   A custom amongst the Torres Islanders though not invariably followed, is for a widow to become the property of the deceased husband's brother. I know one unfortunate man who thus inherited a shrew, and it cost him the whole of this banana patch to bribe a fool to marry her. Widows amongst various island groups are generally married by honest but poor men, for here, as under civilisation, economic conditions bear heavily on Love's affairs. A young girl's parents ask a heavy price for her, but a widow, especially with a large family, can be had cheap. Under native custom, the marriage of a widow is a highly dramatic affair. The ceremony is always conducted in twilight and most of it in intense silence. The spirit of the dead husband is impersonated by his best friend on earth. In one ceremony I witnessed, the flitting figure of the best friend was so wonderfully dressed that his body was hard to glimpse among the shadows and patches of tree-thrown light. He constantly appeared just behind the widow. At the finish of the ceremony (IANAGUD) the spirit faded away and the widow wailed for the last time for her lost husband. I've seen the new husband's eyes protruding like door-knobs on such an occasion.

5 January 1928
"Up Top": A Sydney shrewdie has been trying unsuccessfully in Thursday Island a game that scored him many a free meal at home. With a cockroach in his pocket he would betake himself to a restaurant and negotiate a meal; at the conclusion he would bury the 'roach in the final spoonfuls of pudding and then quietly inquire for the manager. He would inform that worthy in a pained tone that he was no entomologist and anyway, what was going to be done about it? He was invariably bowed out, uncharged for what he had consumed, with abject apologies; in fact, he boasted that for three solid months in Sydney he had lived on 'roaches. But the old stunt failed to work in a Chinee chop-suey joint at T. I. John Chinaman merely smiled benignly at the murdered insect. "Him all light. Him alla same beetle. Me no chop him up fine, tha's all. You pay him all li. Two chillin, please!" And the shrewdie was so dumbfounded that he paid. No doubt he will presently be telling his Sydney cobbers that Thirsty Islanders really do live on stewed cockroaches.

12 January 1928
"Gouger": "Dog's-eye" is an abo whose one optic blazes red when near firelight and melts into liquid-green in the dark. This greatly-feared possessor of the evil-eye recently joined a canoeing party along the Gulf. The voyagers experienced hard times. Hostile nomads had taken temporary possession of all the "good lands" along the coast; and on the barren stretches the canoe-men could find neither sugar-bags nor bandicoots. They captured one goanna, but its ribs stuck out like the knobs on a pineapple. Things were looking serious, and glowering faces suggested thoughts uncomplimentary to the sorcerer, when a whopping kingfish leapt from the water and plonked into the canoe. After a second's astonished silence "Dog's-eye" planted his foot upon the flopping fish; then he lifted up his face to the sky and solemnly said "Tank you for the fish, God." By thus publicly renouncing his old faith "Dog's-eye" did the missionaries a good turn.

12 January 1928
"Gouger": Speaking of gruesome relics on church premises (B. 24/11/27) Sibui Pui (the Tree of Skulls) shades the church door on Boigu Island, Torres Strait. On this huge tree the head-hunters hung their trophies for unknown years, festooning its branches after every successful raid. And lying beside the church now under construction at Cocoanut Island is the sawn-off half of a

canoe. Several of the old die-hards now laying a brick for Christianity will still tell you with a certain pride how many heads that canoe brought back from successful raids in the good old days. It is now used for mixing mortar in.

19 January 1928
"Sea Nomad": Wackett's 'planes have been responsible for some sever fright. Flying low over the Home Island group, one swooped just above a trochus-shelling cutter. The whole crew dived overboard, one lad hopping off from the masthead. Another plane caused consternation when cruising above the waterway separating Moa and Badu islands, the approaching noise puzzled the villagers, as "thunder longa Nor' – West season never come up that feller way before." A boatman fishing offshore was the first to spot the "great pelican" and shout the tidings. As the "pelican" roared nearer he made a beeline for the shore and ended by sweeping his boat up on the sands. The women of Poid village took to the bush, leaving their squalling picaninnies kicking beneath the coco-palms. The men ran too, and even the fowls raced for the shelter of the houses. One girl alone stood her ground and jeered at the flying villagers. She was the school-teacher's assistant and had seen the picture of a 'plane in the teacher's mail. A woman washing among the rocks hid her baby under her clothes, then knelt down and prayed. These Torres Strait natives are civilised, but if Wackett flew over the Tugeri country in New Guinea, he'd be responsible for many heart-failures amongst those unsophisticated head-hunters.

19 January 1928
"Up Top": The Torres Islanders have evolved a strict code of land laws, especially on the fertile islands where cultivation means such a lot. The land on Darnley, Murray and other islands is marked out in plots which are known even to the youngsters. Trees, piles of stones and shells are the recognised boundary-marks. The land is handed down from father to son; should a man die without sons, there is generally a row when the relatives swoop down on the estate. Almost as valuable as the land is the great reef which surrounds so many of the islands, for the islanders depend on fishing when the seasons and gardens are poor. The foreshores are all owned in little plots, and the rights in most cases extend straight out over the water across the reef. All fish, turtle and dugong within any given man's area belong to him exclusively. Should a pirate encroach on the right he is liable to be knocked on the head. Where two islands lie almost together there is an imaginary boundary-line drawn across the water between them. To trespass on the opposite island's fishing rights means war. On a like principle the various

island groups have distinctive fishing-rights over lonely sandspits and reefs miles out in the open sea. Although the Islanders have no written records, they know the rights, chiefly hereditary, of every man, woman and child.

19 January 1928
"Sea Nomad": It takes many thousand bêche-de-mer to make a ton. Some species, though 3 ft. long, boil and dry down to 10 in. To avoid the deadly slow and hard work of swimming after the fish in deep water, the men straighten out large fishing-hooks and plug a pound weight of lead at one end, to which is attached a line. In clear water the big slugs can often be seen on the sandy bottom. As the dinghy drifts, the driver lowers his plum-bob, hovers it just above the fish, then lets the weight drop and the quarry is harpooned. It is hauled to the surface very quickly, otherwise it bloats and balloons and slips off the barb. Escaped and on the bottom again, it blows itself into a ball: no amount of jabbing will then fix it, as the barb seems to slip through and out of the fish as though the skin were of the finest silk. There is a knack in this harpooning. The slugs may be nine fathoms deep and objects on the sea bottom are very deceptive, especially through many feet of water. Then the tide may be running; this will carry the lead weight many feet beyond the marksman's aim, which means that the dinghy has to be pulled back to get another shot. But the "boys" become wonderfully expert; they can allow for distance, deception and current with uncanny precision. The harpooning method in clear, deep water saves a great amount of time and physical exertion.

25 January 1928
"Sea Nomad": To the Torres islanders Babat, the turtle-stone was sacred. It rested within a gigantic clam-shell, sheltered by a grove of sacred trees; wherein were stacked the bones of thousands of turtles. As the season approached, the zogo-le with much ceremony evoked the will of the divine spirit to send them plentiful turtle. The deity was brought into immanent touch through the medium of the babat-stone, which was anointed with oil. The invocation of the season followed the Zugabul (Pleiades), which sheen the tropic skies in early November. When they first appeared a song was sung in their honor; sung by a thousand voices throughout the night until the stars faded

25 January 1928
"Sea Nomad": A fat starfish with fingers two feet long thrives in North Australian waters. The Jap pearlers are particularly fond of him, and with

a pointed stick stab him among the reefs at low tide. Young Nippon, when necklaced with a score of these fish, whose twisting fingers flame in every conceivable color, is a fantastic sight. Around each starfish hole lies an empty stack of shells, which are its tucker tins. Poke into this hole, and a head appears. It may be white or blue, or may change into red if dissatisfied with your face. It sports a parrot's beak for a mouth; this strong beak crushes the shellfish on which it dines, and is the only portion resembling a bone in the starfish's body. These fish have seven, eight and nine legs. Those with seven or nine are poisonous, but eight legged ones are luscious eating. The bêche-de-mer fishers boil them in kerosene tins, having first soaked them in salt water or scrubbed them on a rock to abstract a foaming liquid they secrete. When well boiled they make a delicious curry.

1 February 1928
"Up Top": House-building presents no problems in the islands of Torres Strait. The rafters and supports are of mangrove tree. This is canoed long distances to islands which do not grow the timber, but as tomorrow is as good as today and next week does not matter, the carting of the timber is regarded as a picnic. The roof and sides are of cocoanut matting, woven by the women. This matting excludes rain and is delightfully cool in summer, but is not waterproof for more than two years. A species of long grass growing on the sandbanks will, however, when carefully woven, make a roofing material with a life of seven years. Much of the building is done on the communal system. If a bridegroom finds the material the crowd will shove up his house in a day. Latterly, since the islanders have been making money out of trochus-shell, the ambition is to possess a house with an iron roof "alla same white man".

1 February 1928
"Sea Nomad": Torres Strait canoes can beat the fastest lugger afloat; and some of the Strait luggers are swifter than coastal steamers. The lightness of the canoes cannot be altogether the secret of their pace, because the luggers also are light in proportion and carry a far greater spread of sail. I often think the canoe outriggers materially help the speed. These torpedo-shaped billets of buoyancy, well out from each side of the canoe, are continually smacked and bounced with a forward impetus by the waves. It is only in a rough sea that the outriggers actually touch the water.

8 February 1928

"Sea Nomad":   Recently a Daru magistrate bewailed the loss of a favourite tom-cat. For reasons conveyed to him he pulled out to a visiting cutter and implored two Frenchies aboard to restore his cat. Volubly they protested that they had no knowledge of the spirited animal. They hadn't either, personally, but they'd eaten the body. Hung up by the cook for five hours to get rid of the smell, then stewed slowly in wine, tom-cat had provided a delicious dish. For some reason, the meat must not be tainted with water, and for some other reason a she-cat is not good eating.

15 February 1928

"Sea Nomad":   New Guinea canoe-builders are experts who hold their job by hereditary right. Different classes of vessels are built, ranging from the huge war canoes, through the intermediate fishing craft, down to the "torpedo" canoe. The trees generally worked by the tribes adjoining the Dutch New Guinea border are the mah-moro, the goo-goobah, and the matoo-bah. They are of very tough and yet comparatively light, wood. When chipped out and seasoned the shell will stand the action of sea and sun without splitting. The "torpedo" craft are tiny vessels of duar wood, which is exceptionally light. The masts of the larger vessels are of black mangrove. The ropes are very strong, being made of twisted cocoa-husk or, more commonly of the bush vine, a creeper composed of long strands of tough fibre. The sails are of cocoanut matting, very closely plaited, and of great strength and resiliency in the strong winds. The canoes are built for trade with the various tribes and the Torres Islanders, with whom at one time an extensive yearly business was done. In the good old days the price of a canoe was reckoned in skulls, varying in number with the size of the canoe. This time-honored currency is still good in parts of New Guinea, but the Torres Islanders, now being civilised, use shell money, mostly the rare armshell; this is worth in our money from £4 to £8, according to the quality and size of the shells. One average armshell will buy a small canoe, and three a large one. The Torres Islanders now use mostly canvas sails, the purchase money for which they get from trochus-shell fishing. The "torpedo" canoes are similar to our fancy speedboats. They skim along the surface as if made of cork, yet, for all their lightness , are very seaworthy.

22 February 1928

"Sea Nomad":   The Gaili girls may be prettily tattooed ("LAGANI-NAMO," B. 19/1/28), but so are the flappers of the West Division, and for better reasons. Many of the tribes there make the daughter the father's pedigree book and diary. When dad comes home from a raid proudly displaying a brace of dripping heads he tattoos a new design on his daughter's back or thighs; this design assures the handing-down of the tale to his descendents. Any hair-raising exploit that may come the way of the old man is recorded on his daughter's hide. If she happens to be a baby, the mother is responsible for seeing that the design is impressed indelibly. Due to the ingredients used, this often means days of agony for the child, but when she reaches the flapper stage, her most proudly displayed adornment is dad's history upon her body.

29 February 1928

"Sea Nomad":   Mainlanders and Torres Strait islanders tell wonderful tales of the sucking-fish which help them to catch turtle. The fish, they say, warns them when a cyclone is brewing, and gives them a nod when a submerged reef lies in the fairway. It is supposed to know when things are not ship-shape and to come aboard and rebuke the sailors. Occasionally the remora attaches itself to other fish besides turtle – a shark even. When such is the case the men aboard can tell instantly by feeling the fin vibrations along the line. The remora find difficulty in adhering to a dugong on account of the very smooth and sometimes oily hide. The suction-power of the fish is extraordinary, the hold being practically undetachable. They are quite easy to capture, as often a number of them adhere to the sides of a lugger as she is sailing. The natives, who still use the fish, always have a couple in the bottom of their canoes under wet leaves. The Chinese have fished with remora for centuries, but the Torres Strait islanders swear that a god first explained to them their use.

7 March 1928

"Sea Nomad":   Some deer were let loose on Friday Island by a pearler. There they thrived for years, but with small increase; they were eventually removed to Horn Island, mainly because of the intrusion of one sporty buck on lady bathers. "Friday" is a picnic spot, and repeatedly he invaded the privacy of flappers who had retired into the bush to disrobe. One of his famous exploits was the treeing of three maids in the altogether. When, however, the buck took to charging boatloads of landing picnickers, and upsetting dad and the kids into the water,

and chasing mum and the girls up the beach, the deer were banished. For some reason they have not thriven on the much larger Horn Island.

7 March 1928
"Sea Nomad":   I was much puzzled by the innards of a giant banyan-tree on Maubiag (Torres Strait). A "boy" chopped into it and cut through bone. Slivers taken down the side of the tree showed that the root-like trunk was as full of bones as a porcupine of points .I pored over the problem, and noticing Sambo grinning, called on him to explain the joke. It appeared that the banyan was once the centre of a village. The villagers threw all their dugong bones upon and around the tree, and the continually dropping shoots and roots in course of time grew through and around the accumulation. The tree was sacred to a spirit which guided the destinies of the dugong, and the bones were placed there so that the tree could thrive upon them whilst the natives grew fat on the meat.

7 March 1928
"Sea Nomad":   Forbes or "Spirit" Island, just off the Pascoe River, Cape York Peninsula, is worth a visit from the archaeologists. Encircling one of the hills is a stone wall commanding the beach, obviously built for defensive purposes, though long since overgrown by scrub. On a hilltop is a lookout strongly walled with rock, and at the water's edge, hidden by undergrowth, is a big cave showing evidences of one-time human occupation. Some of the great rocks along the slopes are shattered as if by cannon-shot, and cannon-balls of an antique pattern have been found by natives, buried deep in the earth and sand. There is a tradition that the island was once a rendezvous for black-birders, but that would hardly account for the fortifications. The natives are very hazy on the island's history, but they will tell you that "plenty fight" occurred there before and after the black-birding days, and they have a dimly-outlined legend of lamars (white spirits) who came to these parts long ago in a ghost ship, ran on the reef, settled on the island and lingered there for years before the last survivor was killed. There are some details that suggest the old-time Spaniards.

14 March 1928
"Sea Nomad":   Tribes near the Dutch New Guinea border have thought out a clever drill with which to bore the holes in their bone and shell ornaments. The instrument is a stick about two feet long, with a circular disk of baked clay six inches from the bottom as a pressure weight. The tip of the stick is split,

and a needle-pointed piece of flint bound in it with fibre twine. At the top are two long fibre-strings, their ends tied to a loose crosspiece about a foot long. The strings are tightly twisted around the top of the stick; then the crosspiece is pulled steadily downwards, causing the stick to revolve rapidly as the string becomes unwound. The momentum re-winds the string. On boring a pearl-shell for a crescent mia, the drill point is placed in turn on the designed spots marked in ochre, and the palm of the hand or middle finger held gently on the tip of the drill to keep it upright or at whatever angle is required. A great deal of thought must have been expended on this drill.

21 March 1928
"Sea Nomad":   If Dr. Duhig (B. 22/2/28) wants specimens of stone-fish, a letter to Dr. Vernon of Thursday Island, would produce the goods. Stone-fish vary in size and breed. A two-foot specimen would be a monster. A wound from one causes agony, sometimes lasting for months. One remedy is to gash the wound and fill it immediately with Condy's crystals. Binghi uses native herbs. The Japanese and native divers who tread on the spike of the fish are sometimes forced to undergo treatment in Thursday Island hospital. Nothing known in the sea can produce the same agony.

21 March 1928
"Up North":   Dancing is life to black brother. Every dance is significant to him, because it tells the story of how his ancestors lived, how he himself lives, and how he expects to live after death. The dance commemorates an event in his life, or in the lives of the gods that created him and all things. Many dances are stories that unfold to the young men the history of their tribe, the virtues of their ancestors, and make a strong appeal to the youths to mould their lives also to the well-being and longevity of their tribe. Dances at the fruit, vegetable and fish seasons are thank-offerings to the particular deity who controls that season. Every action of the dance has a meaning, and the natives fully believe that the invisible Being looking on knows and appreciates the motives of the dances. Their educational dances also are an appeal to the tribesmen to learn all they can of the queer white man's world and keep abreast of the times. The lugger crews at Thursday Island for instance, on returning to their island homes, staged dances giving in detail the white man's wonderful procession at Jubilee time. When Wackett's seaplanes landed the returning islanders gave a dance in vivid representation of the wonderful "birds" and the consternation they created along the waterfront.

But from the ever popular movies the home-going crews draw their most inspired themes. The dances they act to show their home comrades the white man's way of life would make the hair even of a Hollywood producer stand on end.

4 April 1928
"Up North": A voracious black ant raids the nests of his white brothers in the Far North. Eventually he takes full possession, devours the inmates, then turns his attention to the many storage chambers filled with the fruits of the white-ants' labor. The pirate is an arrogant-looking black ant of generous proportions. Many a deserted nest is proved to have been ravaged by these ants, which in sufficient numbers could wipe out the white-ant pest for all time.

25 April 1928
"Up North": "Carisbrook Jun." (B. 14/3/28) slips badly when he insinuates that the abo. is satisfied with one wife only. One is the general rule in N.Q., but a man will get as many as he can, not for love, but because they come in handy for keeping the home fires burning. Many young men possess no missus at all, because custom ordains that the old men can claim all the maidens and hand over the old women to the young bucks should they feel so inclined. Hence in camp there may be several greybeards with half a dozen wives, and a dozen young Romeos languishing. When such a harem-owner dies the youths rejoice, for there is then a chance of the wives being parcelled out. The youths are getting more assertive nowadays, and backed up by the missionary, are demanding a more equal distribution of female goods. Needless to add, the young gins are backing them up.

25 April 1928
"Sea Nomad": Even island natives, who spend a third of their lives on the water, have never thought of the rudder for steering their craft. The canoe people steer with the paddle as they go along; a well-manned vessel is manoeuvered with perfect accuracy, every man working in harmony with the whole to the exact flick of the wrist. Women handle their canoes almost as well as the men. The great sailing canoes of Boigu, Saibai and Dauan are steered by a long board manipulated in a heavy sea with marvellous dexterity by one man. Various Papuan tribes in the island rivers and swamps never use a paddle, but pole their craft, steering it thus with wonderful ease in waterways where reeds and creepers and trailing branches brush the sides of the dugout. These craft travel noiselessly and can disappear in an instant should the occupant so desire.

2 May 1928

"Sea Nomad":   Few churches possess as many tragic relics as the Quetta Memorial Cathedral (T.I.). The bell that tolls daily came from a wrecked ship; so did the ewer at the font. The same ship's riding-light is there and a portion of the wheel-box forms the top of the credence in the chapel. The compass-bowl of the Catterthun, wrecked on the Seal Rocks, is used as a stand for the ewer. Two benches in the nave are bits of the Volga, which lies on a reef near Goode Island. The Kanabooka left a lifebuoy and a flag as its gifts of remembrance. A tablet commemorates the Cape Melville hurricane, where over 300 men went west. The diggers have endowed the church with a pair of candlesticks used by the A.I.F. in Egypt.

9 May 1928

"Sea Nomad":   In the pioneer days of Torres Strait, when the thousands of reefs and coral passages were uncharted and unknown, hundreds of ships went down as they sought to crawl along those tortuous laneways. In several passages ships have actually piled up on top of another. Most of them are long since forgotten, but relics are brought up every now and then by the pearl and trochus divers. The fact that the 'Windhover' a comparatively modern vessel, is lying underneath a steamer off Bramble Cay was recalled the other day when a native retrieved her brass capstan-head. In some places it is alleged that wrecked ships actually lie three deep, but there is nothing left of some of them except a few copper bolts overgrown a foot thick with coral.

9 May 1928

"Joss Stick":   The comparative respite in the Chinese turmoil, and a consequent improved demand for sandalwood, has considerably bucked the little-heard-of Queensland trade in that romantic merchandise. A few weeks ago two China-bound steamers took some 150 tons of the stuff from Townsville to the Flowery Land, most of it coming from the main range inland. In China, though some of it is used for making the familiar boxes, most of the precious wood is ground to powder and used as the main ingredient in incense sticks for propriating the gods and the souls of ancestors. Sandalwood-getters are not distinguished for their religious tendencies or respect for anyone's ancestors, but, as contributors to the pacification of minor deities and the repose of millions of departed souls, they have their humble uses.

16 May 1928
"Sea Nomad":   A famous shell rests among the zogos on hilly Yam Island. It was stolen from Yam by New Guinea canoe-men. Their return trip was accursed. Fearful storms drove the canoe on a sand-bank, from which the crew refloated it only when all their food had gone and two of their number were missing. Then a calm drove them nearly mad because of thirst. Some of the crew in desperation leapt overboard, hoping thus to appease the wrath of the shell-spirit and so save the remainder of their friends. A remnant in a dying condition finally reached New Guinea shores. But immediately the shell was carried into the village a curse fell upon the people. They were defeated in battle; many of their young women were taken; sickness struck down the children and their vegetable gardens wilted. Canoes loaded with tribute were finally despatched to Yam. But the infuriated chief refused to touch the shell, and it had to be taken back again to await the arrival of a Yam native, who cleansed it of all New Guinea vices and diseases before it could be reclaimed by its rightful owners.

16 May 1928
"Up Top":   In the tropics, for some unexplained reason, mosquitoes and March flies will swarm on a man wearing dark-colored clothes, whereas white-clad humans are partially immune. But many creatures have color preferences. Bees are attracted by a white cloth, and the effect of a red rag on a bull is proverbial. Even fish have their partialities. Kingfish will hungrily bite at a whirling rag of white or red; other species prefer green.

23 May 1928
"Up Top":   Up north there is one vegetable that a man never gets tired of anymore than he would get tired of bread. This is "sweetbuks". It is the bread-like qualities of the tuber that has made it a favorite throughout the north and the Islands. Men have been known to live for months entirely on "sweetbuks" without suffering ill effects. Shipwrecked crews have lived for months on fish and crabs alone. My mate and I did so for five long months on a mangrove islet. We got as wiry as savages and as bad tempered; in fact, we were beginning to develop nigger characteristics when a Jap pearler took us off. The greatest hardship was the absence of tobacco, seaweed proving a very poor substitute.

23 May 1928

"Sea Nomad": Strange that the highly-developed islanders of the Eastern Group (Torres Strait) never hit on the idea of a written language. Their zogo-le on great occasions could demonstrate a complete mastery of telepathy, sending and receiving thought-messages over long distances. Ordinarily, news was passed by word of mouth from island to island, the canoe-man carrying as his bona-fides a specially recognised bow and arrow, known as the TOME. A special TOME was carried when aid was sought to raid a neighboring island. At the approach of the big yearly ceremonial gatherings, these TOME men travelled long distances with invitations. The greater ceremonies took place on Darnley and Murray, as these two islands are the most fertile in the Strait. The islanders' calender was the KUP, a stem of cocoanut-leaves. For each day one leaf was torn off. Thus when a canoe cruised the outlying islands with invitations to a big feast, the leader regulated his sailings according to a preconceived plan, and the zogo-le knew to the day when to expect his visitors.

23 May 1928

"Up Top": I have a mate who shudders with horror when anything touches his neck, even if it is only a drooping vine, a wind-blown leaf or an inquiring insect. And yet he has battled his way through the New Guinea head-hunters' country. It was at Somerset, C.Y.P. that a cold thing dragged across his face while he slept. His shriek awoke me, and the match I lit showed him standing rigid, his upheld hands clenching a carpet-snake. It was near python size, 10 feet long, and proportionally thick. Jim's right hand squeezed the reptile's middle whilst its coils tightened around his neck. His left hand clutched its throat, forcing the big-fanged jaws wide open. He had gripped it in the one position which made it impossible for it to strike. He would have stood there paralysed until the thing strangled him had I not tugged the writhing coils away. Even then he could not move; and, whilst I jumped for the revolver, the coils whipped round him again. When the snake's head had been blown heavenward, Jim collapsed.

23 May 1928

"Sea Nomad": Tutu Island, a patch of mangroves on coral lying beside the famous Warrior Reefs that have made history in the pearl-shelling industry, was once the home of a tribe that terrorised the length and breadth of the Strait right across to New Guinea. Even today the New Guinea men bring tribute to Maino, last mamoose of Tutu. Maino's father was the chief Kebisu, who

forced his people to tolerate big Captain Banner, thus allowing the discoverer of the pearl-shell beds an opportunity to work the find. Kebisu hob-nobbed with Captain Moresby, of the Basilisk, as man to man, when the captain was endeavouring to conquer the islands by peace. The people of Yam Island, near by, who are the remnants of the Tutuites, have their produce gardens on Tutu, but never camp there. Maino, who bears a striking resemblance to King Edward V11, had the ill-luck to reach manhood when the virile whites had just about conquered the Strait. He used his power to protect many a famous explorer and naturalist. D'Albertis, the Italian, got out of most of his scrapes through Maino's influence. For years, Maino was Sir William Macgregor's orderly, and saved his master's life on more than one occasion.

30 May 1928
"Up Top": In the jungles, during the wet season, leeches are a menace. Though for 50 feet around the camp the ground be scraped bare of dank vegetation, and even though a man's bunk be built high, leeches are still liable to find him by night. The baby ones, mere cottony wisps are the most feared. They enter the nostrils and the ears and generally secure a firm hold before their host becomes aware of their feasting. Even if they can be pulled out with pincers, it is dangerous as the mouth of the leech has got a firm grip on the tender membrane and tears some away as it is pulled out, leaving a running sore. If the thing can be seen at all, a heated needle end applied to its stern will cause it to quickly lose its hold.

30 May 1928
"Atherton": Recently a cobber of mine cycling home after a bush dance ran over what looked like a stick. Next second, man, bicycle and snake were playing at somersaults. On moonlit nights, snakes like to take a siesta in the soft dust of a white road. An overloaded citizen of Cooktown was staggering home afoot when one of these sleepers, suddenly aroused, crawled around his leg. The drunken gentleman calmly got a death grip on its neck and zig-zagged on with the thing coiled round his arm. It was the heated argument in the kitchen that brought wifey in to investigate. Hubby was doing his best to induce a frightened snake to enter a bottle by pouring boiling water on its tail. His idea was that if could only cork up this fantod he would know for a certainty in the morning whether others of the species he occasionally saw were dinkum.

6 June 1928

"Up Top":   While horse hunting in the ranges towards the head of the Mitchell (N.Q.) we came on a Myall's storehouse. It was a cleft in a granite ravine, and possible raiders were warned off by a symbolical heap of ochre-daubed stone. Inside were bunk-like arrangements of saplings, forked up to three tiers, neatly packed with dilly-bags, sea-shells, coolamons, fish-spears, paper-bark, bundles of ochres, rasp-leaves and bottle fragments in broken down stages from the shaving rasp to the finished glass spear-point. The storehouse undoubtedly represented an accumulation of traded goods, and out of curiosity we tried to make friends with the bucks, but they weren't having any.

6 June 1928

"Sea Nomad":   Fish snooze at times but always with one eye open. Deep down in a coral crevice, their body camouflaged by plant growths, they will stay moveless for hours. In a river, under a ledge of rock, a fish will regularly take his siesta in the one spot, pressed almost invisible against the rock by the current. On the coral islets when the tide goes out they swarm in the shallow waterholes, and jambing themselves in amongst the countless mangrove roots stay there with only the faintest tremble of side fins, just like the gentle swaying of leaves under water. Should a shark or stingray dash across the pool, there is instant commotion. But as the tide creeps in every fish awakes, for soon the waterways will be flooded, and hungry bellies will call for food.

20 June 1928

"Up North":   A time-honored custom with Torres Strait natives is the wearing of the "love-stick", a little piece of wongai wood beautifully polished, hung at the neck and nicked. Each nick represents the wearer's conquest of a lady. When he marries his bride treasures the trophy; should he die untimely she keeps it and howls over it. She will even show the thing to her next husband, if any, and boast of what an invincible man her first was.

20 June 1928

"Sea Nomad":   A tree growing in the Sepik (Papua) River country should be of value to the white man. The natives make incisions around the trunk, at the bottom gutter placing a spout leaf, which drains into a bamboo cylinder, a clear yellow oil. This is as good as cocoanut oil and they use it as such. It takes a considerable time to fill the bamboo, the course of the oil being protected from the rains meanwhile by palm leaves.

27 June 1928
"Sea Nomad":   A sturdy piece of early-day work stands on Raine Island, home of countless sea birds – a warning tower for ships. It was erected in 1844, the Fly, Bramble and Prince George bringing nearly all material from Sydney and a score of convict labourers as well. Coral rock was quarried out, and lime for mortar was burned from clamshells, but water had to be brought from the Sir Charles Hardy group and wood from near the mainland. The job was completed in about three months, the tower was 75 feet high, the diameter at the base being 30 feet and the walls five feet thick. A tank was placed alongside; pumpkins and corn were planted; then the place was left to the sea birds. It looks very woebegone now.

27 June 1928
"Sea Nomad":   A monster prawn fattens himself in the mangrove creeks of Thursday Island. He averages eight inches long, and is as juicy as a young pig. Half a dozen make a substantial meal> Similar creatures thrive in some of the New Guinea rivers. But the mastodon of all prawns waxes fat in the great waterholes of the Mitchell (N.Q.) where all fish grow oversize. Fifteen inches is the length of well-nourished specimens. They are almost as large as the smaller crayfish in the Coral sea.

27 June 1928
"Atherton":   Plants are continually exercising intelligence and physical energy right under our unobserving noses. In the N.Q. bush a number of trees store their seeds in pods which explode in the end and shrapnel the seeds abroad. On a summer's day, I've ridden under patches of these trees and the continual "pop pop" brought back war-time memories of sniping made more realistic when the nervy prad stopped a whizzing seed with his ear. Another even more ingenious scheme is that of growing hooks on seeds and dropping them on wandering stock below. I've often watched feeding stock pushing by a particular tree-climbing creeper. The moment they were under the vine, down came a shower of evilly hooked seeds, which gripped wherever they touched the hairy hide. I've examined a dead calf and found its mouth full of seeds, whose cruel hooks had pierced far into the roof of the mouth, and even through the tongue. In such a case the plant would attain a double object, for the calf would carry the seeds a considerable distance to fresh soil, and when dead would provide manure.

4 July 1928

"Sea Nomad":   The coming of the white man has entirely changed the habits of Hanuabada and Elevala natives. Nature forced every one to work by making the Moresby district alternately wet and dry. For six months in the year the two big villages were hard pressed to find drinking water, let alone water for the huge gardens on whose produce they mostly lived. The dry belt stops short up the coast east and west and there the foreign villagers grew their vegetables and fruit all the year round, living in plenty while the Moresby lads were half-starved. Around Hanuabada the soil is all clay, and some native Adam Smith decided that trade must be the salvation of the community. Under his tutelage the Hanuabada crowd developed a pot-making industry that lasted for many centuries, right up to the advent of the whites. They traded the pottery along the coast, returning with sufficient provisions to keep them throughout the dry months. Their trading ventures were on a huge scale, comprising fleets of hundreds of giant Lakatois, and the sailing and return of the trade fleets were occasions of tremendous enthusiasm and rejoicing. The once flourishing industry has gone into limbo; but Big Guvvermen sits down longside, so between odd jobs and tourists the villagers probably do better than they ever did in the old days.

18 July 1928

"Sea Nomad":   That cockroach-bitten Papuan of "Orokolos" (B.6/6/28) is no rarity in the shelling boats. After a long cruise they become overrun with 'roaches of a size that is only matched by their ferocity. I shall never forget the disgust of a Jap diver who woke up one morning with bald patches making piebald his nice black hair. The 'roaches can chew hair to the roots without waking a heavy sleeper. I've only met one man who blessed cockroaches. His feet were covered with corns. He woke up one morning to find the corns chipped neatly off; the cleverest doctor couldn't have made a better job of it. Why the 'roaches never chewed right into the beef I don't know. Each year the shelling boats have to be fumigated against the pests.

18 July 1928

"Gouger":   Not always are the white man's wonders viewed with boredom by primitive man. When Wackett's seaplane swooped down the water lane between Moa and Badu, the people of three big villages went hysterical with astonishment and terror. Some mothers even forgot to snatch their babies before running screaming into the bush. A canoe in the waterway was emptied in a trice – its crew leaped overboard. Far south towards the Home group Wackett playfully dropped near a trochus lugger, the crew of which were supposed to be civilised. Every man dived into the sea.

18 July 1928
"Up North":   For liveliness, Echuca (B.11/7/28) wasn't a patch on Burketown (N.Q.) in the days when all the male citizens had to go armed because of the blacks. Burketown's pubs then carried on without a licence; in fact, it did without a police force for years. Finally, fatal fights became too frequent, and the Law was installed. There was no gaol, and obstreperous prisoners were handcuffed to a long chain, which in turn was spiked to a huge log. One evening several bad boys were tethered to the log. When the constable strolled along next morning to see about their breakfast they had picked up their log and walked . He found them and the log in a bar, and had to shout for all hands before they would condescend to carry the gaol back to the proper position.

25 July 1928
"Up North":   The swastika as a symbol of good luck is known to many ages and nations. I've seen it tattooed on the chest of a Malay in Torres Strait; it has been found on the Bronze-age weapons of Britons, Europeans, Asians and Americans; it is carved on the kitchens of Pompeii; and Helen of Troy ordered her slaves to chisel it in stone on the walls of her favourite city. The sun-worshipping Indians have left carvings of it in mountain cities, and some of their descendents still draw it in sand as a way of ensuring good luck at a parting. To this day it is the lucky sign of India. And the swastika is familiar to our own abos.

1 August 1928
"Atherton":   Amongst the gulf tribes the expectant mother is secreted by the old gins in the quite of a tree-shaded creek. A couch is scraped out in the warm sand and cushioned with heated leaves; then the crooning attendants group around the patient and give experienced help. The mother is warmed over a soothing smoke fire, and the little stranger is washed and lathered with an ointment made of powdered charcoal and fat of the carpet snake. A boy is proudly received; a girl is a less welcome arrival. If it's a girl a twine of possum fur or twisted human hair is twisted around the first joint of her little finger with a view to stopping

the circulation of blood, eventually causing the finger-joint to drop off. The same objective is more quickly attained by bandaging the hand in paper-bark, leaving the joint exposed. The joint is encircled with honey and the hand thrust into an ant's nest. I have heard a mother make the bush ring with her howls when baby has been operated on in this manner. The custom is not universal.

1 August 1928
"Sea Nomad": Just west of Darnley Island a black squall suddenly hit the lugger and heeled her rail under. We hove to like a wallowing log in a rain-whipped sea of ink and clung on by the skin of our teeth. Then a crackling row like the static of a thousand wireless sets gone mad broke out overhead. Every stay in the lugger right to the bowsprit was a leaping mass of yellow-blue flame, which, as we watched, sprang into thousands of tiny balloons of frantic life, intermingling with and leaping over one another backwards and forwards along the stays. It was a beautiful sight, but the piercing crackling made the island boys eyes bulge like billiard balls. The fireworks lasted five minutes, then disappeared as the sun shone out in glory.

1 August 1928
"Atherton": Nocturnal creatures mostly have very large eyes. The seeing apparatus of the owl looks like a couple of saucers. A wild dog's eyes appear to expand by night, and the darker the night the larger and more luminous do they become. Animals, other than felines which do most of their sightseeing by day, do not show nearly the same eye luminosity at night as those that forage chiefly in darkness. The Northern Territory bush by night is a lesson in undreamt of life to the quiet observer. A flicker-flash of marble-blue eyes, green eyes, yellow eyes, tiny eyes like a gleam of rubies, medium eyes that for seconds gleam balefully in a liquid light, eyes of swimming gold that glare unwinkingly, and a strong sense of unseen eyes; eyes staring round from an unseen log, from the bushes, from under a tuft of grass, from a tree branch, from the air, from everywhere – in more ways than one "the night hath a thousand eyes".

8 August 1928
"Atherton": I was riding over an ironstone ridge in N.Q. when the earth rumbled hollowly and rose with a distinct shiver. The horse stopped dead in his tracks and trembled violently, rearing in terror as a withered branch snapped from a limb overhead. The business was all over in a minute, but the prad

stepped like a cat on hot bricks for many a mile after. I saw an earth tremor cause much more serious consequences in Cape York Peninsula. The cattle had been uneasy all the afternoon and we found it increasingly difficult to keep them in a mob and travel in the required direction. At evenfall, just as we were debating their queer behaviour, the ground rumbled from a great distance below, then rose in a sort of travelling wave. The mob was away instantly. Nothing could have stopped them, and our horses became just as unmanageable. It took us a week to re-muster the beasts with the loss of over a hundred.

15 August 1928
"Up Top":   N.Q. natives have an ingenious system of trapping eels. The traps are cylinders of plaited lawyer-vine, about six feet long. The centre narrows and the eel, squeezing through, finds himself in a more commodious chamber, in which he takes refuge during the hullabaloo. A score of traps are stretched across a river, the mouths facing upstream, during the dry season, when the volume of water has lessened considerably. Connecting the traps is a fence of brushwood and grass as a camouflage and also to ensure that the fish cannot pass down the river without entering the traps. The tribe then enter the water some miles above and wade down, standing shoulder to shoulder, stirring up mud with their legs and thrashing the water with bushes. All rocks and logs are turned over, spears are jabbed under all ledges, and submerged leaves and mould are disturbed. The fish scurry on ahead of the hunters and are finally yarded in the traps. If the traps are filled the abos stand in a dense line 30 yards back and hurl their spears into the terrified fish that remain

22 August 1928
"Sea Nomad":   Because a sleepy "boy" piled the cutter on a reef, we had a trip across the Strait in an open dinghy. There was not a breath of wind, so we took quick spells at the oars and prayed for the nor'-west to lie low. Night came bringing heavens massed with golden stars and a sea that was a plain of dark-green velvet. On the horizon a star appeared, a red star that grew fast in foaming splashes of green. It spread until it was a pathway, then a road, hundreds of yards wide, with its head tearing towards us foaming with many-colored lights. In a few minutes it seemed as if all the fish in the Coral Sea were flying to smash us down. The gigantic shoal burst upon the dinghy with a hissing of phosphorescent spray and a tattoo of flying bodies on wood. We were forced to turn the dinghy bow on, and found that paddling was impossible against the

impact of racing bodies. Half a dozen shoals appeared all mixed up, big fellows preying on the welterweights, giants on the big fellows and sharks dashing through the lot in luminous streaks of hissing foam. One man kept the dinghy bow on while all hands threw out the glittering fish that otherwise would have swamped us. It was half an hour before that mad fury of fish had passed us, and our arms ached from the labor of clearing the dinghy.

22 August 1928
"Sea Nomad": In a shaded banana-garden in Torres Strait I saw a picturesque emblem revolving from a branch. It was a large but perfectly round stone, painted coral-red, suspended by a red cord of twisted cocoa-husk. It was artistically decorated with palm-leaves to resemble the rays of the sun, the leaves painted in varying shades of crimson – a charm imploring the sun to shine out and warm the cold gardens to life after weeks of rain. The gardens had quite a number of charms, some of them effigies of departed supermen; others bearing queer hieroglyphs. The islanders still remember their old deities, and I don't think they will ever quite forget them.

22 August 1928
"Atherton": Speaking of queer drinks, there was a mysterious decoction that gave Government Resident Jardine a lot of trouble in the early days of Somerset (Q.). Regularly on Saturday nights the marines and water police would abandon themselves to the pleasures of intoxication, and as Jardine was always expecting a massed attack by the natives on the isolated settlement, this intemperance annoyed him. Vainly he threatened delinquents with the triangle lashed to the broad-leafed tree facing the tiny beach; the Saturday night orgies still continued. Vainly the government cutter was dispatched to scour the near-by islands for an illicit still. Jardine could never solve the mystery, but years later it transpired that the rum-runner was an old renegade who inhabited a cave on Albany Island right opposite the settlement. There he compounded his hardtack, a simple brew of cocoanut-milk and molasses, "pepped" with a chewed-up plug of trade tobacco, and brought it over to his customers in a dinghy by night. The marines called it "alligator's milk", presumably from the jim-jams for which it was responsible. Jardine, walking the verandah at headquarters and suspiciously watching the marines' barracks, never dreamed what the cocoanuts held.

29 August 1928
"Sea Nomad":   In the old days the Torres Strait natives preserved the skulls of their parents as well as those of their foes. The skull of a man's father was the best divining instrument that he knew, except the skull of a priest, and priest's skulls were too expensive for the proletariat. Captain Banner was the first man to buy a Torres Strait skull. A Tutu man offered him the skull of his mother for four tomahawks, and he bought, though a stick of tobacco would have been nearer the market value. D'Albertis, the Italian naturalist, was very keen on skulls, and nosed out bargains from Cape York to New Guinea. He got a great haul at Mawatta, then an important native trading centre. These trophies were smoke-dried – some raddled red and others with cheeks and noses filled in with wax and painted to resemble life. Others had tufts of hair glued to the pate. The Germans were also keen skull hunters and got away with some fine specimens. But they were not popular with the natives. They fixed their own prices.

5 September 1928
"Atherton":   After all, man plods a long way behind nature. Up north the thistles fly away on sometimes unbelievable journeys, and each aeronaut comes to earth in one of the cutest parachutes imaginable, drops his seed and carries on with the business of life. There are also spiders in Cape York Peninsula that sail away in flocks of scores of thousands until the air resembles drifting snow. These chaps build an exquisite silken balloon in which to sail, anchoring to the tops of trees as the mood seizes them. Many plants send their seeds abroad in flying vessels; some seeds have dinkum wings attached. Other plants have a fancy for water voyages and launch their embryos from riverbanks to drift oceanwards in non-collapsible and non-sinkable boats. Many are the clever schemes to get the seeds planted in unoccupied land as far away from the parent as possible. Some seeds are gummy and stick to passing animals and birds, thus riding on the cheap for great distances. No matter where or by what method man has travelled, the seeds of plants have shown the way many thousands of years before.

5 September 1928
"Gouger":   The nearest parallel to Edie Creek in Australia was the Rocky River diggings on Cape York Peninsula, where the reefs were 2000 feet above the sea in dense jungle, The Leo and the Rocky are mountain torrents shadowed by dense tropical vegetation. The reefs, though very small, were phenomenally rich. It was impossible to pack the poorer stone down the precipitous range, so

Lakeland, the finder of the field, built a water-wheel in the jungle and for years crushed by water power. Rich alluvial was won in the streams. To get to the field overland meant a trudge of over 300 miles from Cooktown. By sea you went to Claremont Island Lightship, then by lugger to the Chester, finishing with a wild bush scramble up the great range. Lakeland was a fine type of the old pioneering prospector, and was in harness to the last. He went out alone with his team a few years back, and his bones were found by the Coen police.

12 September 1928
"Up North": Old Hans Dehm, a prospector who perished on the east coast of Cape York Peninsula a month back, was in the "Dead Man's Secret" country, which has claimed many victims. Adventurous souls have cut their way deep into that belt, never to be heard of again. The "Secret" mine was found long ago by a party of diggers, all but one of whom was killed by a shower of native spears as they worked. With one horse and a bag of rich specimens, the survivor fought his way for over 300 miles back to civilisation, throwing away everything that encumbered him, as his horse grew weaker and weaker. He reached Cooktown with only one of his specimens left, there to succumb to his wounds and privations. Years later, Jardine Somerset, and Hamilton, an old-time politician, made several attempts to locate the "Dead Man's Secret". Less adequately equipped prospectors have tried just as hard, but all attempts have failed. So far as is known, the location is roughly about 15 miles inland from False Orfordness. The country is densely covered with turkey-bush scrub, quite impenetrable for horses, and almost as bad for men carrying heavy tucker packs.

19 September 1928
"Sea Nomad": On calm, dark nights the Coral Sea nurses living clouds of phosphorus, some on the surface of the water, but mostly in a mass of green illumination a few feet below. Many fish in this sea seem to be able to flood themselves with phosphorescent light at will. Coral plants sometimes appear to be lit up by soft green electric lamps. In the jungles of the North the ground at night for perhaps an acre in extent will seem to be dimly pulsing light, and if the decaying leaves are stirred they will almost flame with crinkling phosphorus. I have seen a rotted tree ablaze with fairy lights, visible 200 yards away, as a result of intense accumulation of phosphoric fungus. Countless insects are phosphoric. I have even seen a phosphoric snake – possibly its scales had collected the phosphorus when crawling over damp leaves.

19 September 1928

"Sea Nomad": Sparta's national training was not more severe than that of the Torres Strait natives. Lads at an early age commenced a most rigid course intended to make them almost immune to hardship and pain, and to fit them to become defenders of their country and worthy tribesmen. Every inhabited island in the Strait had its kwod, or training camp. Some had as many as eight. They were generally secreted in almost inaccessible spots among the hills or swamps, and some were also fenced around with palisades . Once within that grim enclosure, a lad might not see his parents again until he was a young man, perhaps never, as some of the rites were very strict and cruel, and the penalty for cowardice was often death.

19 September 1928

"Up Top": Despite their sharp eyes and good bushmanship, aboriginals have seldom figured in our mining history. In Victoria's early rushes a black stockman "specked" a £4000 specimen for his squatter boss, and Ernest Henry, the discoverer of Cloncurry, made use of the natives by training them to locate outcropping copper ore. But I believe our only genuine abo. prospector was Pluto, who located Plutoville, on the Batavia River (N.Q.) which yielded many nuggets, and Chock-a-block, also on the Batavia. Nuggets from this area ranged up to 120oz. Pluto died in 1916. He was kept in tucker for years by H. Wade Robinson, a telegraph officer, who was a good friend to northern prospectors . Robinson was a Norfolk Island man, descended from one of the Bounty mutineers.

26 September 1928

"Sea Nomad": Needing some shark oil, we slung a chained hook overboard by the Massig Reef, Torres Strait. The line foamed out with a 15 footer in full fighting fury attached. He lit out for the depths and the surface in a series of wheeling dives that circled him around and under the lugger. In a few minutes he was being chased by a score of other sharks whose fins clipped the water and dived in shivering speed whenever the frantic capture catherine-wheeled to escape. The boys were delighted, cheering on the careering monsters from the deck and rigging. Eventually a bullet on the nose stunned the captive. Instantly his whereabouts was a lather of foam, his tail disappeared, his tailless body went bouncing among glittering bodies that were themselves flung out of the water by weight of rushing numbers; then his head vanished. Away swirled the line again amidst the frantic cheering of the boys, for the monster that had swallowed the

huge head had swallowed the hook as well. The water became a seething mass of sharks that suddenly darted off in a vanishing road of foam. One had bitten the line through, and the whole pack were after the hurrying escapee.

3 October 1928
"Atherton": Along the coast of Cape York Peninsula large areas of country become bogs in the wet season, but these morasses are covered with a deceptive hard crust of grass, clay and pebbles. A line of packhorses will be mooching along quite comfortably on solid ground when suddenly the leader throws up his head, making violent efforts to swing up on his hind legs. The following horse then goes down and if the team is inexperienced, in a few minutes every horse is caught. The only way to retrieve the bogged animals is to unpack like greased lightning, cut the girth to get the saddle off if necessary. If the bog is shallow the horse may be rescued by ramming grass, bushes and logs under him to give him a footing. Even then he has often to be helped by a leverage of saplings under his belly, and the mucky job may be complicated by the rescuers getting bogged themselves. In deep bogs a horse sinks very rapidly, and the more it struggles the faster it goes down. When the mud has got over its neck and is climbing towards the out-thrust head, there is no hope.

10 October 1928
"Atherton": In the silent scrubs of the Daintree range there lives a lively lizard who spends half his life in the water. He is 18 inches long, with tall hind legs and a tail that is an excellent rudder. He likes the shaded streams where they ripple over stones. His happiness is in leaping from scrub to scrub across the water, taking flying jumps to the big boulders, but running through the shallow water with his head held very high. He seems to propel himself off the small stones with his hind legs and tail. Water running very fast makes but little difference to him; in fact he seems to get an added impetus by dashing at an angle through swirling water. This lizard is fairly common along some mountain streams, but I have never seen him in the lowlands.

17 October 1928
"Up Top": When the N.Q. Binghi falls in love and the lady is coy, then, if totem relationships are legitimate, he hies to the sorcerer, offering the necessary present. A love charm is made, of light wood about eight inches long and two inches wide, shaped like an eye and smoothed almost flat. Burnt into it are mystic signs which represent the love of the stars for the man, and ochred bars represent an

enamoured he-cockatoo and other fowl. The sorcerer murmurs incantations over the charm and breathes into it, so he says, a feeling of life which will magnetically attract the senses of the girl. At night Romeo retires to a romantic spot some distance from the camp, threads a hair-string through one end of the charm, and commences to whirl it round his head while facing towards his lady's gunyah. The charm vibrates with a soft but penetrating noise, and Romeo speaks with it impassioned words of love while glaring through the darkness. All his mind is on the girl, and the vibrations of the charm are supposed to carry to her his pent-up feelings. The first night she may only stir uneasily in her sleep. The second night if all works well, she should vaguely dream of him. Romeo spells for a week, but at daytime with every opportunity, he says things to her with his eyes. If she is still cold, he tries the charm again. She dreams frequently of him, finally stretches out her arms and call his name in sleep. She wakes up, trembling but deliciously warm, her mind full of the idea of what a fine fellow Romeo is. One night she wakes up, crawls over her father's body, glares unmentionable things at the domestic dog, and sneaks out of the gunyah. Romeo knows she is coming, for a thrill rises from his toes up. He whirls the charm frantically so that his rising love will guide and draw her to him.

17 October 1928
"Sea Nomad":   In the early days a surprising number of white men carved out island kingdoms for themselves in Torres Strait, New Guinea and the Malay Archipelago. They were mostly survivors from wrecks, with a leaven of adventurers and escaped convicts. Only about one in thirty escaped massacre by the natives, but these used their heads and rose on the superstitions of their hosts and the cupidity of their chiefs, and often wound up as boss chief. They ruled with a rod of iron. On large islands shared by different clans the chiefs were often at war, and the lone castaway took advantage of this by training his hosts to slaughter the other fellows with but small loss to themselves. After one such victory the position of the castaway was assured, but he had to step warily to avoid entanglement in the intrigues of chiefs and medicine-men. Large islands occasionally harbored two of these castaways at a time. These were given full liberty save that they were not allowed to see one another, the chiefs fearing a combination of whites against the natives. Tales are told of the heartburnings of such castaways when knowing that a fellow white was living almost within coo-ee. On the other hand, convicts, fearful of apprehension by the authorities, ruthlessly opposed the presence of any other whites, even ordering their native

warriors to massacre castaways landing on the beach. Such a one was Wani, of Badu, but there were quite a number of others. These white kings were given regular harems, and the fiercest of them took their pick of the prettiest young girls from each tribe, and left as many children as Methuselah.

17 October 1928
"Two Eyes":   South-west of the Mitchell (N.Q.) the abos. stage a picturesque rain-making ceremony at which many tribes congregate. The show being spread over 10 days the majority of the players are kept busy hunting foodstuffs for the camp. Others build a large gunyah, and prepare stage material. Within a wide circle of the singing people the witch-doctors commence the play. Their naked bodies, well greased, flaunt ochre bars and tufts of dried grasses; they bear armlets of clinking shells and bones. Their mumbled incantations rise from a whining dirge to a crescendo of screaming song as they rush and slash one another with knives. As the blood flows other performers throw handfulls of bird's-down in the air, which, forming a soft cloud, slowly sinks amongst the dancers, clinging to their bloody figures, or being trampled underfoot. The blood symbolises the rain of life, which must dry up if the Great Spirit fails to quench the thirst of his children; the down representing the rain clouds. While this is going on, a stream of workers carries stones into the gunyah, thus signifying the gathering of the clouds. The spectators then arise and circling round the gunyah, dance to a slow chant imploring an answer to the efforts of the medicine-men. The men whose bodies have collected the most down then take some of the stones into the branches of tall trees. Should these drop, it symbolises the falling of the clouds. Should real clouds form, it is a sign that the Great Spirit is responsive. Joyfully the tribes mass in a circle around the gunyah, entwine their arms and with a yell, charge into one common centre and burst through the gunyah. The bursting of the hut symbolises the bursting of the clouds and its fall is the fall of rain.

31 October 1928
"Up Top":   The Cooktown abos. have a legend about the Black Mountains. Big tribes lived around there, one being bossed by a witch-doctor named Maneater. So long as he feasted on lewd fellows of the baser sort, the tribespeople were too scared to complain, but when he slew the chief's son while the lad was asleep they got nasty. So Maneater changed himself into a gigantic snake and took up his abode in one of the innumerable caves of the mountains. Amongst the

rocks there grows a species of grass-tree, whose gum is invaluable for binding weapons, and the gins and piccanninies were sent out each week by the warriors to collect the gum. So the witch-doctor transformed his bad old mother into an eagle and she circled over the mountains by day, signalling down to her snake son the approach of gum-seeking parties. In this way Maneater was able to scoff many a stray gin. The piccannninies he transformed into turkeys for the sustenance of his eagle mother. Then the witch-doctor put it into the minds of the tribes around about to unite and exterminate his own tribe, against which he had developed an intense hatred. So a great battle was fought in the plain below and the remnant of Maneater's tribe fled to the hills, the witch-doctor following in the form of a warrior. But a rival witch-doctor spotted the imposter, who hurriedly commenced turning himself into a snake again. By counter witch-craft his enemy caused a hitch and Maneater became a gigantic goanna which fled up a tree. As the indignant tribesmen filled him with spears he exploded with a bang that shook the mountains and splashed the rocks with the blood-red lichen which grow on them to this very day.

7 November 1928
"Gouger": Thursday Islanders regard themselves as having a special proprietorial interest in Captain Cook, for Endeavour Strait washes their front doorstep, while from the verandah they glimpse Possession Island, where in 1770 the illustrious navigator took possession in the name of King George III, of the whole of the eastern seaboard of Australia. A tablet marks the spot, but few people know that when Cook landed on the tiny shingled beach they stepped over a quartz reef with lumps of gold in it the size of raisins. Surveyor Embley found it when landing to take observations many years later. If Cook and his men had only noticed that gold at their feet – and there was a much larger goldfield within easy distance – Australia might have been populated from the north instead of the south.

7 November 1928
"Gouger": I never saw a man with such a mutilated hide as that island celebrity, the late lamented Nicholas the Greek. There was hardly a square inch of his skin but bore the brand of some desperate encounter with man, fish or beast. In confidence Nicholas used to say, with that wary grin of his, that man was the least formidable because one always met him in his own element. One strip of Nicholas's back carried marks suggestive of the cat-o'-nine-tails (which

he had actually tasted), but these scars were left by the claws of New Guinea alligator. A gash across his thigh was the legacy from a shark, while a neat hollow bitten clean out from a calf of his leg was the work of a sea-snake. His "man wounds" were beyond counting, inflicted by bullet, spear, arrow, club, tomahawk and knife. There were even a few razor slashes, but knife wounds predominated, due mostly to Nicholas's acquaintance with excitable Malays. Although he was usually ranked as a dangerous desperado, Nicholas had quite a number of good deeds to his credit. On one occasion off the N.Q. coast, while trying to save the life of a native girl, he found himself up against 11 colored men with tomahawks and knives, and was badly carved up before he reached shore through shark-infested water. He was sewn up with a packing-needle and thread.

7 November 1928

"Up Top": What's wrong with New Guinea for paper-pulping mills? The island is a mass of timber, from seaboard to seaboard, and the varieties vary from the vine to the giant out of which the natives chop 70ft. fighting canoes. And there are rivers running 500 miles inland, down which rafts could be floated to the sea. A finer field for experiments there is nowhere to be found.

14 November 1928

"Atherton": Many animals and birds are good doctors. The cat and dog have a knowledge of medicinal grasses, and the duck can select the right number of grains of gravel to cure its indigestion. I have occasionally noticed a sick bush bird rooting all by itself for tucker not on its ordinary menu. Though animals have an instinct for what is good for them, they have their poisons too. The camel has his ironwood leaves, the steer his zamia plant, the horse his Darling pea. Occasionally a sort of 'flu runs through the bush, attacking both birds and beasts. I have seen wallabies dead by the score after such a visitation, and the live ones so desperately ill that they would scarcely hop from under a man's feet.

14 November 1928

"Up Top": There is strong reason for believing that diamonds have been found in other parts of Australia besides the Nullagine (W.A.). Old Hans Dehm, a N.Q. prospector, carried with him a small stone of good quality, which he always declared he had got in the dish on the Rocky River diggings. This is a wild spot on top of the coastal range in Cape York Peninsula, all thick scrub. The creek carries blue clay, but it looks like ordinary slate clay. A syndicate was once formed

at Thursday island to see if any more diamonds could be found in the locality indicated, but it met with no luck. Old Hans perished recently on a prospecting trip, after knocking out a shammy for these last 40 years on the Peninsula.

5 December 1928

"Up North":   Is it any wonder that opium-smuggling continues? The recent Geneva report estimates that over 2600 ounces of Government opium are sold per day in Hong Kong. As for illicit opium, that can be obtained as readily and much more cheaply. Three years back it could be bought in Hong Kong for ten shillings a tin, and easily disposed of in Cairns for at least £7. The Geneva report makes it pretty clear that opium was never more plentiful in Hong Kong than it is today.

5 December 1928

"Sea Nomad":   It's surprising what a little thing will retrieve an apparently hopeless situation. Just south of Tutu Island we ran our lugger on a reef. She swung amidships, and we could feel her timbers trembling with every ripple of the outgoing tide. In an hour, at the least, it seemed a certainty that her own weight must break her back. We ran an anchor out astern, and set the boys to the winch, but their utmost efforts only made the lugger shiver slightly to the strain of the chain. We had a crowd of natives aboard, bound for a mission station. My frantic mate ran them to the stern, and set the whole mob jumping upon the deck in unison while he beat time. We felt the lugger quiver, and heard the coral underneath her grinding menacingly. The crew strained at the winch, the natives jumped and howled with redoubled energy and inch by inch the lugger began to slip back towards the deep water. The jumpers were becoming exhausted when the vessel's weight began to tell in our favour, and she went in a slow, crunching glide, slipping back into the sea like a thankful whale.

19 December 1928

"Sea Nomad":   Along those Torres Strait reefs where the edible octopus makes his home the islander identifies the cubby-house under the coral by the doormat of empty shells. The crawler is expertly prodded out of doors, despite his clinging resistance and the native grips him on a certain spot in the back. Immediately the tentacles hang down paralysed. Along these same reefs crawls a shellfish humping a spiral shell. To touch the tip of the shell means a slight yet quite distinct electric shock. Another queer creature that loafs about there grows whiskers. These are really threadlike antennae that enquiringly sway

about under water. They appear to register underwater vibration, for when any fish approaches the whiskers are tucked in under the shell. Occasionally the porcupine-fish bloats here. It looks like a nightmare, and its spines are very poisonous at one season of the year.

19 December 1928

"Fingerpoint":   A favourite method adopted by northern natives to get rid of white men was by marooning. An instance was the case of Toby Leonard and his soldier cobber, who years ago bought the lugger "Young Australia", engaged a native crew and set out from Thursday Island to try their luck at bêche-de-mer fishing. Anchoring just off the mouth of the Pascoe River, the two white men went ashore to look for turtle eggs. The crew whipped up the anchor and sailed away, leaving the two men stranded on a sand-spit, a bare 18 inches above water level, in a lonely sea, without a drop of fresh water and the high tide coming. Providence sent along old Daniel Hodges just in the nick of time. The crew sailed the lugger to the coast, ran her into a creek in Temple Bay, had glorious feasts until the provisions ran out, and then scuttled the vessel and made their way across bush to the Seven Rivers country, to which they belonged. Constables Fergusson and Smith, of the T.I. water police, after a long chase, captured the renegades, who were imprisoned for six months in homely Stewart's Creek gaol. They returned as heroes to incite their tribesmen to further aggressions against the foolish whites.

26 December 1928

"Sea Nomad":   In the Hon. John Douglas's day he took a party in the Albatross on a cruise through Torres Strait. The Bishop of Queensland was aboard (there was no diocese of Carpentaria then). They visited Massig Island where Ned Moseby had carved himself out an Island kingdom. Ashore were Ned and Walker and Captain Dubbins just recovering from a rum bout under the palms. Ned hospitably invited the landing party up to the house, where they were served by Ned's native wife and a bevy of giggling girls, each handing out cocoanut-milk. During the convivialities the Bishop inquired "And what may your denomination be, Captain?" Moseby scratched his head and glared at Dubbins. "I dunno," he said thoughtfully; "what are we Dubbins?" The natives held their breath as Dubbins glared at Walker for enlightenment. "I dunno rightly," Dubbins replied at last, "but I believe I'm a Presbyterian". The question was quite beyond Walker. "Dunno wot I am," he mumbled in a muddled way. "Maybe I am, maybe I aint". "I know what I am now", broke in Moseby brightly," I'm a corroborean!"

9 January 1929

"Sea Nomad": The old "City of Hankow", lately lying off Garden Island, Sydney, was towed from Thursday Island by H.M.A.S. Sydney for repairs. She was a noted tea clipper in her day and sailed in goodly company with the "City of Pekin" and "City of Madras". Looking now more like a huge ungainly box than a ship, she is again to be towed to T.I. to resume duty as a naval coal hulk.

16 January 1929

"Sea Nomad": The floating islands in Aussie waters are mere specks compared with what comes down New Guinea's old-man rivers. The Sepik is a beautiful stream, in places 15 fathoms deep, flowing gently through tropical jungle after farewelling its sombre mountains. Its water is tinged light brown by the sago swamps, but is first-class drinking. Islands often acres in extent float calmly down this waterway. Mostly they consist of about a five-foot depth of soil held together by roots, creepers, tufted grasses and a tropical species of hyacinth. Such islands are slow as the hands of time but quite as irresistable. Voyagers meeting them know they must either get out or go under. I know one recruiter who had Hobson's choice. He ventured up a by-way and found a channel completely blocked by an island that was floating forward an inch at a time. His craft was made up of two huge canoes lashed together, with the usual grass house all over to keep out rain. In desperation he set his boys to chop a channel through the islet. This was much easier than it seems, for the boys had merely to tomahawk two straight lines straight ahead. The sopping earth in between was carried to the bottom by its own weight, thus leaving a narrow channel in which the canoes floated. But the islet, like the river and the country which gives it birth, was remorseless. Slowly the severed ends began closing in behind the canoes. This did not matter so much, but some attraction kept forcing the debris quicker and quicker against the vessel. The boys cut faster and faster, the recruiter worked until he too almost sweated blood, but in three hours they were in the centre of an islet that was pushing against them faster than they could cut. Behind, the channel had closed in as if it had never been. When utterly exhausted the crew watched the earth sog tightly against the canoes. They fell overboard too weary even to stand, the recruiter bitterly conscious that he would be pushed back out onto the main river and swept down goodness knows how far until liberated. Suddenly a boy howled. "The canoes are drowning!" They were. The wet earth was irresistably sucking them under. There was plenty of time to get stores and belongings out of the vessels.

The boys, ashen-grey with fright, hurried the goods ashore and waited there while the recruiter stood and watched his craft slowly, very slowly, sucked under until it disappeared, and the islet, its surface intact, went on its way as if nothing had happened.

23 January 1929

"Up Top": In the north there is an agile bush rat that can climb tall trees at the run. He is very inquisitive, and at night slithers along the branches and peers down at the camp-fire with ruby eyes. He hardly waits for the humans to snore before he is hopping over their blankets, pinching crusts, rattling the camp-oven lid and getting himself entangled in the jam-tin. As the night wears on he becomes bolder, and nibbles the sleeper's hair. The resultant roar scatters him and his cobbers into the bushes, where they peer around, with little furry bodies ready for a pattering scamper up the nearest trees. They live on berries and flower pods and the tender shoots of the wild palms. Occasionally a colony of them take a liking to the cocoanut-trees, compelling the planters to fence the butts of the palms with slippery sheets of tin. There is none of the furtiveness of the house rat about them, and they are often pretty. Owls love them.

30 January 1929

"Sea Nomad": The Murray and Darnley island boys and girls are the best dancers in Torres Strait, and eclipse those of New Guinea. For grace, variety and execution their performances rank high among the terpsichorean efforts of savage races. Their costumes are magnificent – dari head-dresses magnificently plumed, crescentic mias of carved pearl-shell, armlets of clinking shells, kadik bowstring guards ornamented with plumes and colored cowries, and skirts of jet-black cassowary feathers or silky fibre of the fig-tree root. Their dances are seasonal, diabolical or just frolicsome, according to circumstances. The first missionaries sternly suppressed dancing, but the present incumbent is broad-minded, and the natives are encouraged to renew their old-time rejoicings, skull or devil worship being banned. The girls, with their head-dresses of croton-leaves and white and yellow down of the Torres Strait pigeon, with dibi-dibi shells and goa-nut rattles, necklet and armlets of shimmering pearl shell, brown eyes excited and swarthy faces smiling, make a striking picture. The music is the clapping, the crooning beat of the wasikor drum, song and laughter, stamping of feet and occasional plaintive strains from reed instruments. Seen in the moonlight under the palms of Medigee Bay, one of these dances is a sight which lingers long in the memory.

30 January 1929

"Up Top": Years ago an agitation resulted in legislation that no pearl-shell taken from Northern Australian waters should measure less than five inches across. Bennet was Customs then, and when John Cowling of Maubriag sent in two tons of shells some of which was reckoned a little under measure, Bennet seized the cargo. The Hon. John Douglas tried the case, but to the customman's consternation he measured the shell on the rounded side, not the flat, and Cowling got his shell back, because the law did not specify along which side a shell should be measured. A subsequent amendment of the Act settled that point, but not before there had been many squabbles. At one time Tommy Farquhar, the Pearl King, had a consignment in cases on the wharf awaiting shipment. Harbormaster Webster inspected the stuff and found two shells slightly undersize. Customs-officer Bennet formally charged Farquhar. "Show me the shell", demanded Farquhar. The customs man handed the shells over and Farquhar promptly pitched them into the sea. "Now where's your evidence?" he asked. The customs man had the cases opened and the contents strewn over the wharf. In all those thousands of shells, there was not another one under size. Both Farquhar and Bennet were mad – Bennet because he had slipped; Farquhar because he had to have all that shell repacked.

6 February 1929

"Up Top": The inseparable companion of Miss Binghi is the yam-stick. About four feet long, of walking-stick thickness, it is of hardwood, pointed at one end, chisel-shaped at the other and fire-hardened. That stick digs up tons of food before it is worn out. A gin will dig four feet down in hard ground for a deep-rooted yam, scooping out the dirt with a clawed hand. She makes a small round hole until her outstretched fingers can reach no further; then if the yams still go down, she must set to work and widen the hole so as to allow her head to go down with her arm, and if the hole is then not deep enough she must widen out again to allow her body to follow her head. The yam-stick also comes in handy, to thrust into hollow logs where kangaroo-rat, dingo pup, possum or bandicoot may lurk. It is poked into burrows to see whether porcupine, snake or rat is at home. It tears into the rotted grasstree and palm and dislodges the fat white grubs. On the seashore it is plunged deep into the mud in search of hidden crabs and prodded down to discover shellfish. In the rocky pools it searches under the ledges for fish, and into coral burrows for the big mangrove crabs.

20 February 1929
"Up Top": The pack teams of the Far North are dwindling; not because of motor competition either. A few years back there were eight teams of 30 horses each constantly moving to the tinfields behind Cooktown (Q.). Along the Peninsula were other teams, trudging to connect the supply luggers with the little goldfields. The big Peninsula mining camp and cattle station and two score of sandalwood camps were solely dependent on packhorse for the bringing of supplies and transport of their produce to the coast. Over level forest country; up 3000ft jungle ranges; along dry tracks or mountain country intersected by rushing torrents; through bush-fires and floods; dry seasons or wet, the old packhorse got there just the same. With the steady decline of tin and gold yields and the cutting out of sandalwood the picturesque teams are vanishing. The Chinese packers, who once had fine teams on the road, have almost entirely disappeared, while the spider–web of teams that once moved along the Palmer, Normanby, Ebagoolah and the Coen are now but a memory.

6 March 1929
"Sea Nomad": A prized shark was one which ate a wealthy Chinaman who fell over the Thursday Island wharf some time back. The yellow man was en route for China, and missed the gangway in the dark. Next day a shark was caught, and inside was the man's leg. The dead man's countrymen offered £500 for his head, which they desired to send to China for burial. Added to this incitement was the fact that the deceased carried a belt holding 200 sovereigns around his waist. Many of the colored population of T.I. turned out in boats after sharks, but though numbers were caught the one containing the head and the money-belt was never hooked.

13 March 1929
"Up Top": Little Thursday Island, with its one mile of roadway is going in for motoring enthusiastically – the speck now boasts ten cars and eight lorries.

20 March 1929
"Sea Nomad": A thrilling sport vanished from the Coral Sea with the passing of the clipper-schooners that mothered the pearling fleets. At the laying-up period throughout the cyclone season a representative vessel of each fleet would be chosen to carry its colors in a race down Endeavour Strait, around Woody Wallace island and back to T I. Intense rivalry existed between the fleets,

which had a personnel of 1500 men all told. All Thursday Island, including its seething mass of colored humanity, lined the shores as the racing craft came in sight heading up the strait. The colored blood, always hot, was apt to become uncontrollable even before the finish of such a race. At times knives were drawn by keen partisans, tomahawks flashed and there was battle, murder and sudden death while the result of the race was still in doubt.

20 March 1929
"Gouger": Captain Alf Gale, retired mariner, hates to have his memory revived by newspaper reports of rich ambergris finds. When a boy he used to play bushrangers with other choice spirits on Bondi Beach. One day the gang stacked a heap of driftwood for a signal fire, and finding a big lump of dried fat, added it to the blaze. Much to their disappointment, it did not burn well though it sputtered a lot. Alf regaled a chemist friend with an account of the experience, mentioning that there were "little black wicks" in the melting fat. Next day the chemist accompanied him to the beach. They raked out of the ashes one little lump of unburnt fat. It was first-class ambergris, and had apparently been a corner of a piece six pounds in weight. "You've burnt a thousand pounds", said the chemist.

27 March 1929
"Up Top": Watched a new chum "blackfellowing" a tree. Instead of cutting a scarf in the orthodox way he nicked the huge trunk completely round, deepening the nicks for half a day. It was a beautiful stick, the barrel going straight up for 60 ft. without a branch. Of course it was as hollow as a drum or it would not have been left there for chummy. That day was breathless, and the amateur found it hot, gazing up in puzzlement again and again as the Sphinx-like tree refused to fall. He had cut completely through its shell and the vertical weight of the tree in that still air balanced it there. Spitting on his hands, chummy tackled the "blackfellowing" all over again, like sharpening a gigantic lead pencil. When it he was just about exhausted, the great tree gently sighed and telescoped slowly down into its own butt. And there it still stands, like a candle in a candlestick.

27 March 1929
"Sea Nomad": Four Japs are now diving in Torres Strait waters clad in the usual helmet and weights. They **have** discarded the remainder of the cumbersome suit for an ordinary pair of engineer's overalls. This leaves them very free to work. They

have fished shell from 30 fathoms and have suffered no ill effects. By all the old theories, they should have been dead men, or at least crippled by diver's paralysis. Possibly it is the brain only that is affected by water pressure.

27 March 1929
"Sea Nomad":   I was anchored for a week, during a cyclonic blow, off Darnley Island, and came to the conclusion that the lugger was haunted. Every evening a faint but unmistakable knocking would commence and echo right through the vessel. All efforts to trace the noise failed. To make the mystery more mysterious, the ghostly tapping seemed to come from below the water-line. All was explained when, on the last night, a grinning islander slid overboard and came up with a vigorously-protesting crab. Its claws had done the knocking, burgling the barnacles on the vessel's copper-plated bottom. I've listened to an almost similar noise in the deathly quiet of the Valala River. The local natives say that in the latter case it is the stubby horn-like nose of a big river fish that does the knocking. He sheers off, then charges the picked barnacle and crushes its shell with his battering-ram beak. Such little tricks played on a lonely human while in a savage country don't improve one's nerves.

3 April 1929
"Up Top":   A gland goes wrong – hence the giant man or woman. So say the scientists. Nature applies the same rule but just as sparingly, in the animal kingdom. I've known a pure bred wallaby to grow as large as moderate-sized 'roo, while an old duck I met up north was the size of a goose. If this particular gland could be located and developed, a powerful blow would be struck at H.C.L. We could grow fowls as big as emus with corresponding eggs; sheep as large as cows (what a harvest for a squatter and shearer!) and cattle as bulky as elephants. It would be pretty awful though if rats acquired the secret and grew the size of dogs, while dogs that ate the rats grew to the size of tigers, with fleas on 'em as big as blowflies.

3 April 1929
"Atherton":   The N.Q. jungles are a study in vine growths. These range from a thickness far exceeding that of a ship's hawser to a thread as fine as a girl's hair. The thick cable growths loop from tree to tree over a distance of hundreds of yards, sagging heavily. It is these cables that make the scrub-faller's job dangerous, for when they are bringing down a "drive" of trees, a cable may pull the mass in their direction. Another vine has a comparatively slender stem

on which it rises to the tallest tree-top, and then swings out from tree to tree, carpeting the tops in a curtain of delicate foliage. Another grows in a series of spirals. Yet another grows in a bamboo-like clump and sends out long feelers that arch to the ground, only to spring up and search for a tree. The lawyer-vine gives forth many lengths of cane, the majority of which creep along the ground. Sometimes it reaches a low-lying branch and immediately begins to climb to the top, and, not satisfied, keeps on across the tops of the trees.

3 April 1929

"Up Top": Some rocks under varying conditions of temperature, behave very strangely. There is a boulder-covered hill in N.Q. which, after a bitterly cold night followed by a fierce sun, makes sounds like rifles popping. It is flakes of granite bursting out from the boulders. The boulders are almost round, and fallen about them are countless flakes about a quarter-inch thick. The great rocks seem to be built in layers, like gigantic stone onions. A particularly nasty type of rock was encountered at depth in one of the Hillgrove mines. It was liable to split suddenly and violently when bored with a drill. On one occasion the whole wall of drive burst in, killing one man and injuring several. There are rocks which, when brought to the surface from a depth and left exposed to the air for a few weeks, crumble up. This stuff is liked by miners, for it is easy to crush. Some rocks can be softened by burning; others explode with a belch of sulphurous fumes.

10 April 1929

"Sea Nomad": It was through a Rossel Island native called Ge-Ke that John Macdonald, recently retired Master of Works at Port Moresby, learnt the Rossel Island dialect, which accomplishment eventually led to the taming of those turbulent savages. Ge-Ke lying aboard the "Merrie England" with a bullet in his leg, looked to Macdonald as his one friend in a world peopled by demons, white, black and brown. Each time the cook passed the wounded savage's bunk, he would scowl fearfully at the patient and sharpen his knife noisily. The terrified Ge-Ke would scream for Macdonald. The native crew, who dearly would have loved to cut the alien's throat, scowled in through the porthole on every possible occasion. Finally, Macdonald had practically to live beside the wounded man. Sir William Macgregor, who was on board, appeared to notice nothing, but the canny old Scot was calculating all the time on this chance that young Macdonald would learn Ge-Ke's difficult lingo, and deliberating as to how he would use his subordinate's knowledge later.

8 May 1929

"Fingerpoint": There have been many attempts to open up the country where the Southern Cross came to grief. As far back as 1837 Lieutenant (afterwards governor) Grey landed at Hanover Bay and did some exploring around the Prince Regent and Glenelg Rivers. An expedition left Champion Bay (Geraldton) in 1860 in a small ketch, and cruised the Lower Glenelg and Regent rivers in quest of grazing country. On their return they boosted the district as carrying "thousands of acres of magnificent grass 7ft high"; unfortunately it proved to be useless "spear" grass, although if the party had got past the coastal belt they would have found magnificent grasses inland. The Camden Harbor Association was found in Melbourne in 1864, and an attempt at settlement made. But the rough country, niggers and isolation caused the abandonment of the enterprise. Twenty years later the "Victorian Squatting Company" sent out an expedition with 2000 sheep which landed on the west shore of Cambridge Gulf. But it took two years before the rough coastal range was penetrated and by that time few of the stock were left. In 1889 all that remained of the company's assets was sold up at Wyndham. Still, a practicable route had been opened around the head of the Cambridge Gulf, and this was utilised in 1901 by F.S. Brockman, who mapped a considerable area of the country.

8 May 1929

"Up Top": Much is said of the hardship the Southern Cross crew had to endure in the way of mosquitoes. Why on earth they did not camp on one of the hills surrounding their landing-ground beats me. They would not have had to climb high to get rid of the pest. Skeeters naturally keep to low ground and are particularly fond of a mangrove flat. Any night breeze that is going fans the hills, and it takes only a very feeble draft to blow the pests away. Up north in the skeeter season no bushman would dream of camping on a flat if there was even the smallest ridge within reach, let alone a hill. I don't know to what height a skeeter can rise, but I've never met them in hilly country in N.Q., even when the flats below were swarming with them. Incidentally, smoke from a mangrove fire is extremely unpopular with the biters.

8 May 1929

"Sea Nomad": Jimmy Mills, a Samoan Giant, was one of the colored men who made history in the early pearl-shelling days of Torres Strait. He was six foot two with a chest like a draught horse and a fine intelligent head. He

imbibed learning from the pioneer missionaries, then went on deep water ships and completed his education as a bos'n, sailing several times around the world. When the islands and pearl-shell claimed him, he had lurid experiences among the blackbirders, and afterwards saw a good deal of the "hell-ships". He finally settled on Naghir Island, below the needle-like peak that overlooks both Strait and Barrier. He was a born trader, had a command of eight languages, and knew how to work on the superstitions of the islanders.

15 May 1929

"Up Top": in the Kimberley (Nor' Westralia) gold rush in 1886 a crowd of ruffianly nomads made a lasting name for themselves, the "Ragged Thirteen". They were a cosmopolitan band of cattle duffers and worse, who on being kicked out of Queensland, lit out for the policeless spaces and the pickings of a gold rush. They crossed the McArthur; then went on to the Bar and kept that already lively place terrorised by revolver play until the rest of the gold-seekers combined and kicked them out. Then the "Thirteen" raided shanties and stores and held up travellers whose parties were weaker than their own. The only thing they never stole was soap. After raiding the shanty at Abraham's Billabong the combined diggers ran them clean out of the Roper, though as the crowd passed on they drifted back again. A favorite game of theirs was to dress as Custom officers and collect the poll-tax from Chows who followed up the diggers, and who were scattered throughout the mining camps of the territory. Only two of the "Thirteen" were brought to book by officialdom. Three others were quietly shot and the others drifted away.

15 May 1929

"Up Top": Organisation for pioneering jobs was first-class in the old days. When Chares Todd, then P.M.G., had charge of construction of the middle section of the North to South Overland Telegraph Line – the two end sections were let by contract – some of the working parties had to travel over 1200 miles through unknown country before they got to their job. They trekked for months in waggons loaded with wine, materials, rations and tools, over unknown areas with water scarce in parts. They had to make their own roads, construct bridges and sink wells, scale precipitous ranges and negotiate desert sandhills. The parties, to their surprise, found that, instead of being all desert, quite large areas of Centralia were well grassed and watered. The greatest difficulty was in finding suitable posts. Scouts were sent out in all directions, and some loads of posts were carted a hundred miles. They are all iron now.

The centre parties did their jobs well and finished before time. The north and south sections, particularly the northern, had endless trouble and had eventually to be taken over by the P.M.G.

22 May 1929

"Up North": In the early days of the Palmer (Q.) diggings the freight from Cooktown soared to £130 a ton for 165 miles. There hurried into Purdie's Camp one day a packer whose horse had cast a shoe, rendering him useless for travelling over the stony ridges. The packer offered any price for nails for the shoe; Billy Yates, a carrier, jocularly undertook to supply five for their weight in gold. The packer agreed, and the nails and gold were evenly balanced on gold scales. The packer hurriedly shod his horse, loaded his team and whistled them off. He was getting 1s. a lb. for packing goods 11 miles, and the horse carried 150lb., so he could afford the price. But the incident was responsible for the report all over the North that the packers of the Palmer shod their horses with gold.

22 May 1929

"Gouger": The latest A.I.M. (Australian Inland Mission) hospital is the Eleanor Symon nursing home at Innamincka (S.A.) which owes its being to the benevolence of Josiah Symon and others. This is its eleventh refuge for the sick, all in places far remote from ordinary medical assistance. It has been suggested with regard to Innamincka that in operations and urgent cases the nursing sisters should communicate with Melbourne, where Doctor G. Simpson would advise them as the case proceeded. At present the nearest phone is 300 miles away, but the mission people hope soon to have wireless. An appliance is now obtainable for about £50, the outfit including transmitting as well as receiving sets and hand generators. One of these, in conjunction with the "Flying Doctor", will revolutionise conditions.

5 June 1929

"Up Top": The so called "desert" of Centralia carries possibly the most nutritive grass in the continent. It grows most prolifically, strange to say, in sandhill country, where as far as the eye can reach stretches a replica of the Sinai Desert. Parakylia, as the natives call the grass, is almost a shrub with stalks full of water. The bucks crush it between stones and squeeze the moisture out into bark troughs. It is drinkable when allowed to stand for the night. Camels are fond of the grass, and will go on indefinitely without water when fed on it.

Stock which have broken away from Territory stations have been known to live in this desert for four months without a drop of water, and when found have been almost too fat to move. At the end of the season the parakylia dries up and loses its water, but stock eat the dried plant ravenously. It has been suggested that underground in Centralia is a vast artesian sea from which the parakylia draws its moisture.

26 June 1929
"Up Top": If the Sal'army cared to start missionising in New Guinea it would leave all the other denominations without a single convert. Papuans and Kanakas love music, and the combination of drums, blaring brass, tambourines and red jerseys would send them into transports of delight. Every tribe in the dark continent would come down from its mountain fastness and follow the blood-and-fire folk to Hell, if the big drum led the way. Head-hunters, woman-eaters, child-slayers, Ku-ku Kukus, Duk-Duks, Kiwaians, Orickavas, swamp-men – every colored heathen in the Possession would flock to the rattle of the tambourine. It would mean the holus-bolus conversion of a continent; but I hope the army won't take my tip, for the Papuan is contented and happy as he is, and has plenty to eat. Missioned en masse he mightn't be so well off.

26 June 1929
"Up Top": It pained me when I saw that "Hamer" (B. 12/6/29) had taken my name in vain in the course of his controversy with himself. The dinkum facts are these. We had dug in at the Doo-Drop Inn in George Street, Sydney, having dug out Major Haveaspot whom we honoured so long as he did the honors. A dog strolled into the bar and scratched a shower of fleas. These insects flew up and drank our beer. In no time they were as big as wallabies. By the time they drunk all the liquor in the bar they were foaming at the mouth and had grown to the size of kangaroos. They then began to chew glass, and became fightable, gnashing their teeth in anything but a mild manner. The dog was torn to shreds and the barmaids fled in terror. I crawled under the sofa but "Hamer" was there already, trying to disguise himself with Major Haveaspot's eyeglass. Police were routed with ignominy and firemen were defeated by the fleas gnawing holes in their hoses. A squadron of aeroplanes arrived three weeks later, when the fleas had grown to the size of elephants. A general massacre of Sydney was averted by a little barmaid with big brown eyes who sprinkled salt on each flea's tail which was fatal. "Hamer" had since, I am told, gone in for fiction; Major Haveaspot has gone into liquidation and the barmaid into hysterics. I expect to be out next month.

26 June 1929
"Sea Nomad": Joe Forbes sailed in the schooner Statescombe in 1824 for the Timor Islands. The crew was massacred by native pirates, the vessel looted and burned, and Forbes and a lad taken prisoner. The lad soon died. Forbes lived through tortures and mutilations until rescued in 1839. While crossing the Arafura Sea, Captain Watson of the ship Essington, heard from a Dutch skipper that an English prisoner was held by the native pirates at Timor Laut. When Watson sighted the place he hurried most of his well-armed crew up into the foretop where they hid with a good view of the deck. The brass guns were rammed with grape and canister and covered with tarpaulins. The ship looked an easy prey to the spy canoes that soon boarded her. Watson watched until a big chief in bird-of-paradise regalia came aboard then hospitably declared that the chief must be his guest for the night. He gained the haughty one's confidence, and eventually learned that the white captive was at a near-by village. At sundown the other natives were shooed overboard, and the chief was invited to sit on the skylight while Watson showed him presents. One present was a brightly-polished handcuff. Watson slipped a link around his own ankle, showing the chief what a fine ornament it made. He then tied it on the chief's ankle, and slipped the other link onto a handy ringbolt. "Now", he said, "hand over the white man or I'll string you up to the yardarm!" When the canoemen came back in they found their chief standing bound on a crate with a rope around his neck, with hefty sailors holding the other end of the rope as it swung from the yardarm. Armed men were up in the rigging and cannon frowned from the decks. The cut-throats surrendered the captive, or rather what was left of him. Forbes couldn't walk. Among other tortures, his captors had put red-hot coals on his belly. He was many months in Sydney hospital before he could hobble about, and he was never again quite sane.

26 June 1929
"Up Top": The big engineering feat of lifting the Victoria bridge for the removal and repair of rollers has gone practically unnoticed in Australia. In fact, comparatively few Brisbane people even know that the City Council has completed the contract. America is more observant; engineer Gilchrist has been asked by the publishers of "Engineering and Contracting" for permission to reproduce plans and photos. The drawings for the lifting apparatus were the production of W.J.Doak; the steelwork fabrication was done by Harveys. The job was an unusual and a very big one, but as neither girls in bathing costumes nor moving-picture magnates nor the razor gang had anything to do with it the stunt press ignored it.

3 July 1929

"Sea Nomad":   Thursday Island didn't overwhelm the German visitors on the Emden with gush; the little island lost too much sleep over the war than to be more than polite. Perhaps no part of Australia had better reason to remember the war years. It was the centre of the naval activity that guarded our north-eastern and northern coasts and the straits and passageways. At different times every T.I. civilian was under arms, quite apart from the big percentage of men who went overseas. The lads who are generally in the naval reserve were soon aboard craft of all descriptions, chasing after reported raiders, sneaking up jungle-clad New Guinea rivers in search of suspected submarine bases, and spying the steamer passageways through the reefs for mines. And T.I. was kept at it right to the very last. There was quite a lot of work that obtained no publicity done in those reef-strewn waters, and quite a number of Australian-loaded ships were saved from a wet grave by the unceasing vigilance of T.I. men, who saw too much of enemy methods to forget them readily.

3 July 1929

"Atherton":   A sheep-dog story comes from Maoriland, where the truth is respected. The tyke was yarding the sheep in a "pull, head and yard" event when a rebellious jumbuck charged him. The dog neither barked nor bit. He simply gave the sheep a straight right on the nose with his paw. The sheep came again and stopped a left cross to the muzzle. It "baa-ed" ferociously, lowered its head and charged again. The dog reared up and delivered a left and right straight to the point. The dazed sheep took the count and rolled backward into the pen.

3 July 1929

"Sea Nomad":   Recently I visited a most desolate spot on the Great Barrier Reef – Raine Islet, a half-mile strip of coral and sand hardly 15 feet above water in its most mountainous part. Fossicking for guano, we dug down some six feet in the coral-sandshell rock, and unearthed a nest of 85 petrified turtle eggs. They looked like shrivelled ping-pong balls badly in need of a wash. Some were merely a thick hollow shell, turned to solid limestone. Apparently the islet has been growing for centuries, for when those eggs were laid the spot was pure beach sand. Now there is six feet of rock above it.

3 July 1929

"SEA NOMAD": A bread relished by Tongan Islanders is made out of the fermented paste of the breadfruit, which, along with other fruits is buried in pits and kept for months. The paste is then rolled into balls and cooked. It is tasty but smellfull. There is a legend that once upon a time there lived on Eua a young man named Vainuku, most marvellously handsome. The princess Tui of Tonga, canoed across with her maids to have a peep at this prodigy. On landing on the islet beach the princess packed the maids off to gather firewood for the billy. One of the girls strayed and found her way into Vainuku's palm-thatched house. A man knelt there making bread. The curious one snatched off the baker's headgear and out rolled the ravishing hair of Vainuku. Although he was warrior, he secretly delighted in the woman's work of making bread. That night under the sighing palms, the sheik sneaked out to do a little courting. First of all he glided to where the princess lay on her couch of fronds. But she rose on her elbow, covered her body with her hair, and held her nose. "Pooh" she lisped. "Get!" – Vainuku was treated with similar disdain by all the girls until he bent over the one who had seen his hair that morning.

10 July 1929

"SEA NOMAD": The Japanese are wonderful sailors as I have cause to remember. I was marooned for seven months on No.1 Howick Island, and at dawn one day saw three sails rounding Cape Melville. On my lookout peak I burned smoke fires all day nearly howling as the wind gradually freshened, which meant that my possible rescuers might not be able to make the narrow passage-way. But they came on. Great combers were pelting in from far across the Barrier, the sea was grey with fog that again and again hid the battling craft. The wind increased until the grass on the hillside was flattened like a mat, and I had to cling to the huge pile of rocks that I had erected as a distress beacon. Sundown came early, and the first little ship bobbed fearfully into the mouth of the passage. I danced a jig and waved a tattered blanket that was immediately snatched from my hands. The boat came flying up the passage and I howled and shrieked, while the wind tore the sound from my mouth. Far below, skirting the very edge of the reef, she passed, and a puff of smoke was whisked away from her stern. I heard no report but danced deliriously, knowing that they had at least seen me. She slewed and raced for anchorage at tiny Coquette Island opposite. Presently the following lugger also fired a signal shot. By now it was almost dark and huge waves were crashing like a foaming cauldron over hundreds of yards of reef. The last lugger

was a blob on the tumbling waters. I clung to the very peak of the lookout trying to make a silhouette, and saw, or imagined I saw, - I couldn't say which – that a dot had been flung overboard as the lugger flashed by into the night. Running down the hill I rushed straight out onto the reef and was picked up and flung back and rolled and rolled and rolled among tons of clinking corals. Shocked and bleeding I rushed out again, jumping the waves yelling and straining into the night. A dinghy appeared and disappeared in the flying spume until talons gripped my hair and I was flung aboard. It was a masterpiece of seamanship turning that dinghy safely upon a thundering reef. Then we had to battle back again through the crashing breakers. Four sweating islanders strained at the oars while a calm faced Jap gave quiet orders from the tiller. Once in the passageway the struggle was nearly over; it was simply a matter of keeping the dinghy bow on to the great waves. For an hour through the dark the lugger cruised up and down running parallel with the reef, seeking a chance to pick us up. It came at last. The lugger flashed past as a huge wave rolled us up to dash us on her deck. Unseen hands reached out, the dinghy was slung bodily on the deck, and the lugger sped on in the darkness with me slithering across the deck clinging to the neck of a lashed-down turtle.

24 July 1929
"SEA NOMAD":   The niggers recently scared off Ambryn Island by a volcano have taken refuge on Malicolo. This would have meant a great feast for the Malicoloians only a very few years back. Even now, in the interior, they are not averse to long pork. A few years back the chief of the most blood-thirsty crowd, the Amac gang of Bignambas, was Rumptner (I believe he is still alive). He had then 117 wives and eight favorites. He must have a thousand by now, for by hereditary right he appropriated the widows and daughters of all his brothers and male relations. The tough old bird had a particular set on Gaspard, a French blackbirder. Rumptner never got Gaspard, though he laid snares for him a dozen times. Into one such trap walked Andre Naturel of the trader "Bienvue", and came within an ace of being scoffed by Rumptner's men. The presence of all these nigs from Ambryn must be making Rumptner's mouth water.

31 July 1929
"UP NORTH":   Whatever truth there may be in the persistent reports received at North Australian police stations that two white women are held captive by the myalls of Caledon Bay (B. 24/7/29), there is plenty of precedent for such happenings. Close to Thursday Island is Prince of Wales Island, where Mrs

Barbara Thompson was in the hands of the Murralug men for seven years. Her husband had been in charge of the cutter "America", and she was saved from the wreck. Deliverance came to her by the merest chance, when a party of officers from H.M.S. Rattlesnake went ashore on a pigeon-shooting expedition. The wife of the captain of the "Speerwee:" met a worse fate in the same island, after her husband and the crew had been murdered by the natives. Ill treatment caused her death. Lower down the Queensland coast, where the "Stirling Castle" smashed up, Mrs Frazer, the captain's wife, was saved from the general massacre. She suffered horrors for two months, when a Government ship rescued her. The fate of a white woman who was with a castaway crew on Moa Island can only be guessed at. For years old natives used to tell how, while the white men were being clubbed, the woman ran screaming up the densely clad scrub peak of big Moa. The head-hunters let her go for the time being, and never found a trace of her again. So far as Caledon Bay is concerned, it is the wildest spot in Australia, and its natives are the most savage and bloodthirsty.

31 July 1929

"Sea Nomad": Kenny was a Lousiade nigger six feet high and as thin as a telegraph pole. His head had been cone "Malicolo fashion" as a piccaninny, with the result that his long forehead sheered straight back from his eyebrows. He was always laughing and from the white man's point of view was just as silly as he looked. But he was as loyal as his shoulders were round. When Allen Innes, the manager for B.P. on Misima, had the natives carrying his precious household goods up to the new house on the hill, Kenny insisted on transporting the big basket of crockery, much to Mrs. Innes's terror. The usual rains had made the clay sticky, and there were just 1000 steep, slippery log steps rising sheer out of the creek. Kenny negotiated half the steps joyfully and then poised himself and shouted a song of praise of his own strength. He was still singing when he slipped and the crockery went crashing down these 500 steps to the very feet of the agonised sinabada. Kenny picked himself up, hurried to the sinabada, and with his own big smile unbroken laughed cheerfully, "Now we can make-him plenty-fella jug belong put-him umbrella alla same Lady Clunn longa Samarai!" But Mrs. Innes much preferred her crockery whole, despite the prettiness of Lady Clunn's drain-pipes covered with broken crockery and used as umbrella stands.

14 August 1929

"Gouger":   The isle of Niuafou, of the Tonga group, where some of the mostly somnolent volcanoes have been mildly playing up, is ruled over by Queen Salotte, a tall and handsome young woman of Samoan type. She was educated mostly in Maoriland and has paid several visits to Sydney. Nuku'alofa is the capital of the tiny kingdom, and the picturesque palace, which looks like glistening marble, though it is merely wood painted white, is a tropic dream among the palms. The sovereign is surrounded by all the pomp and ceremony and little brown toy-soldiers that the Tongans love; but there are no frills about the miniature parliament. I have seen the Prime Minister attired in a faded white lava-lava, and smoking a huge evil smelling cigarette, dangling his big, brown bare feet over the end of the tiny wharf while he dreamily gazed at a fishing-line. Niuafou is a British protectorate, and naturally, Australians have poked their way in there, as traders, officials and missionaries. A missioner of big tonnage is a brother of Earle Page, the Commonwealth treasurer.

28 August 1929

"Atherton":   One of the most unique bands in the world soothes the savage breast at the Lutheran Mission by Salamau Bay (Mandated Territory). There are 17 instruments, each a conch-shell of different tone It took the missioner 12 years to collect shells of perfect pitch. They came from all over the South Pacific. The score is written not in notes, but in numbers, and each player has his number and his note. The performers are mostly Morabe tribesmen. They revel in hymns, but have been known to indulge in such lively ditties as "A life on the Ocean Wave".

28 August 1929

"Up Top":   The expression "humping the drum" is of respectable antiquity. I can trace it back to the Cancona (Q) rush. When the Crocodile field was booming, gold was located on Morinish station. The prospectors were the Smith brothers; the find in 1866. Morinish township sprung up like a mushroom. On Williams Gully, which was exceptionally shallow and rich, there worked a certain Alick Forbes, brother of the well-known Archibald, war correspondent. Alick was something of a poet; a book of his was published, "Voices from the Bush". When Morinish collapsed in the early seventies, the digger-poet downed his pick and wailed:

> Weep, Moranish, weep, the hour has come
> When Alick has to hump his drum.
> He went south and died in Maryborough.

28 August 1929

"SEA NOMAD":   The finding of a Ma State committee of inquiry on the shark menace, that the immunity of dress-divers from attack is due more to their unappetising appearance than to the flash of the bubbles from their helmet, almost hits the mark, but not quite. In the Coral Seas a shark will often circle around the diver at a distance, drawing gradually closer and closer. A cheeky specimen will eventually nose right up to him. A stream of bubbles from his sleeve cuff or from the air escape valve on his helmet and the shark almost kinks its spine in its convulsive back-kick to escape. But such bubbles continually bursting from a line of pipes across a beach would lack the terror of the unexpected. The sharks' curiosity would lure them closer and closer – and familiarity breeds contempt.

11 September 1929

"SEA NOMAD":   Marienberg, where Administrator Wisdom has been honoured by the greatest sing-sing ever accorded a white man on the Sepik, is a Government sub-station 35 miles up river. It is a cluster of native houses set on a big coral-limestone ridge. The P.O.'s quarters, the police and native barracks, are perched up on the ridge. Cocoanut palms wave above the bulk store, petrol dump and rest-houses. Patrol officer Eric Robinson was in charge when I was there. Fifteen police-boys were under him, representing the power which keeps in check the thousands of natives who inhabit the Lower Sepik. About a mile from Marienberg is a big R.C. mission, very picturesque under rows of palms. Father Kirchbaum has been in charge for 15 years. A few miles further on is an oil-boring plant, which has recently suspended operations. The flat banks of the river lie under a wide sea of cane-grass of gigantic proportions. "Sac-sac" (sago) palm swamps alternate with dense scrub patches. Just below Marienberg is a spot noted for its floating islands. I have seen them come creeping down there with a full grown tree upon them.

25 September 1929

"GOUGER":   Bligh, the explosive old naval gentleman who long afterwards was "deposed" from his Governor's job in Sydney, was one of the first navigators to find a passage through the Great Barrier Reef. In his open boat he heard the surf roaring at midnight, and held off until morning, when he found the narrow opening which meant so much to him. Carrying on, he got his first glimpse of Australian land, and gave its name to Restoration Island. The big rocky hill is covered with bushy scrub right to the water's edge, and has one miniature sandy beach. Bligh's crew nearly went mad with delight at stepping on land again.

They searched the rocks for shellfish, and light scrub for berries and birds' eggs. On the second day a horde of hostile savages appeared on the mainland only a stone's throw away, and shortened their stay. Quite recently, Queensland erected an automatic light on Restoration Rock. I was one of the gang. We camped on Bligh's beach. History repeated itself a few days later when natives appeared on the mainland opposite. But they weren't hostile; they merely rowed across and offered to trade their gins for tobacco.

2 October 1929
"Sea Nomad": The Sepik River (Mandated Territory) is no place for a shy man. The traveller, once he steps ashore from boat or canoe, is the centre of attraction for the nigs. of the nearest village, and men, women, flappers, children, tykes and pigs watch him with all their eyes. When a man washes himself, they stand round at a distance watching his every move and passing remarks as the soap lathers his ears and eyes. They seethe with excitement when he shoves a toothbrush into his mouth. Some argue that he is eating, others swear heatedly he is sharpening his teeth. But the most bashfull business of all is taking a bath. A man must either go without his tub or carry on in full view of the public. The old hands carry on. As for me, I have never enjoyed a bath on the Sepik with that gaping crowd gazing fascinated at my every movement. The women are a darn sight more curious than the men.

9 October 1929
"Sea Nomad": Native skin divers in the Northern pearling fields are forced to adopt a spartan diet, for on a full stomach they can neither dive deep nor stay under long. Tea without sugar and a hunk of dry damper is generally their breakfast and midday meal. At night they have a more substantial meal. Eating an excess of sugar is blamed for causing a man "short wind". When a man works at such a depth that pressure is telling "bell him ring longa ear!" Should he disregard the bell there comes a crack as if his ear-drums had burst. Brought up on deck he bleeds from nose and ear, and sometimes spins round and round like a sick fowl. If left to himself he cuts the tip of his nose, which then bleeds profusely and relieves the pressure in his head. After a long spell on shore it comes very hard on a boy to again get his ear-drums "tuned up". He accustoms them to under-water pressure by taking the first week steady, descending to a slightly greater depth each day, and gradually staying under longer.

9 October 1929

"Atherton": If the white man, as the saying goes, must eat a peck of dirt before he dies, the abo. must eat tons. No wonder he has got the digestion of an ostrich, for from babyhood he is used to eating gravel and charcoal. He gets this in his tucker. All food is thrown on the coals and collects its quota of grit. Vegetable food collects the most, for the native flour is moistened, chucked on the coals and often covered with warm sand. Seed foods, nuts and roots are pounded up in various ways, with hands and feet, smashed on wood or ground between stones. Shellfish is smashed and eaten on the seashore with hardly any trouble taken to spit out the grit.

23 October 1929

"Up Top": Thursday Island – a woody spot set amongst blue waterways, two toy forts upon two grassy hills, the residency below, palms on the beach and a little township. Attractive bungalows nestle by the neat hospital. Alongside is ragged Chinatown. Then comes disreputable "Yokohama" with Japs efficiently building luggers to sail Australian waters in search of Australian pearl-shell. Walking the tree-lined street a sprinkling of whites coolly dressed. A few pretty white girls, as nice as their southern sisters. Chinamen leaning against their store doors, dressed in singlet and breeks. Sharp-eyed Japs in flannels and bare feet. Broad-chested island boys. A cow and 20 goats grazing near a horse. A fowl complacently scratching in the street. A Rotomah man ambling down the footpath with strips of turtle meat dangling across his shoulders, Papuans wearing a smile and a lava-lava, grinning abos., shrewd little Malays, intriguing China girls, buxom Island lasses, a smart-looking missionary, the tall doctor in a hurry, a policeman and a soldier. A fleet of luggers in the bay, a rattling of winches as the wharfies load pearl into the Taiping. The pilot launch chugging through the current around Hospital Point. Jack McNulty yarning to Tommy Farquhar, the pearl-king. Rugged hills of Prince of Wales Island across the waterway. Blue sky and a sou'east breeze.

23 October 1929

"Sea Nomad": On the verandah of the old house on Massig Island there still lies the "magic stone" of old Ned Moseby. His sons keep it as a much-prized relic. When Moseby took over the island he was a lone man beset by tribes of bloodthirsty savages. Experienced in native superstitions, he made the most of his knowledge and his great physical strength. The "magic stone" was his instrument

for calling up the winds. The natives knew that should they annoy him he was liable to retire to his magic stone and mumble a few incantations. Then the next time the canoes were at sea, a cyclone would wipe them out. Moseby, deeply learned in sea-lore, used to stimulate this superstition by waiting for the symptoms of a certain blow, and predicting it. His word was never doubted after one or two experiences. He was accepted as the man who could call up weeks of storm so that the tiny island was lashed day and night by thunderous seas, making fishing impossible. He was credited with being able to protect Massig too, and habitants of hostile islands believed that should they canoe across for heads, the white chief would call up a wind that would wreck every canoe. Although Moseby never told them so, the natives believed that every wreck, whether "white man big fella canoe" or just a native craft, was engineered by the magic stone. By such a means and his own striking personality did Moseby keep his head safe while retaining chieftainship and rearing a particularly virile family. To this day no native dares to touch Moseby's "magic stone".

30 October 1929

"Up Top":   Chinese diggers in isolated Queensland camps sometimes possess a community joss. Such a camp was hidden in the jungle ranges of the Starcke. The Chinese lived in grass-thatched cubby-houses, built so low that the inmates could not straighten up inside. My mate and I stumbled on the settlement while prospecting. In the centre of the camp was built a miniature temple, with a grass pagoda-shaped roof. Within, on a dais of sandalwood, squatted a clay joss. The Chinese grouped around it at sunrise and sunset, reciting prayers and reverently bowing. By day, should a man pass the place, he always bowed. It was a queer settlement to find on Australian soil.

30 October 1929

"Sea Nomad":   The storms of the Barrier are continually forming sandspits among the Torres Strait reefs, sometimes only to wash them away again. But when an islet has come to stay it sprouts a surprising variety of life in a wonderfully short time. Such a bank was formed among the Howick Group about 10 years ago. I visited the Group recently, and could scarcely recognise what had been a bare patch of sand heaped upon coral. It is now much larger, with a covering of rapidly-growing trees – mangrove, casaurina, pandanus palms, tea-tree and several others whose names I don't know – 20 varieties of shrubs, numerous creepers and vines, and three kinds of tough island grass. There were

flowers and a sprinkling of birds from the neighboring islands, together with centipedes, crickets, rats and fairly numerous insects. Much of the plant life had been washed ashore by seed from the sea, which must carry surprising numbers of prospective plants looking for a settled home. The flower and creeper seeds may have been brought by the birds. Possibly driftwood carried the insects and lizards, as castaways.

13 November 1929

"ATHERTON": The abo. makes his own twine, hair being the most prized raw material - his own wool, or the missus's, or a possum's. The wool is saved up until wanted then washed, dried and rubbed well between the hands. Then it is teased out into a sort of skein and wound round a stick. Then Binghi gets his crochet-needle, a slender twig about seven inches long with a barb on the end, and, guiding the skein along the needle, works the point backwards and forwards between the moistened fore-finger and thumb of the left hand, which twists the hair into a string, which is wound up into a number of balls. Finally he gets the ends of two lengths, fastens them to the end of the needle, runs them along his thigh, and with flattened hand twists them into one long strong string.. This is used for ornamental headband and waistbelts, armlets or sacred ornaments. For dillybags fibre twine is usually used, but I have known mothers carry their piccaninnies in bags made of human hair. Goodness only knows how much labor and love went into the making of such bags.

18 December 1929

"SEA NOMAD": The easy going Tongan Islanders have decided after thinking about it a long time, that the white man is a curse. Besides inflicting their island paradise with himself, he has introduced the missionary, the tourist, the Government officials and other sticky-beaks, work, Epsom Salts and soap. And worst of all – grass –seed! Paspalum was brought over by a Clarence River man, who imagined he was doing the Tongans a good turn. So did they, until they found it over-running their gardens. Johnstone grass came over as saddle stuffing. When the saddle was cast aside, the seasonal rains transformed the contents into a green carpet of grass. The Islanders were delighted, whites and browns alike. But now Tonga-tabu, the largest isle, is over-run with the stuff waist high.

1 January 1930
"Atherton":   While fossicking behind Barrier Point, Cape York Peninsula, my mate and I saw a huge old man 'roo surrounded by a mob of 50 joeys. The unusual family fed in a grassy plain overshadowed by abrupt hills. The joeys constituted themselves sentinels for the old man, enveloping him in a widespread circle as he fed. A party of bucks which visited our camp explained that at a recent successful 'roo battue they had concentrated on slaughtering the old 'roos and had let the youngsters go. They assured us that it was quite usual for a number of orphan 'roos to fasten on to an old one for guidance and protection.

15 January 1930
"Atherton":   The Australian abo. must have kept himself in a state of grand isolation from time immemorial, otherwise the bow and arrow would have been more generally introduced among them. Only on the Fingerpoint were these weapons used, brought across as barter by the Prince of Wales islanders. There was a yearly trade from the Fingerpoint across Torres Strait to New Guinea at one time. The Strait islanders were always the voyagers, coming in huge canoes bought from the New Guinea Kiwai canoe-builders and paid for with human skulls. The universal abo. weapon, the boomerang, is seldom found in the Strait or New Guinea, for the majority of the islands are too small for it to be of much use, and in New Guinea the jungle doesn't permit its use. On Prince of Wales Island, the largest in the Strait, boomerangs were used, always bartered from the abos. just across the water. Another abo. invention, the womera, is used in the Strait, but all I have examined were undeniably made by mainlanders. But the latter never took to the favorite Torres Strait weapons, the bow and arrow and the gubba gubba. Possibly Binghi feared that the instruments had been bewitched.

15 January 1930
"Up Top":   Binghi, except when he loses his temper, when he is liable to throw his offspring to the ground, is an indulgent father. Throughout the toddling stage he makes toys for the baby: balls of clay in which are thrust brilliant parrot's feathers, wooden discs which roll funnily down hills, toy spears which can be thrown accurately enough to kill a bird or bush-rat. As the youngster grows up education is cunningly intermixed with play. A favorite game is "catch the lizard". The child is shown the track of a lizard across the sand, and in a state of suppressed excitement watches every move of its father, as with puckered

brow, he traces the lizard from grass tuft to grass tuft until it is finally run to burrow under a sheet of bark. After a few years of such training the child can track anything that walks, hops or crawls upon the ground. Then he goes out with the women, learns to distinguish between edible and non-edible roots, how to "smell out" a sugar-bag and note the flights and nesting-places of birds. Long before he is a man he knows how to win a living from the bush.

29 January 1930
"Sea Nomad":   Northern shelling boats are all "luggers" to Sydney dailies. At present there are no luggers actively operating up Torres Strait way; the vessels are cutters or ketches. Pearl-shell vessels are invariably ketches. A lugger is a lug-sailed boat scarce now so far as the pearl fleet is concerned. The ketches are under jib, mains'il and mizzen, though (due to a nautical distinction of names in various waters), often termed jib, fores'il and main. The "Quita", one of Tommy Farquahar's boats is the largest ketch in the Coral Sea; she has, I read, been blown ashore near Cape Flattery, Cape York Peninsula. She carries 22 men and is equipped with five dinghies, several with outboard motors for towing.

5 February 1930
"Sea Nomad":   E.W. Chinnery, the Government anthropologist, who has spent 21 years in New Guinea, reports to the discovery there of stone pestles and mortars similar to those of ancient Egypt. After this I suppose that ordinary observant blokes who have suggested in the BULLETIN that Egyptian expeditions have visited most of the islands wont be so universally laughed at . My own humble opinion is that by far the strongest proofs of association with the land of the Pharaohs are to be found on the island of Mer, Torres Strait. Before the missionary came the men of Mer were spiritualist and astrologers. They had mapped out the stars and could sail by them. They were agriculturalists, and knew to perfection the seasons as affecting the crops and the sea. All these subjects were specialised in by the Egyptians. Another very strong link in the chain was the mummification of the dead; the Mer method was practically identical with the best-known Egyptian process. And might not the vast walled fishtraps round the shores of Mer an Eroob have been the work of forgotten Egyptian colonists.

26 February 1930

"Up Top": One of Australia's forgotten pioneers of aviation is George Hardacre, a farmer in the Central Bucca district (N.S.W.). Over 30 years ago, in between bush toil, Hardacre invented a flying machine, and all Coff's Harbor and the Bucca turned out to witness the trial. The umbrella-like contraption attached by a running wheel to a steel cable stretched between two trees, did its work perfectly when the inventor stepped aboard and handled the levers. The machine not only rose in the air but stayed there with its passenger pumping like a Trojan: then the jealous wind took a hand and smashed him and his machine into a tree. Hardacre emerged from the wreckage bubbling with enthusiasm. A syndicate was formed and patents taken out, but the idea was a decade before its time and the necessity of making a living soon took the inventor back to the bush again.

26 march 1930

"Atherton": I wonder at my cheek when a kid. I was horsetailer to the "pony drover", well known in the Coonamble, Narrabri, Walgett and Goondiwindi districts (N.S.W.) – every prad in his outfit was a white pony. Each little horse was trained in jumping and show-ring tricks. At every country show the arrival of the pony drover was an event. And his outfit scooped up prizes for many years. My specialty was thieving grass. We lifted 5000 wethers from Been Baa and set out for St George across the Queensland border. The stock route was a long narrow lane almost destitute of grass, hedged by fences behind which grim horsemen, selection after selection, watched the hungry flock go by. When we were camped at night the nearest cocky would send his raw-boned sons to do sentinel-duty on the fences. It was my duty to see that the horses got a bellyful of grass. Night after night I'd sneak down to the ponies in the dark take off their tinkling bells and muffle their hoofs. They knew what was doing. We'd go a few miles down or up the stock route; then the ponies would crowd silently round while I snipped through the wires, hanging on to each wire so that it would not "telephone" or twang, and twisting it round the post. The wires cut, the ponies would file silently into the luscious paddock and lose no time getting outside the cocky's grass. I would roll up my blanket by them and have them out of the paddock in the chilly dawn. Repairing the fence was a matter of minutes. The escapes I had make my blood run cold but I was never caught

9 April 1930

"SEA NOMAD": I can't say whether the march of science has evolved a more scientific process of "pickling" Chinamen who die at sea, but in my time it was by the injection of formalin. A vein was opened and formalin was pumped in as the blood ran out. The chief officer used to collect £20 a nob for each corpse. Many old Chinamen returning to the Flowery Land to end their days used to oblige by expiring at sea. Our Chinese carpenter got a terrible shock one morning as a man emerged from the stokehold, staring dreamily, the pupils of his eyes like pinpoints – a confirmed opium-smoker. He stared queerly at the horizon, then dropped dead at our feet. When the chief pumped in the formalin the corpse opened his eyes – wide! The carpenter ran away screaming, and afterwards refused to make the box.

2 July 1930

"GOUGER": There is a strong movement in Papua to try and induce the Australian Government to include rubber among bounty-fed products. Only the most favourably situated estates can continue producing at the present prices. Some reductions in costs have already been effected by amalgamations and centralisation in the two heaviest producing districts, but even if the process is carried a good deal further the outlook is the reverse of encouraging, Unless Government assistance in some form is forthcoming.

23 July 1930

"SEA NOMAD": E.W.P. Chinnery, Government anthropologist, states that circles of standing stone, resembling the relics left by the Druids of ancient Britain, have been discovered on the Sepik River, New Guinea. I have seen several of these traces of an older and more advanced civilisation. At Angerman village is a long cleared space banked with earth three feet high. In the centre is a circular mound about seven feet in diameter grown on now by cocoanut-trees and hibiscus. Like sentinels around the mound are great splinters of stone. The natives could tell us the name of each stone, but they had not the haziest idea of who put the stones there or what they symbolised. Again, near Malangei is a huge space surrounded by earth mounds – possibly the grandstand from which dusky worshippers watched awful rites. These mounds are now lined thick with towering palms. In the centre of the clearing are finger-like slabs of stone four feet high. Moss covers the blackened stones. Malangei village cherishes a very curious chair. It is hewn out of a solid log and is about three feet in diameter and

five feet high. The back is carved into the similitude of a face, wonderfully well proportioned and colored. The seat is supported above the base by four well-carved figures. But who made it, and why, Black Brother can't or wont tell.

6 August 1930
"Sea Nomad": The water spout which was observed near Perth the other day is a rarity in that locality, but further north it is a fairly frequent phenomenon. I've seen the spout in the Gulf of Carpentaria in all its terrible glory. On an almost calm day an inky cloud will reach deliberately down to the waters like a clutching hand. Underneath the cloud the water is agitated and soon commences to form itself into a column which is joined by a column dipping down from the cloud. Then the sea fiend's dance commences. The water column is a huge spinning spiral; its broad base a mound of sucking wavelets frothing high above the bosom of the sea. Its roof is the ugly, frightening cloud which seems alive as its wings soar skyward in an endeavour to tear the column into the sky. But the sea clings grimly to its own while the cloud rushes away at terrific speed. The column stretches and bends and howls as it is forced to follow. Ill fares any small vessel that fouls the erratic course of the monster. The spout breaks in halves at last, sometimes with a sound like a thunder-clap. A big spout rarely lasts more than half an hour. At times in the Gulf as many as 20 of them are visible at the same time, all rushing about on their own eccentric and unrelated course.

13 August 1930
"Sea Nomad": The lepers of the Dutch East Indies live alternately on the heights of hope and the depths of despair, played on by ever recurring rumors of new cures for their dread disease. Many a cure has been tried upon them, and for some psychological reason they actually improve for a time under the treatment, but after a while relapse. A £5000 X-ray plant has recently been installed at Pelantoengan, the European colony. There are four leper colonies in the Dutch East, and the Salvation Army has taken them all over.

10 September 1930
"Sea Nomad": Outback camps occasionally tell a grisly tale. Last month George Hallwood, prospecting near the antimony mines along the lonely Mitchell, grew curious as to a weather-beaten saddle outside a humpy door. He pushed in and found a skeleton lying on the floor garbed in decayed dungarees, with a rusty gun

lying by its side. The Mt. Molloy police went out to investigate but it is unlikely that they found any clue to the cause of death, which may have been starvation, suicide or murder. Many dead men have been found that way in lonely places, not always with a gun for company either. Several skeletons were dug up some while ago in a guano deposit on lonely Raine islet, home of seabirds. Whether they represented a massacre by natives or a fair warfare among the early pearling crews, no one can tell. Some of the skulls showed neat round bullet holes and others were cracked, suggesting acquaintance with the disc-shaped clubs of the islanders.

5 November 1930
"Up Top":   The champion banana-eater of Australia is Cooktown's Mick Flynn, a little man with a tangled red beard. I've seen him eat 13 dozen bananas without stopping. He is a teetotaller. "I never mixes 'em," he confided to me: "the fermentation in them bananas makes all th' brew I want."

17 December 1930
"Sea Nomad":   A rumpus that will make the South Sea Bubble explosion seem like a squib in comparison is due any moment in the South Pacific, and the missionaries will make the detonation. For long the various denominations have been at loggerheads. With the rapid progress of settlement in the Islands in the last 20 years, the position has become acute, with new bodies rushing in to labor in vineyards already tilled. The old established missions resent the intrusion of the newcomers. They feel that the claims staked by the pioneer padres, who risked fever and the cooking-pots of the cannibals, oughtn't to be jumped in this fashion. "Why", ask the older missionaries, "don't these fellows open up new territory as we did?" The niggers, who watch the fight with increasing bewilderment, have given up trying to understand it. Their philosophy is that the best creed is that whose mission offers the best price for cocoanuts. Meanwhile planters, recruiters, miners and officials watch the gathering of the storm with unveiled delight. They don't love missionaries.

17 December 1930
"Up Top":   On top of a dump at Lightning Ridge stood a tall, stern, grey-bearded man, a double-barrelled gun in his hands. He meant business. He roared down the shaft for the young chap to come on top. A muffled shout floated up, "Go to Hell!" The greybeard laid aside the gun and upended the windlass, allowing the top logs to go thumping and bouncing down the shaft.

Then he commenced methodically shovelling the dump down. A crowd of diggers collected, but there were reasons why they didn't interfere. The young chap below desperately shovelled the fast-falling dirt back into the drive behind him, but the toiler above formed a chute and simply poured the stuff down. By midday the lad below was bogged to his waist in dirt, and the drive behind was choked up. He called "Enough!" It took him a long time to climb up the shaft; he stood there, trembling at the knees, a fine young figure, stripped to the waist, caked in sweat and dirt. The greybeard tapped the gun held loosely in the crook of his arm. "What are you going to do about it ?" he growled. "I'll marry her," said the youngster sullenly. He did.

24 December 1930
"Sea Nomad":   There is a grim black cliff on Mer (Torres Strait) known as "Geedee's Leap." Geedee was a lovely slender little thing with clean bronze skin and eyes like black stars: the belle of Maiad village. Came along a blackbirding schooner. The crew landed in a steel-grey dawn, half a dozen whites and a swarm of Polynesian and Asiatic savages. Before the palms threw shadows they burst upon the village, and flames leapt skyward and showed where the dinghies waited as men dragged screaming women across the beach. The females fought like wild cats. One sixteen year-old girl fastened her teeth in a Chinese throat and she and her captor died together. Geedee ran swiftly. The mob headed her off as she fled through the scrub, seeking refuge in the Valley of the Dead at Deaudapat. She twisted and turned but at last they penned her to the long grassy spur that runs out into the sea. She sped along this and stood poised on the furthermost rocks, panting and distraught. Then, as the pursuers drew near, with one last wild scream she leapt out of life.

31 December 1930
"Sea Nomad":   The Siwai people of the Solomons are uncanny musicians. They tune in, so they say, to spirit orchestras, and play melodies which they claim they derived from worlds millions of miles away. Their most impressive instruments are carillons of up to 20 huge, deep-toned wooden bells with a rich rolling sound. The chief ringer is invariably a solemn person with a ring through his nose and a library of allegedly occult opuses in his head. At that, heard under the right conditions, the music of these natives is weirdly appealing. Some student of musical evolution should go out and get a few gramophone records and sort out their scale.

31 December 1930
"Up Top":   Civilisation is a matter of bingy before brains. You can't have a big brain unless your ancestors had the opportunity of growing big bingies. Take our desert abo. and the "swamp-rat" of New Guinea. They are skinny little devils who haven't any arts or culture. But in both countries, in regions where game is plentiful, the natives are a finer type, physically and mentally. The well-fed savage squats by his slow fire, and with wrinkles on his beetle brow painfully fashions a better-poised spear. He invents a method of hardening the wood. His hunting now takes less time. With the leisure at his command the well-nourished native thinks out still more efficient hunting devices – the womera throwing-stick of the Australian abo., the bow and arrow of the Papuan. Coastal tribes are the most advanced, because when the hinterland is drought-stricken they can take their food from the sea. A few hundred generations of that and they have houses, gardens and well-built canoes. Also they have leisure not only to laugh and make love, but to make songs, stories and plays about the love and the laughter and the hunting. And there's the whole epitome of human evolution.

7 January 1931
"Sea Nomad":   The sea around the Great Barrier Reef is the breeding-ground of clouds of scum, which float in acre-wide patches. These rolling oilily in the lazy waves are seaweeds. A shipmate of mine was a microscope enthusiast, and he showed me under the lens drops of the scum – whole forests of plants, growing limbs and vinery and folding leaves of magic delicacy combined with atoms of dancing animal life of wondrous colors – wriggly, spiral and star-shaped things. Funny thing about that conglomeration of vegetable and animal life is that the whole acre or so of slime can move concertedly – wriggle ahead, glide back or move sideways like a vast flat snake. Fish feed on the stuff avidly, and it might supply nutrient for humans for all I know.

28 January 1931
"Up Top":   The wild sow grunted uneasily as she sniffed her scampering piebalds and blacks and whites. There were only eight of them. One was missing. She squealed in frightened doubt as if mistrusting her eyes; then nosed the jungle loam and ran swiftly back upon her tracks. Propping suddenly, she was bumped by the trotting piglets as with nostrils distended she smelt the missing progeny. She peered over a precipitous bank that bordered a scrub-clad

ravine. There he was, the ninth piglet, squealing up from a ledge immediately he twigged his mother's snout. In snorting relief she wheeled and charged her inquisitive brood back from the depth. Sinking on her haunches she carefully worked her forequarters over the edge. She might just do it, but if she slipped! Straining hard down she just touched noses with him. Carefully she coaxed him up till she could fasten her teeth in his hide, then struggling backward she puffed and heaved and dragged herself back clear from the edge. She lay gasping while the piglets romped and squeaked around their rescued brother. Then she staggered up, snatched the errant one by the scruff of his neck and, eyes blazing, shook him until the jungle rang with his squeals.

11 February 1931

"Up Top":   The candle-nut tree grows to a great size in N.Q., and its fruit ought to have a good market value. The kernel tastes like walnut; the nut contains fully fifty per cent oil of an amber color. Pioneers assure me it was once generally utilised for candle-making, and that after the oil was extracted the cake made excellent fodder for cattle. I've seen niggers pack the stones together with reeds as torches, which burnt steadily for hours.

25 March 1931

"Sea Nomad":   There is no reason to doubt that the Newnes shale-field in N.S.W. is a dinkum deposit, but there are some outcrops of shale along the coast that weren't put there by Mother Nature. In the old days several ships went ashore in Torres Strait waters, loaded with oil shale for treatment overseas, and this shale has been picked up on quite a number of islands. Coal, planted in the same fashion, is even more frequently met with, and has been responsible for raising a great many false hopes.

1 April 1931

"Up Top":   One of the identities of N. Queensland in the days of long ago was "Break-a-Leg" Charlie. He'd blow into Cooktown every Christmas. It took a barrel of beer to mellow him, but when he was quite full he was very happy. He stood only four feet ten, but he was a mass of bone and muscle, like a wild boar. He never wore boots, his dress suit being pants with an open-necked flannel out of which poked grey hair, like the pelt of a goat. When drunk he went from pub to pub seeking to "break a leg". He had been a wrestler in his day, and must

have plied that art in a very rough school. His small size and surprising strength made him an awkward foe. He would unexpectedly charge a man's knees just like an overgrown bulldog, and if he heard a bone snap his cup of joy was full. He was always all smiles, even when seeking to break a leg. He said he lived "up th' Peninsula where the wild gins grow," and that's all the address he ever had.

* * * * *

Ammunition carts at Gallipoli.
The 5th Light Horse at dinner - Trooper Idriess on the left.
Photographs by Barney Haydon, courtesy Haydon Archive.

Gouger
of
The Bulletin

World War 1

The second part of the book contains the WW1 articles and reinforces Idriess's well-known ability to detach himself from his immediate surroundings at the end of each day (or at stolen moments during a lull in the fighting), to briefly record in his diaries what he saw and felt at the time. -- These to be expanded at a later date to become the articles presented here. Included also are the few WW1 snippets from the first 'GOUGER' in the interest of maintaining continuity and keeping "like" articles together.

25 July 1918

"Gouger":   Ever hear of that little scandal at Rafu? Well, shortly after the mounted men had taken the place, an English infantry division came along and camped by the Bedouin village. A little apart was a mud hut in which resided old man Amalakite, his buxom young wife and two fine, wild-eyed daughters. The whole lived in harmony with the ancestral melon-patch, the mangy camel, the little donk. water-carrier and 78 billion fleas.. But as the weeks went on, wifey found much favour among the amorous Tommies and made a fine collection of their piastres in the same way as her sister Delilah had done only 20 miles away with warriors of a long-forgotten army. At last old Amalakite, bitter wrath, hied himself to the O.C's tent and demanded action for his sullied honor. Result, a guard with fixed bayonets placed around the Bedouin's home, which even the Tommy Romeos dared not face. Mrs A. did not take the sudden cutting off of her nickel harvest in a penitent way at all. In fury she stormed to the O.C's tent, demanded the interpreter, and spake thus: "So the old dog has despoiled me , has he? Then by the beard of my father I'll see the mongrel grilled on red-hot iron. Dig up the floors of the hut and see what ye will find." With a final glare all round she spat twice on the O.C's treasured carpet, whizzed around on bare heel and was gone. A fatigue party was quickly formed, the flabbergasted Amalakite bundled out of his home, and the earthen floor dug up. Stacked in neat rows underneath were 43 Anzac rifles, with a miscellaneous collection of ammunition. The last I saw of him he was disappearing in a cloud of dust in the direction of the Red Sea.

15 August 1918

"Gouger":   Three Light Horsemen were blotted out in a curious way shortly after the occupation of El Arish. Seeing something floating close inshore, they stripped and swam out to it. The first swimmer put his hand on the shiny thing, and there was an awful explosion. I was joy-riding in one of our old 'buses at the time flying low inshore, and that terrific report made me think all the Archies out of Sheol had burst just under the old 'plane's tail. Some pitiful tragedies happened along that old shore. To one chap in particular. Seeing four Frenchmen in difficulties, he swam out, pulled ashore three and returned for the fourth. But his strength was gone and he was drowned. Two of the Frenchmen he brought to land died. The French troops thought a great deal of the deed and recognised it in chivalrous fashion. An officer of the 2nd Light Horse met his death like a man close to the same spot. While riding along the shore he saw two of our fellows washed out. There was a very heavy sea running. Plunging his horse in he managed to bring out one of the drowning. Swimming the nag back to the second man he managed to get him mounted, but when close in shore a huge wave broke over the two men and the horse. Out of the sand and foam the laboring beast at last struggled, with the drowning soldier's arms still clasped around its neck. The heroic officer was washed away and drowned.

15 August 1918

"Gouger": Have you ever seen a large body of men look aside to laugh boisterously, with the fear of imminent death close upon them? It was on the second Gaza battle (19th April, 1917). The Light Horse Brigade were guarding the rear of the attacking Light Horse brigades and the cameloes. About four in the afternoon, over the tops of the low hills all around, suddenly swarmed thousands upon thousands of Turkish cavalry. Their numbers and their quick attack upon our rear was a complete surprise. Only one brigade to withstand such a multitude! Let our thin line be broken and woe to our comrades already heavily engaged with the infantry ahead of us. What a rush to the shallow trenches we had just dug! A galloping away of led horses to cover. Feverish jambing in of loaded strips to the Hotchkiss guns. The quick order from Brigade H.Q. that the line was to be held to the last man. The whine and crash of shrapnel as the Turkish mountain guns swung into action against us. A little distance away, in the dry wadi bed, a field company of Engineers were peacefully digging wells and erecting water-troughs. In the flush of the excitement a hatless officer galloped up, yelling "get for your lives! All the Turkish cavalry are on us!" Down went the engineer's tools. A rush for horses. Into the limbers went the scared animals. Some men attempted to pull up the already filled troughs. Others shouted to let the troughs go to Hell. The drivers leaped into their saddles. The men rushed the limbers. The officers and non-coms. steadied their horses. And in a swirling cloud of dust the swinging limbers were off. All that portion of our line which had witnessed the little interlude laughed and laughed until the tears came with satiation. It was a great swing-away.

19 September 1918

"Gouger's apology": – I used to think the donkey tribe the most useless, laziest and senseless animals the High Command ever put cussedness into. Now I humbly apologise to the donk. All through Egypt the poor little cove plods the livelong day under whole haystacks of bersene (lucerne). He carries two great panniers of vegetables, loaded to the ground, daily to market. He

carries all Abraham's family on his back simultaneously, and often the family's water-jars as well. He is yoked to the plough side by side with the tall, mangy camel or the ugly, big-boned Nile buffalo. He acts, also, as the plain riding horse. To see a big, 6ft. Gypo, with his toes touching the ground sitting astride a little donkey and belaboring it with a thick stick, is to feel like lifting the big loafer one under the ear. In Palestine the donk helps the women bring in all the grain from the fields and between times carts his master all over the country. But it put the finishing touch on things when we used the donk ourselves. From Beersheba and onwards many of our horses were shot, and to keep up with their hurrying comrades many of the luckless riders secured donkeys and followed the fast moving columns. To see a bunch of small donkeys plodding up towards the firing-line through the dust each with a brown, disreputable-looking Australian on its back, armed to the teeth and carrying 36 hours' rations, was always enough to bring a big laugh and a cheer from the line. But, as the boys said, after they'd painfully lifted their sore bodies from the donks and dropped under cover: "it's better late than never".

26 September 1918

"GOUGER":   A few days after the fall of Beersheba our brigade was pushing the Turkish rearguard hard on the extreme right flank. For three days we had been pestered by snipers harrying our rear. On the fourth morning a persistent marksman had shot three of our troop horses, and finally a man through the heart. Six of us were told off to settle him. We started him from the rocks on a little hill to our right, but not before he had shot another man through the thigh and killed another horse. He proved to be a Bedouin, and he made straight for the Turkish lines. But we galloped him off, and in despair he turned and jumped down a large dry well-hole. These holes are hewn out of solid rock, the opening being just large enough for a man's body to go down, but widening out into a considerable chamber underneath. One of our hot-headed lads galloped up, jumped from his horse and before we could stop him, peered down the narrow hole. Immediately he was shot through the head. It was impossible for us to lean over and shoot down, because we were then outlined against the blue sky – an unmissable target to the rifleman in the dark chamber below. We called out in Arabic for him to come up, but the only reply was a hoarse snarl. So we laid aside our rifles, and each man collected a huge pile of stones. We stood a little way from the hole, and then methodically commenced to throw the stones in. Except for the steadily falling rocks, there was silence for half an hour; then the

man below commenced to shoot upward as the stones closed around him. The chamber below was 14ft. deep, but in an hour's time we had nearly filled it. The gentleman below must have begun to climb on the heap as the stones gradually filled the chamber, because suddenly his rifle muzzle showed out above the small opening. He was trying to hold the gun so that his bullets might chance to hit one of us, but we held ourselves very low and threw in the stones faster. The man fired until his arms must have been wedged tight with the stones; but he never surrendered. The last we saw was his rifle muzzle, now silently showing over the edge of the hole. Soon that was covered and we came away.

10 October 1918
An Australian Light Horseman, back from the Holy Land, put it to THE BULLETIN this way; "I have seen something of dirty people in the last twelve months – people who make a hobby of sheer dirtiness – but Egypt produces the champions. I give you my word, the natives there know by the whiff of a man what district he comes from."

10 October 1918
"G.L.I." A group of Australian camel-men were surprised by a taube while waiting to attack at Beersheba. Instantly every man had jumped to the ground and scrambled under his camel's belly. Down came the bombs. One landed squarely, burying the man underneath a shapeless welter of what had a second before been a camel. The man himself was unhurt. An hour later I saw a bomb drop almost underneath a mounted camelman. The beast was blown to a pulp and the man dashed to the ground 30 yards away, but, except for being a blithering idiot for a couple of hours he was unhurt. Saw where a camel-man scout had put up a great fight for life one day. His corpse was lying behind his mount, his rifle still clenched in his hands, sighted over the camel's back. There were 49 bullet-holes in the carcase. The man had one bullet-hole, clean through the heart. Beside him lay a little pile of 80 empty cartridge cases, mute testimony of a fight to the bitter end.

17 October 1918
"Gouger's" Novelette: – I was with a party of Light Horse scouts who were reconnoitring near an Assyrian village, when from a clump of rocks came a rifle-shot that killed one of our horses. Now the owner of that horse would rather have been shot himself than see his beloved prad killed by a lurking sniper. So

with a furious oath he picked himself from the ground and ran straight for the rocks. The rest of us put spurs to our horses and also made for them. The Turkish sniper jumped up and ran, as only a man with death at his heels can run, straight for an Assyrian village. He dashed through the open doorway of a large hut, the door of which we found very strong and heavily barred. Some minutes were spent in breaking it open, and we were in a room, empty but with another closed door at the end. This was also broken open, and in the darkest corner of the room was the sniper. There was also a woman, but she covered up her face and, screaming, ran out as we rushed in. The corporal in charge had his work cut out to stop our infuriated comrade from shoving his bayonet there and then through the prisoner. Out in the sunlight the horseless man said: "It's no good, Corporal, I mean to have that man's life. My old horse has carried me these last two years through thick and thin. He was killed by a cowardly shot. It's six miles back to Headquarters. It is impossible for you to prevent me shooting him on the way. Far better to get the job finished now." The corporal looked undecided for a minute. Then he angrily said: "Oh all right; have it your own damned way." Rough hands pushed the Turk against the wall, the man whose horse was shot stepped forward, and with hard eyes lifted the rifle to his shoulder. The sniper suddenly screamed, clutched off the military cap on his head, and pulled down a fall of jet black hair. "He" was a young Assyrian woman. She had swapped clothes with the hunted man in the few minute it had taken us to reach him. The "woman" who had slipped away was the sniper. We never got him.

14 November 1918.
"Gouger":   In the desert fighting in Egypt and on the fertile Palestine plains there is not even a twig of firewood. The Light Horse crossing the desert used to eagerly rush the scanty desert shrubs in search of precious dried roots with which to boil the quart-pot, and the empty cases of bully-beef were carried on horseback for days. Those lucky ones who possessed a few sticks of wood would carefully light up to boil the billy and their less lucky comrades would scramble to get their quarts as near the blaze as possible. As soon as a quart was on the simmer the tea would be thrown in, the pot hurriedly removed and another took its place nearer the scanty flames. I have often seen as many as 40 quart-pots in one line, their owners standing anxiously around, alternately hoping, praying, cursing that their tin would come near the boil before the blessed fire burned down. When we drove the Turks back to Bir-el-Abd we cut the Turkish telegraph line, and a man from each section of two brigades, some hundreds

in all, broke out from the line and rushed the posts. Innumerable instances occurred for months where men risked rifle and shell-fire just for the sake of a few sticks which showed somewhere near the enemy's lines. When we got into Palestine we found that a lot of the Arab's hovels were held up by wooden rafters, and as these fellows used to snipe our stretcher – bearers we used to borrow their rafters with pleasure. A good few men were stabbed and found a lonely grave in Arab wells after entering these places on their own. Still it did not stop the rest of us.

5 December 1918
"Gouger":   Have you ever been in a signalling corps? Neither have I. Don't ever want to be now. In the old training days – ever so long ago it seems – we used to envy the signallers and throw malicious borak at them. They never did a picquet, never did a guard, never did one solitary fatigue duty. Just stood all day long waving flags, and at night played with flash-lamps. But in the desert campaign things were different. There we would see a troop of signallers, under shell-fire, gallop full belt across the open to the nearest hill from where they could flash back intelligence to H.Q. And on that hill they would have to stand, splendid targets for the concentrated fire of Turkish guns. As men fell they were replaced by reinforcements in the early part of the campaign, but soon the reinforcements dwindled and dwindled and at last failed to come. I have seen some of these troops reduced from 30 to eight men, and these, exhausted by months of fighting , great loss of sleep and desert hardship, had to carry on the work of the 30 that make up a full troop. It was impossible to have done it, except for the men's sense of honor. Out there it was the unwritten law to "Carry on" until a bullet put an end to all things, or a man collapsed physically or mentally.

26 December 1918
"Gouger":   A scorching burning heat rose from the desert sand all through the never-ending day of the Bir el Abd battle. All along the far-stretched line the one thought was water. Could it not be got from somewhere? Surely there must be some little oasis close by where a man could make a sudden dash with the troop's water-bottles. But the Turks suddenly attacked in great force. Our rifle and Maxim fire swelled to a quickening roar, and all chance of a long cool drink was finished. The barrels of our rifles, already burning hot from the sun, quickly got hotter from the rapid fire, until it was almost beyond human endurance

to hold a weapon. The attack was finally beaten down, the firing steadied to independent firing with sudden outbursts of machine-gun fire, and the never-ceasing long-drawn whine and crash of bursting shells. It was then I began to notice dully, the man lying behind a sandhill on my left. He was continually turning his head and looking behind him, then facing forward again, for all the world as if he hated to look behind but must. I thought he was trying to stop himself from making up his mind to rush back across the desert for water. Suddenly he did jump up and run back. I looked over my shoulder as he ran, for I thought he might know of some well quite close. But he ran back only 50 yards to his fallen horse. We had galloped into action under shrapnel fire, and scattered horses, with here and there a tumbled form of a man, testified to the accuracy of the Turkish batteries. Their shrapnel bullets were still biting the sand, searching for our led horses some little distance away. The trooper standing by his horse half raised his rifle and slowly lowered it again. The poor beast, wounded three hours before, was still feebly writhing. Its mouth was open and the long, black swollen tongue had dropped between the jaws and was lying helpless in the burning sand. Slowly the man took his water-bottle, pulled out the cork, and emptied the precious contents down the horse's throat. And I thought not a man in the line had a drop left! His great act of charity done, that splendid sportsman suddenly took off his hat and laid it across his charger's eyes. Then, holding the muzzle of his rifle steadily for a second in his mate's ear he pulled the trigger. Then he ran back bare-headed to his place in the line.

23 January 1919
"Gouger":   Two days after the battle of Bir-el-Abd our regiment was watering its horses at one of the small oases about twelve miles from the battlefield, when someone called my attention to a riderless horse, saddle on and bridle dangling, coming across the desert. The poor beast must have smelt the water, for he stopped, pricked his ears, and catching sight of our thirsty horses pressing eagerly around the well, neighed shrilly, and came across the sand at a full gallop. He dashed among a group of horses, knocked one man backwards down the shallow hole, and thrust his nose in a canvas bucket of water that one of the boys was holding out for his own horses. It took 14 buckets of water before we could get any control over this thirst-maddened animal, which by this time had been recognised as belonging to one of the men missing since the battle. There was dried blood all over the saddle, and big patches of dried blood down the horse's neck, showing that a desperately wounded man had clung there. "I'll take

the poor beggar back to the camp and give him a feed," said one of the lads. He mounted his horse and catching hold of the riderless horse's bridle rein, tried to lead him towards the camp. But the horse was of another mind. He walked very slowly, continually looking around the way he had come, and whinnying. Finally he stopped altogether. The man leading him, getting impatient, jerked the bridle. The horse reared, the bridle fell, and off went the charger at a tearing gallop the way he had come. Several men went after him, but it turned out to be a 10-mile ride before he stopped. When they caught up, the waler was standing quite still beside his rider. The man was lying face downward in the burning sand, shot through both lungs. He was not quite dead, but went west before the ambulance sand-cart could get him into a dressing station. That's why the boys shoot their horses rather than see them sold into slavery.

10 April 1919

"Gouger": "Centurion" (B. 27/2/'19) says that septic sores were painlessly cured in Egypt. His M.O. must have been a genius. Too well I remember the long line of poor devils in my regiment standing outside the M.O.'s bivvy each morning. At times 5 p.c. of the brigade had these festering, painful outbreaks. Each man in the line would have taken his own bandage off waiting for the M.O. to pass along. Those with sores just coming would have a wet bandage slipped on lively, but for those whose afflictions were ripe out came the dreaded scissors, a point was jabbed in and a long cut made. The scissors were then run in again and a cross-cut made. Then the M.O.'s steel-like fingers squeezed the sore until a man's belly felt as if it had gone up out of his mouth. A Red Cross orderly slapped a bandage on the half-paralysed leg or arm, and hurried off to the next victim. Our M.O. seldom used a lance; the scissors were quicker and through much use the damned things got blunt. It was on the long marches that the experience was the worst. Often when fighting all day, riding all night, food nothing but bully beef and biscuits, insufficient and brackish water, these sores could not be attended to for weeks at a time. Then perhaps the column would pull up for a couple of hours, the doctor and his orderlies would hurriedly unpack their medical stores, and the hurry-up surgery would commence all over again. These septic sores want constant care. When they got all over a man's body, especially between his legs, the constant riding in quick pursuit of the enemy was hell.

30 October 1919

"Gouger": The Digger in trouble was not always without a friend. The O.C. of our regiment was a solicitor in civil life, and a devoted father to the hard cases of the family when they were in trouble, which, as a rule, was every pay-day. When the regiment was stationed at Bir-el-Deuidar, the so-called "48 hours' leave" was initiated. At that time Tommy M.P.'s were swarming in Port Said, and they lost no time in running in the leave men almost as soon as they hit the disreputable city. The Tommy Provost sent in such lurid reports about the behaviour of the Aussies that at last G.H.Q. threatened to stop leave altogether. Then our O.C. took a hand. He refused to convict his men on the written evidence of police many miles away, and somehow managed it that the M.P.'s and the witnesses had to come to Bir-el-Deuidar to give evidence. This meant a train trip to Kantara, then a 12 mile ride across the desert to the regiment. Most of the M.P.'s had never been in a saddle in their lives. Of course we picked out the quietest horses for them. The first trip these policemen had they gave us such an exhibition that we almost forgave them the errand on which they had come. M.P.'s were littered all over the desert. After that they generally preferred to walk. When they got to the camp disillusionment No. 2 was with them. They were faced by an O.C. who knew every trick of the law. Faked charges, which went down so easily with their own Provost, were in a few minutes pulled to pieces, and M.P.'s and their witnesses were soon floundering. Result: No convictions, and the dreary trip back to Port Said again. The boys were so embittered against the M.P.'s that we all went to the further end of the oasis, intending to say a few words to them. But the O.C. got a whisper at the last moment, and he came down on us like a school of pyramids. And of course we knew he was right. I trod the mat before him once, and when it was over I felt the sand burning through my boots and melting my spinal-chord. That talk had more effect in keeping me on the narrow regimental path than three month's pack drill would have done.

11 December 1919

"Gouger": What treacherous dogs the Arabs of Egypt and Palestine are! Throughout the desert campaign the Bedouin tribes hung on our flanks, watching our small mounted army struggling across the great wilderness. On every engagement with the Turks the Bedouins chipped in with long range sniping, paying particular attention to the unguarded Red Cross carts. They waited patiently for the defeat that never came, because then they could have swarmed in between us and our scanty water supply. Later on, in Palestine, when

the big British army came in, and the Turks rolled up from the Caucasus with their German divisions, the vermin used to hang on the flanks of both armies, watching the battles and waiting to chip in against the loser. They were in tens of thousands there. For 20 miles along the rocky hills of Hebron, the black-shawled vultures used to sit watching day after day the bursting shells and the galloping squadrons. When at last the Turkish armies were smashed and forced to retreat, the Arabs swooped down on them, only to find that the cornered Turk could still bite, and died very hard. For our part we were glad at this. It was all right to smash a brave enemy in fair fight; but no soldier likes to see him torn to pieces by a pack of mongrels when he is down. Later on, when the big Turkish relief armies came up, the Arabs hung ominously around us again: but when the Turks were routed, the birds of prey left us for another harvest. Many stray bodies of Turks surrendered to us simply for protection.

18 December 1919

"GOUGER": During the afternoon of the second battle of Gaza, while dodging the ceaseless shell-bursts, I flopped down behind a dead camel as the only shelter available. Two other men were there before me; but they needed no cover now. One was a Maorilander, the other a hard-faced Aussie. Both men had been shot through the temple, and they lay with their faces turned towards each other. Between them stood a water-bottle, and lying on the baked ground was a penny. No need to tell a man they had tossed up for the last drink. Perhaps in the excitement of the toss they had forgotten. Anyway, there was a little round hole in each man's head.

11 March 1920

"GOUGER'S" BATTERY: The armory of the Arabs was often infernally interesting. Some of their old guns fired a bullet the size of a small shell, and were dreaded on account of the ghastly mess they made of a man. The British rifles they had were, of course, looted; and Turkish and German weapons were supplied to wanderers friendly to those nations. The rest of their guns represented nearly every make on earth, from the muzzle-loader firing broken-up chains and bolt-heads to the latest Winchester repeating-rifle. The very ancient weapons had their stocks barbarically carved, and in many cases were inlaid with silver. But the horse pistols were the souvenir-hunters' joy. Many of these, hundreds of years old, had butts of pure silver. Some were fired by the gunpowder-in-the-pan; others by the percussion cap. Numbers of the very

old Turkish and Greek pistols were inlaid with precious metals, but I wouldn't have fired one of them for a thousand piastre note. Most of the tribes had six-chambered American revolvers, and one surly-looking camelman whom I searched surprised me by drawing an automatic "Star". The cutlery was also very ancient and assorted. One splendid blade a chief possessed was a relic of the Crusades. The hilt was in the shape of a cross and was heavily inlaid with gold. The blade was ornamented with scroll work and a Crusader's motto in Latin had been etched into the steel. The blade was so pliable that when bent the point would just touch the hilt. Double edged swords were numerous and cavalry sabres were in almost every mud hut. The ancient curved scimitars particularly took our eye. They were nearly always decorated with silver, and sometimes the hilt was inlaid with gold and precious stones.

12 August 1920

"Gouger": Speaking of fantods when no liquor was available, I had them badly on Gallipoli, due to incessant alarms and loss of sleep. They were particularly strong and fear-inspiring during the small hours when our very souls were crying for sleep. These were the hours, too – particularly those just before the first cold peep of dawn – most favored by both sides for attack. Time and time again I have clenched my rifle and, staring through the loophole across the still darkness to the dim, rock-silhouetted line that marked the Turkish trench, have seen shadowy forms crawl cautiously over their parapet, and quickly disappear into the inky darkness of the gully that lay midway between the two trenches. Should I sound the alarm? My mates would have the agony of awakening from their precious four hours' sleep, to stand with their bayonets at the loopholes with every straining sense alert, waiting for the attack that perhaps would never come. Would I wait until I heard the Turks climbing up the gentle slope to our parapet? But by then a shower of bombs would fly into our trench, and simultaneously with the explosions would come a fierce, triumphant yell of "Allah!" and hundreds of furious bayonet-jabbing forms would be jumping down upon the sleeping regiment.

And so it went on all through those terrible seven months. No wonder each outgoing hospital-boat took with it a heavy quota of mentally-deranged cases. Birdwood knew when he appealed to Australia to be very patient even though on resuming civil life the returned Digger failed and failed again.

2 March 1922

"Gouger": On a Digger's foursome:--- We had been on Gallipoli a fortnight when four mates in my regiment decided that the chances of a man seeing Australia again was one in four. So they arranged that none of them was to touch his deferred pay and that the survivor on reaching Australia was to receive the lot. Two days later a Jacko bomb claimed the first. In the following month two of the others were wounded; but they played the game, and were back in the line before their wounds were thoroughly cured. The fourth was then badly gashed by a shell splinter. He was sent away to hospital, but was returned to Anzac Cove two days before the general evacuation, and had hardly set foot of the beach before a shell from Beachy Bill sent him west. Months later a spray of machine-gun bullets registered the third man beneath the date palms of El Quatia. That left only one, who was now entitled to collect. Fate gave him his chance, for a bomb-dropping taube wounded him again at Bir el Abd, and on coming out of hospital he was offered a cushy guard job. But he refused to take it, and fell at last in sight of Jerusalem, sniped by a miserable Arab. So death won the wager thumbs down.

15 May 1924

"Gouger": As an offset to the malingerers, army doctors could tell of many Diggers who concealed their wounds, or tried to. In the Egyptian Government hospital, Alexandria, the man in the next bed to me had been brought in with a bullet in the lung. Under the X-rays they discovered also a bullet in the fleshy part of the thigh, the wound completely healed up. The patient told me later across the beds that he'd got the bullet in the thigh three days after the Landing at Gallipoli. It had not given him much trouble, and had soon healed up, so, as he "didn't want to leave the mob" he said nothing about it. Another man in my regiment carried a bullet in his arm right through the Peninsula. It "shifted," and was extracted at Maadi eight months later. But to ignore even the slightest wound on Gallipoli was to take a big chance. Our m.o. had repeatedly warned us to come to him, however trifling the injury, on account of the germs in that graveyard of centuries. I got the merest flick across the kneecap from a tiny flying shell-splinter; it raised one drop of blood, which I wiped away. "What a fool I'd look to parade to the doc. with that scratch!" I thought. But, three days later I was carried to him with a septic leg, which it took him all his time to save.

15 May 1924

"Gouger":   I had a mate in the good days who could see as well by night as by day. On the darkest of nights his eyes would occasionally glow as if covered by a film of phosphorous. Some hereditary relic, I suppose, of the ages when his ancestors used to forage under cover of the darkness. He was invaluable when travelling over rough bush country by night. He once told me his brother also had the same gift – or curse, as he called it. In Palestine I always felt quite secure when on night outpost duty with him. No prowling Turkish patrol could get within 300 yards of us. He fell within sight of the walls of Jerusalem, worse luck! He was very tender about his feline sight, taking it as a sort of slur, and I doubt if any man in the regiment but myself knew about it.

12 June 1924

"Gouger":   Wonderful what an attachment often arose between men and horses in the Sinai and Palestine campaigns. I remember three cases in my own regiment where horses actually pined away and died when their masters were killed. I can recall lots of nights during the hard rides of the desert campaign when "Halt!" having at last been given my horse flopped on the sand and I laid down beside him, and, snuggling up against his belly for warmth, fell straight asleep. On one cold night during the Romani stunt, all our regiment and a regiment of Maorilanders slept thus cuddled against their exhausted horses, under the brilliant desert stars.

26 June 1924

"Gouger":   It is a fact that a big-gun shell in full flight can sometimes be seen by the naked eye (B. 5/6/1924). On Gallipoli a howitzer used to fire from near the beach straight over our regiment. As the flying shell passed immediately over the crown of the big ridge on which we had our trenches, and providing there was a low, darkish cloud right above, keen eyes could distinctly see the shell in its crescendo flight. The eyes had to be fixed on the exact line of flight; in the same way one could at times follow the course of a bomb dropping from a plane. I suppose thousands of men saw the hand-grenade coming that hit them. I know I did. Or, rather, the sparks of the fuse. The one with my number on it was a jam-tin bomb from Jacko in Lone Pine, and it came through the dark night like a hissing Catherine-wheel, only it seemed the size of a comet to my lively imagination.

7 August 1924

"Gouger": The Turk had the draw on us for a long time in the desert campaign because of his wonderful sand-resisting rifle mechanism. He could fight all day in a sandstorm, and his rifle breech-block would not choke through sand grit. Neither did the steel require oil. On the other hand, our breech-blocks had to be swathed in special canvas covers, which had to be whipped off before we could fire a shot. The bolt also always needed a film of oil. In action it was hell when the finely-drifting sand combined with the burnt oil and intense heat to jamb the firing-bolt. Then a man had literally to sweat to keep his rifle talking, while Abdul coolly whistled along five bullets to our one. Centuries of desert-fighting have made the Turk familiar with every phase of sand, and, for all the disparagement thrown on his intelligence, he has had the brains to manufacture steel which defies the choking action.

7 August 1924

"Gouger": I sometimes doubt if African dates would be such a popular article of diet if consumers could see the processes some of them go through before being shipped. The date oases of the Sinai desert are mostly owned by Sheiks whose harem walls front the Nile valley. Each season the nomad desert tribes get a "contract" to wander over the desert stripping the dates. The fruit is picked nearly green, and thrown into pits dug in the sand and lined with palm leaves. The fire of the desert sun heats the sand, which gradually ripens the fruit. Afterwards big brown and black men, with flat, sand-cracked feet that have doubtfully ever touched water, jump into the pits and stamp the dates down to compress them for loading. When an oasis is picked bare, the dates are generally packed into palm-leaf baskets and slung on to the mangy camels and carried to Port Said, which has acquired the name of being one of the filthiest places upon earth. Isn't it time Australia grew her own dates?

23 October 1924

"Gouger": "Moe's" New Guinea natives with red hair (B.25/9/24) may have an explanation, though I would hate to insinuate anything. I remember well when the Desert Column marched into El Arish we unsophisticated Australians were surprised to see a proportion of the Arab population with both fair and ginger hair. Curiosity, of course, got the cat out of the bag. They were souvenirs of Napoleon's troops that had occupied El Arish about a century ago. At least, that was the Arabs' proud explanation

18 December 1924

"I.L.I.": When the argument was quiet in Palestine some lucky regiments had a ride down to Rujin El Bahr, where the sainted Jordan runs into the Dead Sea. The water, 25 per cent salt, is so buoyant that an egg will float in it; the horses, used to a dip in fresh water or even the Mediterranean, seemed comically astonished at floating so high. Some 6½ million tons of water are supposed to flow into the Dead Sea daily from various streams, and the whole of it has to be carried off by evaporation, which gives some slight idea of the intense heat under which fighting took place in those parts. In that same Jordan Valley a horribly prickly shrub abounds, from the formidable thorns of which the native Arabs will tell you that Christ's crown was made. I often used to wonder, when riding through the choking dust-clouds of the valley, or crouching among the burning rocks with the bullets chipping sparks from the boulders, whether the day was hot when *He* toiled up the valley under the crown. Close by old Jericho grows a small shrub with broad, green leaves woolly-looking on the under side. The fruit is the famous Apple of Sodom.

22 January 1925

"I.L.I.": I think the native gains unearned credit in the matter of superior eyesight. It was wonderful to note in the Desert campaign how in a couple of years the eyesight of the Aussie troops developed. At the outset an Arab would contemptuously point out to us smeary brown things creeping among smeary brown hills on smeary brown horizon, and count correctly their number and give their names, to the confusion of the white soldiers. In two years the white soldiers, if still alive, could do exactly the same. It was simply a matter of the development of the vision in open-country fighting, where if an outpost's eyes were not continually alert their owner was likely not to want them any longer.

2 April 1925

"Gouger": An Aussie pal in Gallipoli was passionately fond of a little furze bush which struggled for life just atop of our parapet. He built sandbags round its possy, and watered it every day from his own scanty ration. And the water ration was scanty. One morning the plant delighted its benefactor by sporting a little green bud, which presently blossomed into a bright scarlet flower. A few days later a whole bunch of flowers flaunted cheerily against the hard brown of the parapet. One day when the soldier was in the support-trenches the sweating water fatigue trailed along. The Aussie drew his ration and hurried into the

fire-trench to his beloved vegetable. It was a blistering hot day. I was oiling the catch of my bayonet on the firing step, and I remember he smiled as he leant up towards the cheekily bright petals and poured them their ration. At that instant a Turkish shell caught him through the chest, and his blood kissed the drooping scarlet of the flowers.

7 May 1925

"EMU CREST":   At Maadi one dull day a berseem camel-driver promised us a tale for a half-piastre. A very rich old sheik, he said, wished to die and be gathered to the Prophet. Despite all his yearnings he continued above ground, unable to appreciate the joys of life and love. The tribe decided that he must have offended a camel, for it is well known that within animals reside the souls of djinns; so the chief camel was requisitioned to put the sheik's worry before the herd, and see if there wasn't any way out of it. The boss camel came back from the meeting and said: "Sheik, you may now ascend to rest – we have forgiven you. But before you seek the Prophet, learn why you have so deeply offended us. We suffered the drivers' whips and heavy loads, for such things are the gifts of Allah. But you played a dirty trick on us when, after having strung us out for the caravan trip, you placed a miserable ass at the head to lead us". We gave Ayoub a whole piastre.

28 May 1925

"GOUGER":   One of the best friends I made in the war was a little pony that carried me for three long years over blazing sands and mountain snows, carried me safely through many a hail of Austrian shells and Turkish bullets. I've shared my iron rations with her in the hard times, and my water-bottle on the awful desert marches. On the Khan Yunus stunt the regiment had halted for a hasty meal among low hillocks close to an evacuated Bedouin camp. We slung the scant nosebags on the hungry neddies just as I was called away. Twenty minutes later I got the strongest feeling that my pony needed me. I cannot explain it, but I was sure she was in trouble. I grabbed a good-tempered orderly to carry on with my job, and ran back to the squadron. The pony was missing from the lazing troophorses. I ran straight past over the hillocks, feeling sure she had wandered back to the Bedouin camp. The nomads often buried barley grain about their camps, and I was in the habit of fossicking for the big earthen jars and giving the good belly-fodder to the mare. She'd remembered all right, and in the course of her quest had fallen down a Turkish rifle-pit. As I raced I could

see her head plunging frantically just above the level of the pit. There was a black shroud struggling about her neck. It was a Bedouin girl with a horn-handled knife, and the brown devil was trying to cut my pony's throat.

4 June 1925
"Gouger": I remember being very hungry one bleak morning on Gallipoli. We'd just been warned to be very careful of our bully-beef and biscuit ration as the submarine campaign might prevent the landing of stores altogether. As I passed along Shrapnel Gully, subconsciously running low past the bad spots. I remember musing dolefully on the prospect of semi-starvation being added to our other hardships. Suddenly, on the side of the gully, I saw a hand, a very brown hand, a very shrunken hand, smelling evilly and with a cloud of flies humming around it. Maybe I wouldn't have noticed it particularly for these fragments of humanity were always cropping up in unexpected places, but in this hand was clenched – an army biscuit! As I looked, I could almost see the humorist's strained smile as he placed the good biscuit in the dead man's hand. A horrible idea was telegraphed to my brain by my empty stomach; but I shivered in disgust and passed on quickly.

9 July 1925
"Gouger": It was two days after the Bir-el-Abd stunt, and the fierce sun whipped the crowns of distant sand dunes into shimmering tiers of light. In a far flung line some hundreds of us were cautiously scouting in pairs long distances apart. From a rough gully, drab with desert bushes, came the faint wail of a mouth-organ. The tune was "Annie Laurie". Thoroughly surprised, my mate and I turned our horses' heads, and the hoofs ploughed deep in the sand as the animals rolled and stumbled down the hill. At the bottom lay a Tommy, his head trying to capture the shifting shade from a meagre bush. His body lay in the sun-haze, with puttee bound bushes around his blood-stained thigh to keep off the flies. The quavering notes ceased as his blue eyes looked up in quick apprehension. We could read his thought plainly: "Turks"! And then the relief that tried to smile from his sun-cracked lips as he saw instead two browned Aussies! He was only a kid, a remnant of Kitchener's army.

But he was game. Two blazing days of thirst and nights of bitter cold and loneliness he had spent there with his mouth-organ!

"Ah was afraid ah'd go clean barmy. Chooms, when mah lips cracked too much to play," he whispered when we'd emptied a water bottle down his throat.

23 July 1925
"Up Top": Sun heat, like everything else, has its soft side if a man only learns to adapt himself to it. For instance, at times it is actually cooler to be out in a blazing sun and walking about than it is to be lying under an inefficient shelter. I remember oppressive days, unbearable when lying in a sweltering hut that became quite bearable when I got out in the open and commenced working. From shelter I've watched men toiling in the hot sun with pick and shovel, and felt sorry for them, but later experience has taught me that they were actually cooler than I was. To lie in the usual bush shelter on a broiling day is misery indeed. Get up and do some work, either mental or physical. I believe that physical is the better. I don't know whether it is that a man's mind is taken off the heat and his hard-luck worries, or that physical movement in some way sets up a reaction that cools the body, but it is a fact.

The troops noticed the same thing in the desert. The halts in the march were always the hottest, and when on the move the unbearable oppressiveness of the heat seemed to relax. So long as a man wears few clothes and loose ones at that, the act of movement creates a draft that cools the body.

17 September 1925
"Gouger": Clarry was a decent sort of youngster with the one vice of always going into the firing line in a clean uniform and with a fresh shave. As he'd seen Gallipoli and the Sinai Peninsula right through, we knew he was not a Kiwi soldier, but how he'd managed to carry another uniform and have it always spotlessly clean and ready for use over the drearily long desert trek set us all wondering. It was Long Brad who came nearest to what I believe was the truth. Clarry, sweating and dusty in knee-frayed breeches, lumbered along. Long Brad straightened his back and wiped the sweat from his brow. "Wisht t' hell Clarry had his Kiwi togs on now; a scrap'd be better'n this. I s'pose if 'e gets knocked he wants ter go to the angels nice and pretty." I thought of Brad's words when months later I was helping to dig a hasty grave beside the long white Hebron road. Clarry looked wonderfully neat and clean. Though we'd had a solid week's fighting there did not seem to be a speck on his uniform. Only on his forehead was there a dusty band where he had kissed the ground as he pitched forward. With the boy's own handkerchief Brad brushed the dust away as we lowered him; and somehow he seemed to smile his thanks for this last small service.

7 January 1926

"Gouger":   Our mob's first experience of aeroplane efficiency was when the 5th Light Horse, camped at Bir-el-Duidar, had been hurried out on an all-night desert stunt on the chance of capturing a herd of camels believed to be not far away. At dawn we were at the rendezvous, but there were no signs of our quarry. Suddenly a plane came droning above the sandhills, skimming the tops, nosing into the still-black valleys, buzzing over sun-tipped ridges. Then it swooped, and with a flash of metal came straight at us. The head of every man and horse was turned aloft, the message it dropped was: "The camels are in a valley two miles to the east; Bedouins are hurrying them off." The whole regiment leapt to saddle, and the metal falcon hummed away. Without the 'plane we should never have got near those camels, for the beasts were fresh, unloaded, and in charge of men born to the desert, whereas our horses had already gone 36 hours without water. Presently in the hazy valleys ahead we heard the excited stuttering of a machine-gun, and when the leading horsemen ploughed down the last sand-ridges there was a mob of some hundreds of camels noisily "ringing", while viciously circling just above was the 'plane. Never did sheep-dog guard his mob more vigilantly pending the shepherd's arrival.

14 January 1926

"Gouger":   I noticed in Palestine during the war years that in some respects its birds, like our own, took the man-hawk seriously. At the sight of a 'plane they would swoop to earth, scuttle among the barley or green leaves of the orange groves, and there crouch until the winged menace had sailed past. They seemed to sense a 'plane fully 10 minutes before we could either hear or see it. When camped near trees for any length of time, the uneasy twitterings and quick apprehensive flight of the birds, warned the more observant of us that a hawk with egg-laying capacity was drawing near. Then we, like the birds, became uneasy. Familiarity, however, soon bred contempt, and birds whose home grounds were taken over by aerodromes became used to the whirring machines and treated their noises with contempt.

25 February 1926

"Gouger":   "Cranky Joe" came from a N.S.W. North Coast home where Dad had nailed a horseshoe over the cow-bails for luck and Mum had nailed one in blue plush over the door. Joe himself had always solemnly alighted when he espied a cast-off shoe, and spitting on the iron, had faithfully thrown it over his

shoulder for luck. Consequently, when as a solitary scout he drew a shrapnel burst on himself and the bullet-hail did no damage except to neatly chip off the nearside shoe of his old charger, he hopped off quick and lively and collected it before galloping for cover. For weeks after, unknown to his cobbers, he wore that shoe upon his flannel, just over the heart. Two days before the attack on Beersheba he developed a sudden cold sweat. It struck him that the shoe only framed his heart, and did not shield it at all. It was, in fact, an invitation for a bulls-eye, and Joe felt certain he was going out. The night before the stunt he sought the farrier-sergeant and explained his trouble. The farrier was old in service and understanding, and almost within echo of the Beersheba redoubts hammered the shoe into a not un-shapely shield. Padding it with flannel, it neatly covered what Cranky Joe considered was his heart. He slept soundly that night. Next afternoon he was one of the first men in the galloping charge to sway and roll from the saddle. He came-to a couple of hours later with the doctor examining his chest curiously. Over the heart in ugly blue was the shape of the shield, and on the shield itself the remnants of a flattened bullet. Joe put in a fortnight in hospital recovering from shock, but to-day he is serenely milking cows next to the old home with the blue plush horseshoe over its kitchen door. Over his own mantelpiece is a little roughly-made shield splattered with Turkish lead.

18 March 1926

"Gouger": "Sleep means muscular relaxation," says the wise man. But I've watched men, animals and birds asleep in positions that necessitated muscles being kept alert. I've seen hundreds of men sitting asleep in their saddles, and I've watched birds and animals asleep in positions that made muscular relaxation impossible. When disturbed by something not hostile they simply regained poise without awakening. Wild ducks will keep paddling while asleep to avoid being carried downstream by currents. Some men without waking can actually perform well-practiced mechanical work. I remember one personal experience. The troops were weakened by hard fighting, sickness and woeful lack of reinforcements, and were so nerve-strained as to be physical wrecks from want of sleep alone. I was armed sentry on a shell-magazine, and any breach of duty was punishable with death. Sound asleep, I stood stiffly erect, with hands clasped around the rifle-muzzle and bayonet-shaft. The officer of the guard came noiselessly in the pitch darkness to the pile of shells and stood within three feet of me. Automatically my rifle jerked up, the bayonet-point resting quite steadily within an inch of his chest. He remained absolutely quite for several minutes,

then said softly: "Sentry, you are asleep." "A lie!" I replied as my eyelids opened: "there is a bullet in the chamber, my finger on the trigger has taken the first pull, and if you had made the slightest suspicious movement you would have been a dead man." "Then why did you not challenge me?" he asked quietly. "Because we had been repeatedly warned of the spies who go among us in officer's uniform. I could not be absolutely certain until I recognised your voice. If you had been a spy, and I had challenged you, you would have melted into the darkness on the instant. But I had you at my mercy, whether friend or foe." After a pause he said: "But your eyelids were shut!" "No," I replied emphatically. "The left eye was closed, the shooting eye was ready for instant action." I do not understand it, but it was one of those things we learnt we possessed during the war: to sleep and yet retain our mental activity.

6 May 1926
"Gouger":   Outside picturesque Duran the Palestine Imperial troops built a tremendous supply-dump, with edible stuffs and rum for its valuable centre. It would have taken a brigade to guard it, and the O.C., who looked on all Australians as born thieves, hit on a little device of his own. Immediately the fatigue parties had drawn rations, the guards would rake a circle around the vulnerable supplies. Thus, any "Australian boots" would be seen on the soft sand at daylight, and the Tommies reckoned there would be no difficulty in tracking the depredators. (They had heard quite a lot about tracking – from Australians.) But though stores mysteriously did disappear, the guard o' mornings could never detect any sign of the Australians having invaded their master-piece. It was only last night that some old pals and I had a reminiscent laugh about the row our q.m. kicked up over missing a miserable hand-rake.

27 May 1926
"Ili":   The war years made death so constant a companion for millions of us that I believe a gifted few glimpsed through the veil. One sensitive friend of mine saw his loved brother blown to pieces. A month later, during duty, this man shouted, "Jump, Jack! Quick!" As we landed in the trench-bottom the shell burst on the very spot where we had been working. "I didn't hear a sound," I said curiously; "what gave you warning?" After a momentary hesitation, he said defiantly, "Wally's voice." He went on to tell me how his brother had appeared to him, just as he was in life, the night after he was blown to pieces, and how he had twice heard the dead man's voice distinctly. He continued to hear it to some

effect, too: more than once his strange intuition saved those close around him. He came to be called "the Witch", and an idea grew that every man who stuck close to him would live to see Australia again. He several times told me of some unlucky one whose number was called. And he was always right.

8 July 1926
"GOUGER":   Here's another for THE BULLETIN's tally of coincidences. The column had halted, and my cobber became interested in a wobbly lark on the roadside barley-field. The songster was plainly in distress, and the bird-lover hopped off his horse and ran the disabled flutterer down. There had been rain, and sticky red clay had caught between the bird's toes. Fluffs of thistledown had adhered with more clay, and as the bird floundered still more had accumulated until its feet bulked like two tomatoes. It was a tedious process freeing the exhausted sufferer, and while my cobber was doing it a Turkish shell landed below his browsing horse and blew it to pieces. Only a fortnight ago he rescued a Queensland peewee in similar mud-laden distress. And, to prove that truth is stranger far than fiction, he then lost his second horse - a snake bit its nose as it browsed awaiting the return of the Samaritan.

8 July 1926
"ILI":   I wonder if a wad of rejected verse (it was THE BULLETIN that did the rejecting, too) ever landed another man into such a mess as this. She was a fascinating lady who I first met in a Cairo casino. All being fair in love, I had posed as an officer to become better acquainted, and was soon meeting the enchantress at her own house, where there was a rose-garden surrounded by towering walls. The clever questions about military matters she asked me in such a childlike way set my brain working overtime, but I gave her a good run for her money, and if the heads had heard me they would have been staggered at the military knowledge a humble private can fashion into plausible lies. One starry night her pink finger-tip strayed within my tunic and came in contact with an envelope. She tried to withdraw it, but I begged her not to and confided that they were documents relating to mobilisation orders that I should have locked up, but had been in such a hurry to meet her, etc., etc. Her persistency deepened my suspicions about her and I shied at a parting drink, but I fell when she produced an unopened box of Turkish delight – the genuine stuff is delight indeed. I suppose it was 18 hours after when a beastly native policeman kicked my ribs in the Esbekiah Gardens. My head suggested to me that I was in Hell,

and my stained face and arms and the filthy fellaheen gabardine covering my otherwise naked body tended at first to deepen the conviction. I have never been able to look on Turkish delight since without a shudder. Of course I never saw that wad of MS. again, either.

15 July 1926
"Up North": It is risky to suddenly wake a man who has fallen asleep with danger on his mind. Once after we had been sniped at all day, I roughly woke my mate at mid-night for his turn at picquet duty. He was up and lunging at me with drawn bayonet even before he stood properly upright, and our yells startled a mile of outposts. A party of us volunteered for the risky job of blowing up a Beersheba bridge. We managed to creep between the Turkish outposts and rested in a donga. Instructions were whispered that each man not watching should sleep if he could, but in the event of a patrol stumbling across us we were to go to it as silently as possible. Two hours before dawn one of the "suiciders" woke his mate. Instantly clawing fingers fastened on the bending man's throat, and he came near never seeing the sun rise. In later peaceful days, while prospecting towards the wild west coast of Cape York Peninsula, the niggers persistently dogged our tracks. One of the party became "windy" of this unseen foe, and when awakened to help round up the horses he fired from his blanket. The bullet, catching the third in the thigh, ended the trip.

16 September 1926
"Gouger": In the Gaza hills, after Beersheba, we came on a tragic group: a Tommy sergeant, his hands tied behind him, two Turkish soldiers, a Bedouin and a donkey. All had been dead for months, and the atmosphere had sun-dried them. The details of that grim tragedy we never knew. Close by was a nomads' camp which provided us with another riddle, less sinister but equally insoluble. She was a remarkably beautiful Arab girl, with lily-white skin, black eyes all ablaze when we excited her and a mane of auburn hair that fell to her knees. The Arabs swore she was a full-blooded desert queen, but the romantic theory that they had captured her as a white baby during some midnight raid found some supporters among us. One Light Horseman, a bit of an ethnologist, contended that she was a throw-back to the Phoenicians; my own view is that she was indebted to one of Napoleon's cohorts for a male ancestor. She was a woman, anyway, right down to her dainty little toes, and enjoyed immensely the close interest the barbarian Australians took in her, to the fierce jealousy of her swarthy countrymen.

23 September 1926

"Gouger":   Watching a lizard the other day, my mind flew back to a whole line of men just as motionless, and our greenish khaki merging as easily with the soil and crushed barley. Fronting us lay hundreds of other men, their bluish-grey uniforms making them just as invisible until some nervous movement betrayed a presence. To the everlasting credit of the trainers of the Anzacs, the Aussie beat the Turk at making a chameleon of himself; probably the greenish khaki with its not too clean-cut lines was superior to Jacko's bluish-grey, in that it dissolved just a little more perfectly into any color-scheme underneath. And many of the man soon grasped the knack of continuously firing a rifle without the slightest visible movement, right in the face of the foe. Nature, coupled with the threat of death, is an unbeatable teacher.

10 February 1927

"Gouger":   In the early Gallipoli days the Navy captured a Greek barque loaded with eatables and softgoods. The worth-while things not being sufficient to go round among the Diggers on Anzac Cove, lots were drawn and there was much grumbling when a hungry man would find himself the possessor of a pot of Vaseline instead of the eggs or cake he had been hoping for. A character in the 9th Battalion, familiarly known as "Cock", was approached by Lieutenant Arnold, with "What did you draw, 'Cock'?" "I'll bet me tot o' rum against your water-bottle that I beat *yous*," was the reply. "Right," said Arnold, and he held out a tin of tooth-power. "And over ya water-bottle," "Cock" rejoined. "See me 'ead?" he demanded, slinging off his old slouch hat. "Is there a skerrick of 'air on it?" "No," Arnold admitted. "Well, 'ere's wot I drawed!" And "Cock" triumphantly held out – a fine-tooth comb!

3 March 1927

"Gouger":   Some men get all the thrills. A cobber of mine was on the northern pearling fleets before he enlisted. His first experience of war was when he mixed it with Abdul at the Landing. Later on he and a mate, between bombs, sneaked out one night into No Man's Land and tended a wounded Maorilander amongst the bushes for two nights and days. They bayoneted three men, portion of a Jacko patrol, before they finally succeeded in dragging the wounded man, foot by foot, into our trenches. My cobber was next blown up at Quinn's Post, but survived to return to the Peninsula. After several more hair-raising and hair-breadth 'scapes he was taken prisoner, and put in a harrowing time under hard task-masters in the interior of Asia. Eventually he returned to Aussie a rather

quiet man, and we reckoned his thrills were over at last. But we were premature. He married a little red-haired girl with shiny eyes, and his latest thrill came the other day with the arrival of twins.

7 March 1928
"Gouger":   Our own General Chauvel's fighting advance with the Desert Column might fairly give him a place among the great figures of the Great War (B.22/2/28). The advance was made over a hundred miles of practically waterless desert, with no steam train or train of lorries to carry supplies, against an army of trained militarists, veterans of a dozen campaigns, savagely contesting every mile of the way. And Chauvel was leading comparatively raw soldiers, thousands of whom had not even shot a wallaby. The Sinai Desert campaign, not including Palestine, was a war on its own, though, of course, completely overshadowed by the operations in Europe.

6 June 1928
"Gouger":   I often wonder if any of our poor old Light-Horse neddies are alive in Egypt; there were never gamer animals or stauncher mates. My last fell stone dead during the hectic weeks of the great final Palestine "push". He had three shrapnel bullets in his back, and must have carried them for a week at least without my knowing it. During that dreadful desert ride from El Katie, at long intervals a wailing howl would float down the plodding column, "Dismount!" Men would just fall off, horses would sink to their knees and then stretch straight out with the man coiled up between their legs for warmth, till the whole column lay like a huge snaky cloud shadow up and around and over the white sandhills. What agony it was for horses and men to flounder up when that wail floated along, "Mo-unt!" Poor prads! Luckier those that fell in action than they that fell into alien hands.

20 June 1928
"Gouger":   The most exciting road in the world to negotiate was Shrapnel Gully, before the great sap was dug. On commanding cliffs at the gully head waited the Turkish snipers. Across the track at short distances apart we threw up sandbag traverses. The mode of travel was to run hell-for-leather to a wall, have a breather, sneak to the end of the bags, bend double and take a long breath with the fear of death in it, then rush out and tear to the next wall, hearing the viscous hum of bullets meant expressly for you! To proceed at a walk was certain death. When platoons and troops were going up it meant a mile of gasping

runs, intermixed with death-speculating halts. Half a troop of men would rush around a traverse and fly; the next crouched a minute longer, knowing that unseen rifles were levelled awaiting their dash from cover. And so on, and so on. To strike a light in that valley of death by night brought a shower of curses from unseen comrades and sounds of hurried scrambling to dodge the bullets that came whistling down from the owl-eyes away up the gully heights.

27 June 1928

"Gouger": I wonder if primitive forms of transport will ever die out. I was knocked among the Jericho hills, and for painful miles was rolled down to the motor-ambulances in an old two-wheeled cart. No motor could be trusted to cover that ground. Many a wounded man will never forget the lurching camel-ambulances of the Desert and Palestine campaigns. With a wounded man slung on each side, those dromedaries would clamber up and over and across interminable sandhills, carrying on from sunrise to sunset where motor ambulances could not venture. A terrible trip for wounded men was the grim journey back from Magaar. Having ridden all the afternoon and night, hedged in by ghostly sandhills, we attacked at dawn and fought all through a blazing desert day without water. We retired that night still without water, shadowy columns of desperately tired and thirsty men and horses. The wounded rode back on wooden sleds!

11 July 1928

"Gouger": Small bodies of troops occasionally got lost on the far-flung lines of Syria and Palestine, especially in the Sinai desert. At Bir-el –Abd, when the scrap was at its height, two troops of helmeted yeomanry came trotting along to where the 5th Light Horse were blazing at the on-coming Jacko. Our squadron-leader promptly annexed the perspiring Tommies, who confessed, that they had mislaid themselves, and they wormed gratefully into the sand beside us and opened out on the Turk. The Tommies stuck to us while the fighting lasted, and galloped away with us at evenfall, except some who lay quite still on the crown of the hill. In the fighting after Magaar several Tommy troops were bushed for a couple of days. Australian troops sometimes got lost, too. Many a light horseman can vividly remember his regiment riding all night following its own tail. On one such occasion we circled all night about the Turkish guns. They let us have it at dawn, and the whole regiment galloped hell-for-leather for home and breakfast. This particular regiment wasn't the Fifth; that crowd had got in out of the wet much earlier.

25 July 1928

"Gouger": A crippled mate revives memory of a snappy little British destroyer that loved to let Hell loose on dark nights opposite Chatham's Post. At any old time that destroyer would sneak close inshore, hurl her eggs and then dash off. The Turks in the trenches she favored must have hated her. But a day came when she hit us too. The regiment hopped the bags and attacked the Turkish trenches in broad daylight, with the sole object of stopping their reinforcements from attacking the troops charging Achi Baba. While we lay out in the open under hellish rifle-fire, that blasted destroyer raced inshore and enfiladed us with shells. The Turks got their own back that day.

25 July 1928

"Jack Hall": During the days when the Light Horse trailed Jacko across the desert my cobber Bill, who was the possessor, contrary to regulations, of a camera, decided to do his own developing. He had everything but a red lamp, and there aren't any red lamps in the desert. On being consulted, I made several inane suggestions that were received with silent contempt, and then I had a brain wave.

"What about this?" I asked, winding an old Bulletin cover round our makeshift lamp. The glow through the sheet gave the desired effect, and later on Bill's grunts of approval from beneath an old blanket propped up on sticks gave assurance that all was well.

8 August 1928

"Gouger": It happened at El Katia. The 5th Light Horse had galloped into the oasis under a hail of machine-gun bullets, tumbled off their horses and charged across an open clay pan towards the Turkish guns. Right in the open a malevolent spray of bullets cut through Darkie's belt and set his strides tumbling about his knees. He struggled up and started in pursuit of the regiment, one hand gripping his pants, the other his rifle, haversack and bandolier, while his water-bottle thumped around his neck. He fell again and a mouthful of earth smothered his curses. Then a fresh idea struck him and he rolled about trying to extricate himself from his impeding nether garments, but despite frenzied efforts, he couldn't unlace the knees and get them over the leggings in time. Then the bullets began to spray around him and he realised that he was being made a target. He struggled up once more and saw the tail end of the regiment disappearing under cover of the distant palms. Darkie sturdily took-up the chase, though it looked to us as if every

rifleman in the Turkish army was trying to get him; the sand and clay around the hobbling man was torn by bullets every moment. Miraculously he reached cover and flopped down, weeping tears of sheer rage.

29 August 1928

"Gouger": Is there any older road in the world than the great caravan route from Egypt into Palestine? The Phoenicians traded along it and cut the Amalekites' throats when they could catch them. David camped on it and disciplined the Bedouins. Samson trod it where it branches off into Gaza. Cleopatra and Anthony drove along it, Joseph and Mary carrying Christ walked it. It was our Desert Mounted Column which pushed the Turks back along the same track. The "road" wanders from oasis to oasis, there being no water elsewhere, and the wells are from 20 to 40 miles apart. Our engineers cleaned and repaired several reservoirs of stone where the ancient Romans had stored water. In more modern times one of Napoleon's armies left their bones in the sands around El Arish. They also left some red-headed kids.

19 September 1928

"Gouger": During the desert campaign there were far more curses wasted over watering horses than in the actual fighting. The oasis wells, used by the Bedouins from time immemorial, were farcical to a brigade of thirst-maddened horses; and even at permanent camp, where wells had been dug, hand-pumps erected and long canvas troughs installed, one might see struggling men being dragged over the sands by animals frantic to get at the troughs out of their turn. Often the operation took hours, and when he got a chance the unspeakable Turk would make it worse by sniping. Even when he had been driven well back by the patrols, you could never feel sure that Abdul wouldn't get his guns to work from miles away and lather the clustered horses with shrapnel. I have seen men sitting by their dying horses and crying; there were few things more poignant than seeing the poor brute that had carried you far and faithfully struck down by an unseen enemy when waiting its turn for water.

7 November 1928

"Atherton": In the desert campaign it was easy to get lost at any time, but I well remember one night when a mist blocked us even from steering by the stars. The whole regiment rode like shrouded ghosts, the only sound being the shuffle of hoofs, the squelch of sand, and an occasional softly whispered curse.

Each horse of the 500 plodded on with his nose thrust against the leader's tail, for it was impossible to see further. We rode right up a sloping bank on to a screaming medley of "Allah!" "Allah!" "Allah!" "Austral-ee!" "Austral-ee!" "Austral-ee!" As the foremost horse stumbled down into the redoubt, heavily-coated figures staggered up with arms upraised. Three sharp revolver shots, one shouted order, a machine-gun stuttering into the air, and the electrified regiment had wheeled as one horse and were galloping like a thundering avalanche. We pulled up a mile away, mustered in marvellously quick time and ascertained with the minimum of vocal sound that not a man was missing. I have often wondered whether we or the Turks got the worst scare.

12 December 1928
"Gouger": There was no safety zone at Gallipoli. All landing troops were under shell fire before they touched the beach, and thereafter were under all sorts of fire. All day long bullets fired from the Turkish front line were whizzing over our trenches to hum across the space behind and eventually plonk in the sea. The tiny beach was always under shrapnel fire from "Beachy Bill". No square foot of ground was immune from falling missiles. Whether a man was slinging bombs from the front line, carrying wounded to the beach, or landing bully beef from the waterfront, he was under fire night and day. Gallipoli was all front line. In fact, the front-line trenches were sometimes the safest place to be in. Up there at least a man did have a sort of trench as an apology for protection against the rain of missiles.

20 March 1929
"Gouger": In Egypt, the concentration of our war dead into suitable cemeteries was a vast task. There were no fewer than 55 graveyards that had formed temporary resting-places; in addition there were thousands of scattered graves in the Libyan, Sinai and Hedjaz deserts, with thousands more in Palestine. The graves dotted along the Suez canal were easily found, for we always held the canal; their occupants now sleep in Ismailia. But along that great unmarked highway across the Sinai desert towards Palestine, we fought for two blazing years and many men lay where they fell. Others were buried by their cobbers in shallow holes in the bullet-swept ground. Yet, years after, most of the dead were collected and now sleep at Kantara by the canal. Those who fell in Palestine are mostly now in cemeteries in Jerusalem, Ramleh, Gaza, Beersheba, Din-el-Belah and Haifa. The Jerusalem cemetery on Mt Scorpus, hard by the Mount of Olives, is one of the most beautiful in the world.

24 April 1929

"Gouger": I don't think the Turk troubled overmuch about the tabulating of his dead,; he may have reckoned that some of them, particularly his colored allies, were better dead anyway. On Gallipoli more than any other front, he had every chance of mustering those who had answered the call to Allah, but I never saw or heard anything to make me think he did so, even in the case of those poor devils who lay out with our own for those long months in 'NO MAN'S LAND'. The Sinai Desert must hold the dust of thousands of Turkish "unknown soldiers". Abdul fought willingly enough there, but in the end there was a vast retreat that covered hundreds of miles. The British buried the Turkish dead after the attack on the Suez Canal, but after that the drifting sand of the desert was the only undertaker. I have ridden over dead greycoats in the lonely oases extending from Romani and from El Katia, and among the dismal sandhills on the long, dry march to Bir-el-Abd. Whenever possible, our chaps buried their fallen foes, but there were times when we were too hard pressed to give our own dead sepulture.

19 June 1929

"Gouger": Touching these war medals.

Some months after the evacuation of Gallipoli our O.C. was notified from G.H.Q. that a limited number of medals were available for each regiment, and was asked to send in a list of men who deserved them. The O.C. (General L.C. Wilson, then in command of the 5th Light Horse) replied that he wanted none, for the reason that every one of his men had earned a medal. I have often thought that the answer aptly applied to the whole army on Gallipoli, and for that matter in some other theatres of war as well. I'm not a medallist myself, though I admit to having been recommended on more than one occasion, which perhaps, impressed on me how hard it was to land the trinket that meant so much. Most of our O.C.'s disliked recommending unless one of the numerous deeds of heroism that might well have earned one had been brought to the notice of the G.H.Q. by some Imperial officer of high rank, or possibly a French "brass-hat" who happened to have personally seen it. That was how most of medals came to be granted, and even those recommendations did not always hit the bulls-eye.

17 July 1929

"Gouger": When our transport reached Aden we were greeted with the glad news that 100 cigarettes could be bought for a bob. I loaded up my kitbag with 2000, and before we reached Cairo it was full of a fine yellowish dust consisting mostly of camel's dung. At Cairo we bought alleged Turkish cigarettes, made in filthy mud hovels out of street bumpers, straw and other ingredients, with a trifle of genuine tobacco thrown in as a makeweight. They smelt abominably, and would make any tram or restaurant hum like a dogbox. There were good brands of tobacco to be had, of course, if you could pay and knew where to buy. The Gyppo girls were always ready to tell you. I can see the little henna fingered devils now, coiled on those divans like gilded kittens, with wisps of smoke daintily ascending from their tiny gold-tipped cigarettes.

4 September 1929

"Gouger": Hebron, where Arabs have been massacring Jews will be well remembered by survivors of the 2rc Light Horse Brigade. After the capture of Beersheba we headed for the precipitous Judaean Hills near Hebron. The Turks rushed up some batteries of German artillery, posted them on top of the hills and gave us particular hell as our horses struggled below in the rocky gullies. We scrambled towards the enemy over the roughest country, but the Turks lined the hilltops across the valley and forced us to take shelter amongst the rocks on the opposite side. No man dared cross that long, white, age-old Hebron road, once trodden by Christ. In the fighting days that followed, cowled Bedouins squatted like silhouetted vultures on the hills directly behind us, and betrayed our sheltering position to the Turkish artillery across the valley. As a shell would fall near us, a white-cowled figure would stand innocently up, and the distant enemy would know exactly where to aim the next shell. But with our murdered horses the bones of some of those vultures lie rotting among the Judaean hills.

4 September 1929

"Gouger": Fresh from the scorching heat of the Jordan Valley, we reached Jerusalem in a bitterly cold wind, and noted a few Jews by the Wailing Wall, so much mentioned in the cables of late. They looked shivering bundles of rags. Then we returned to the Valley of Desolation by descending 3000ft down the old Roman Road, and found some humans who had even more to wail about. Even the Bedouins clear out of that hell in summer, but there was curious tribe of scrags or strays left, a forlorn crowd of derelicts who always reminded me of our own mulga abos. They were a hybrid mob, said to be descended from African slaves imported by the Arabs in their days of conquest. They seemed to live mostly in holes in the ground, and snakes, spiders and sandflies look to be about the only things that could furnish them with food. The official military handbook of Palestine has placed it upon record that "nothing is known of the climate of the Lower Jordan Valley in summertime, since no civilised human being has yet been found to spend a summer there". And yet our boys stuck it, and how many paid the penalty!

9 October 1929
"Jack Hall":   Diggers that have tramped and ridden on desert sands will remember the scarab beetle. This little fellow will roll a piece of offal into a ball and kick it along from sunrise till sunset. One of the species did a good deed at Moascar when a trooper attached a cigarette to him by a thread and headed him for the "birdcage" filled with defaulters. The trooper's cobber inside gave a gasp of relief when the little chap scrambled through the netting, and the guard noticed nothing.

27 November 1929
"Gouger":   The horse was of paramount importance in Sinai and Palestine and Farrier-Quartermaster Cook was the magician who saw that the 5th Light Horse never lacked remounts, even when a dozen neddies were wounded by the one shell burst. His method of obtaining "spares" was to annex every horse suspected of being a nomad. It was said of the 5th that they faked more hoof-brands, dyed more coats and pinched more horses than any brigade among Allenby's crusaders, but that was mostly jealousy. Anyway, Cook did not mount the complete regiment on his own. My third horse I acquired myself when the Indian officer's groom who was minding it was asleep.

6 August 1930
"Gouger":   The bravest man I knew in the war was a little weed of a chap who fought his native cowardice for three years and never let it get the better of him. On Gallipoli the broomstick bombs were his special horror. All day he was a bundle of nerves, waiting tremulously for the night to come. By sundown he was abject but he would stick to his post all through the night. In the desert fighting and in Palestine the bursts of shrapnel sent him nearly imbecile. I have seen him livid, crouching under the belly of his horse while the regiment was awaiting

the order to go into action. He would lose all control of his physical movements except that he never once ran away. Long after he had proved that he was no malingerer, the squadron-leader tried to persuade him to accept a job back at the base, but he resolutely refused. He lived through three years of war without a scratch – and I wonder how many deaths he died!

17 December 1930
"Hadahoss":   The Brigade was hurrying through a valley in Palestine, the horses frantic at the smell of green things after 12 months of desert sands. Our job was to root out Ali El Hassan and his band of cut-throats. Suddenly Harvey, a nice chap but impetuous, caught site of a field of poppies. He confided to me that his girl, back in Nimmitabel, gave him one of those flowers when they parted. When an old crusader's church came in view above orchards and cactus hedges there suddenly echoed the "plip-plop!" of sniper's rifles firing from Beni Sali, immediately chorused by the roar of a heavy shell from Weli-Sheikh-Nuran. The squadrons galloped across the barley fields hastened by a rattle of machine-gun fire as the Maorilanders charged Khan Yunus. Our regiment fired only a few shots. Only one man was killed – poor Harvey, and he clutched a scarlet poppy in his hand.

* * * * *

SS Newcastle, Newcastle Harbour.
Rev. W.H. Macfarlane - 'The wandering Missionary of Torres Strait'

Gouger
of
The Bulletin

Short Stories

This third section contains 11 short stories from THE BULLETIN that have not previously been published in book form. Also included are two additional stories from THE BULLETIN'S subsidiary magazine THE LONE HAND. These stories are the "Black Opal" and the "Tin Makers". They are included here in order to complete my collection of all his contributions to the Bulletin during the main period of his involvement with that magazine from 1911 to 1932.

THE BLACK OPAL
How Australia's Unique Gem is Mined at Lightning Ridge

About 500 miles north-west of Sydney and near the Queensland border, is Lightning Ridge, the home of the black opal. The workings stretch for miles around. The only semblance of order is where the scrub has been cleared away to make room for a couple of streets, along which are the hotel, post office, police station and a few wood and iron stores.

At present there are about 300 men working on the field, but few of them are on opal. The shallow workings of the field, where the opal was got from the surface downwards, are all worked out. Those were the good times, when a shaft could be bottomed in a couple of days, the opal taken out, cleaned, faced and sold within a fortnight. That is, if the miner was lucky enough to "bottom" on opal. The men are now working on what is known as "The Hill," where the depth of a shaft varies from forty to sixty feet, and parties of two, three and four now work together.

The claim, consisting of one hundred by one hundred feet, is first pegged out as close to a payable claim as possible. A site is selected for the shaft, and work commences. The shaft is about five feet long and about two wide, and usually goes through solid sandstone from the start. Given good sinking, two men will bottom a forty-foot shaft easily in a fortnight, using explosives when necessary.

When the sandstone strata has been gone through, the opal dirt, which is really fairly soft rock, commences. It is generally separated from the sandstone by a thin, very hard band of rock, varying from two inches to a foot in thickness. The miners call this the "steel band."

When the miner reaches this band he begins to speculate. Will it prove another duffer? Or will his pick unearth a nest of the beautiful gems that he has been spending months, or even years, of hard work seeking?

In the "steel band" have been found some very beautiful opals, but it is usually underneath it, pressed hard between the opal dirt and the band, that the best opals are found. At times they cluster like oysters, so close to one another that the blade of a pocket knife can hardly be pushed between.

Sometimes the opal is a couple of feet below the band; often it is more, and has been mined as far as twenty feet down. Potch and color are the only traces the miner can go by. Potch is in reality poor opal, but it often leads on to good opal. A dark reddish tint running through the opal dirt is the other guide. But there is no certainty of striking opal. Whole claims have been worked out on potch and color, but never an opal found.

If potch or color shows when the miner or "gouger," as he is usually called, sinks through the opal dirt for a depth of about six feet, he generally starts a drive about four feet high by three wide, and burrows his way in for twenty or thirty feet, following the colors as they twist and turn, until they ultimately "cut out," or lead him on to opal.

Where the opal may be at any depth the men usually work in a six foot high drive, and tunnel their way in for forty or fifty feet, and often more. Much of this driving is done on the "blind," that is, working without a single trace of potch or color---just a bare wall of rock in front. As the men work they way in, they shovel the mullock into the bottom of the shaft, where it is piled up ready for hauling. Hauling the mullock is the worst part of the work, and takes place twice a day. When three men are working together the work is not so hard. Two men are on top, one at each handle of the windlass, while the third stops below and fills the large bullock-hide buckets. Three buckets are used, and are kept going all the time. One comes up full and passes the empty bucket in the shaft going down, while the third is being filled by the man down below. The shaft has to be logged up ten feet from the surface, and this often makes a sixty feet haul.

Men may drive a shaft in all directions, even on the best of traces, and finally have to give up without finding a single opal. The drives stretch out from the mouth of the shaft very much like the tentacles of an octopus. Some are low and narrow, some run so far that their end is lost in the darkness.

In a low drive, the gouger, stripped to the waist, sits in a crouching position, the candle shedding its feeble light around him, and showing in relief the "face" at which he is working. Using his light driving-pick carefully, the gouger's whole attention is concentrated on the face of the rock immediately before him.

"Crack!" A sound exactly like the breaking of glass. The gouger drops his pick, and, bending forward, seizes his candle, and holds it to the face. In the rock is a splendid black gem, a fiery bar of color running through the inky potch.

It is a moment of great excitement for the gouger as he informs his mates of the find. Then they hurriedly join him bellow to view the beautiful thing. And a good black opal seen in the face down below by candlelight, the sand and potch just chipped off the edge by a lucky blow of the pick, is indeed a beautiful sight. The colors flash and scintillate as the candle is held before it, bright orange melting into liquid red, and again into dancing green.

Then the men enter into eager consultation. "Is it solid, or is it sandy?" One holds the candle while the other gently gouges above and below the precious stone.

"Click!" The gouger utters an exclamation, mostly a bad one, and holds the candle at the face. He has struck another stone, a smaller one; and through the sand and dirt can just see the bright colors of another opal. They are "on it" ---- no doubt of it this time.

The first stone is safely got out, and eagerly the men clean the sand from its edges and examine it. With the aid of a pair of snips the potch is cut away from its edges, each snip revealing further color and disclosing the value of the stone.

The first stone is put carefully away, and the gouger sets to work again. If he is on a big patch, with the opals clustering very close together, he may drive for three weeks or more, and cut away only about six inches of ground a day. He works very carefully and slowly, never quite knowing where the next opal will be, and always on the look-out against smashing a good stone.

It is customary when on opal for the men to work all night. This has been brought about by the "night-shifters," or "ratters" ----men without the slightest principle, who live on the miners by finding out who is getting opal, watching them to their camps at night, and then going down the claim and working like demons all night. Many a gouger has knocked off work in the afternoon after striking opal, and going round the stores and among the camp-fires at night, excitedly told of his good luck, only to find on going below next morning a seven foot drive where he had knocked off the night before, a great heap of mullock, broken potch and fragments of smashed opal, evidence of the ruthless haste with which the "ratters" had worked in his absence.

Dynamite caps are often placed in the face by miners when on opal for the benefit of "ratters"; so that if they visited the claim in the night and commenced working, they would very likely strike a cap with the pick, and cause an explosion. But, so far, they have been too cunning to fall into the trap.

In cutting an opal out, another is often dislodged by the pick and falls to the floor unnoticed. When the mullock is sent to the surface, eight or nine men are often seen sprawling all over the dump, examining every piece of potch, and breaking the lumpy opal dirt, on the look-out for stray stone. From one dump, recently over one hundred pounds' worth of opal was thus secured in a month, and the loss to a careless gouger is often considerable.

Opal is classed ready for sale in three grades, and is sold either "in the rough" or "faced." In the rough the opal is just as it was when dug out of the ground, except that it is snipped around the edges, so as to give a better idea of the quality of the gem. The buyers, as a rule, prefer the opal in the rough. For, though it is a gamble, they have a better chance of securing a valuable stone at a ridiculously low price.

A stone, or a parcel of stones (opals are mostly called stones on the field) may be worth (say) eighty pounds in the rough, but when faced prove to be worth one hundred and fifty pounds. On the other hand, when put on the "wheel," a stone may diminish in price to a third of its estimated value. A stone may look beautiful before being faced, but when put on the wheel proved to be full of sand cracks, or its colors obscured by potch, or the face of the stone "scummy."

But mostly it is the other way. Stones have been purchased by the buyers for £5 in the rough, and sold for £30 or £40 when faced. Quite recently one of the buyers bought a parcel for under £20 in the rough. One of the stones when faced turned out to be a beautiful black gem, for which £180 was offered. But stones like that are scarce.

As the buyers give very poor prices for stones in the rough, the gougers generally have their opal cleaned and faced, and sell the parcel on its "face" value. Facing opal is the process of grinding away the potch and sand from a stone, thus showing the opal at its best, and ready for the jeweller. The facing machine is similar to a dentist's lathe, and is worked by foot with a treadle wheel. On the lathe head is a rapidly revolving carborundum wheel. The opal is first held to the revolving wheel until all waste matter is removed, leaving the colors of the opal showing to their best advantage. The wheel is then removed and replaced by a wheel of coarse and fine emery paper, which takes any scratches out of the opal and helps to brighten the colors. The stone is finally polished with jeweller's rouge on a revolving felt wheel, and after being valued, is ready for sale.

Though there are professional opal-cutters on the field, a number of gougers have their own machines, and do the cutting themselves. Considerable experience of opal and the machine is necessary before a man becomes a successful cutter, as one turn too many of the wheel may easily spoil a good stone, and take pounds off its value.

The gouger, if he is an old hand, generally values his opal himself. When a buyer comes to the field the gouger takes his parcel to him. The buyer generally does his buying in an ill-lighted room, and spreads a piece of newspaper on the table, so that the opal may show to the worst possible advantage.

Some of the sellers will ask the price they think their opal is worth; and not all the barracking in the world will get it from them for a penny less. on the other hand, one or two of the buyers offer a price, and will come very little higher.

There are four resident buyers always on the field; and buyers from Sydney, Melbourne and Adelaide make occasional visits. Every now and then a buyer from London, America, Berlin, or at times, France, visits the field; and the

gougers look forward to their visits. As a rule they bring a decent amount of capital, and give a better price for the opal than the local buyers.

The highest-priced stone ever obtained on the field by a buyer was secured for £102. There have been a few stones that brought £100 apiece. One stone in its rough state was sold for £100. Another black stone, when brought to the surface, fell into five separate pieces but proved to be beautiful opal. The five pieces were sold for £255.

About the biggest patch ever mined in Lightning Ridge was struck by a party of three. For years they had had very indifferent luck. They were on the point of leaving the field disgusted, when one suggested tossing up to see if they would sink one more hole. The shaft won the toss, and in the bottom of the forlorn hope they took nearly one thousand pounds' worth of opal. In two months' time they mined a little over three thousand pounds' worth.

The most surprising fact concerning the black opal is its low price compared with that of other precious stones. The dazzling beauty of the black opal has not yet attained the high place in popular favor it deserves. For, though the black opal is found at Lightning Ridge and nowhere else in the world, there is a general belief that it is not rare. As a matter of fact, really good stones are more rare than almost any other precious stone. And the fact that the black opal cannot be successfully imitated is another reason why it should command higher prices.

White Cliffs, in its boom days was a far bigger field than Lightning Ridge. White Cliffs supported over 3000 people while Lightning Ridge at its best only boasted of 1000---but of course, the opal mined is of entirely different kind.

In settling a dispute on the field, such as driving over another man's boundary, jumping a claim, etc., the men all roll up to the scene of the dispute, a spokesman is elected, and the case is tried. Both sides are heard, the spokesman asks a few questions, and sums up the case; and finally the miners vote as to which party they think is in the right.

The men work six or seven hours a day, and find it quite enough. Living is cheap on the field, about twelve to fifteen shillings a week easily keeping a man. The work is clean and interesting, but above all, a man is his own "boss." And for the unlucky beggar driving on the "blind" there is always the hope that he will "strike it yet."

1 May 1912
I.L. Idriess

THE TIN-MAKERS

Thud! Thud! Far away in the heart of the mountain the pick strokes echoed, coming dully from the long tunnel whose black mouth showed forbiddingly right above the creek bank.

At the tunnel end, the grey-bearded miner dropped his pick with a satisfied grunt, and reached for the tobacco tin, for it was "smoke-oh." His mate was examining the "face" they were working at with the light of a dimly burning candle. here and there in the pebbly wash dirt were little seams of what looked like jet black sand, but was in reality the precious stream tin.

"Well," asked the grey-beard, "how's she looking?"

His mate lowered the light, and getting a four-foot prop, commenced to place it beneath a dangerous looking rock in the roof.

"Not much good," he answered, slowly, "there's some good tin there, but the granite boulders keep coming in and cutting it out."

He fitted a wooden cap piece above the prop, and jammed it well home.

"That will hold half Queensland," he said. "There's no chance of that basalt falling now. I wish this hide-and-seek tin would come along through."

"Strange," remarked the grey-beard, thoughtfully, "this wash dirt was once the bed of a mighty river, with peculiar fishes swimming in its waters, and marvellous creatures living on its banks."

"Um!" remarked his mate. "Don't empty that tobacco tin. Thanks!"

"Scientists reckon we was once them fishes," went on the grey-beard, "and in millions of years gradually grew into what we are now."

"Which is two blanky tin scratchers," broke in his mate, sarcastically.

"Yes'" pursued the grey-beard, "and delving for tin in the very river bed we once lived and toiled in."

"Um!" the young man grunted. "How do you account for our finny ancestors living through the molten lava that in bygone days flowed into the river and filled it up. Reckon that kills your precious theory, as it killed the fishes. I wonder under what conditions this tin was first formed all the same?"

The grey-beard looked at his sun-tanned young mate. The old digger dearly loved a yarn, and this innocent-looking boy would at least hear him out, even if he did call him a liar afterwards.

"Well," he said, slowly, "I will tell you a yarn that proves we have lived through the lava, and will and will answer your question at the same time. And as this mountain top is hanging above us, it's the living truth.

"You've heard 'em tell of the Black Swan, the claim I got my big rise out of?" His mate nodded.

"Well, one mornin' I went to work feeling pretty moody, through getting no tin and bein' in debt like. It was in the rainy season, and the water had been slowly leaking through the tunnel roof, collecting in a fair sized clear pool where I'd worked the day before. I stood there wondering if it was worth while to drain the tunnel properly, or to chuck it and go fossicking on the Deep Lead."

After a while I noticed some tiny bubbles rising through the water, right against the wash-dirt. I held the candle over and looked more closely, and there clinging to the water-worn stones, was a cluster of tiny brown eggs, about the size of a grain of tin.

At first I thought it was tin, but while I looked each grain separated from the bunch, and, sinking slowly to the bottom, burst, sending up a wee fairy bubble, before my very eyes hatched a tiny insect.

I rubbed my eyes and looked, feeling a bit startled like, but the eggs had gone, and in there place swam dozens of kicking insects that jumped and swam about like fire-work torpedoes. You see, they must have been eggs laid millions of years ago, before all that molten lava flowed into the river an' made it a river no more. The spark of life was still smouldering in those eggs, and now that the prehistoric conditions of life they were used to living under came to them again, that is moving room and being submerged in water, they just simply hatched. "Wonderful thing, this Nature!"

"Yes'" replied his mate thoughtfully, "I've heard of scientists finding grains and seeds in the old Egyptian tombs, and forcing them to life by artificial means. Go on."

"Yes, that's it exactly," said grey-beard. "Well, those there insects grew till they were about the size of a match head. and in shape like tiny crayfish, all arms and legs. And me kneelin' down there on me knees with the candle, watching them, that interested I didn't notice the water creeping half-way to me knees. After a while I discovered that they were working together at a furious rate, but all with a kind of system.

It took an hour before I drops to what they were working at, an' when I seen through it I nearly fell dead. About fifty of 'em was diggin' out little grains of red sand from among the wash dirt, and swimmin' with it to the fellers at the 'face.' They pounds an pulls an' mixes it, their little legs flyin' like the arms of a windmill, sending up a shower of weeny bubbles to the top of the water.

When the manufacturing process was over, three of 'em catches hold of the

result, which was a single grain of black sand, and swims with it to the 'face,' where they jammed it in a thin black seam. They was makin' tin."

The grey-beard paused, and glanced from beneath shaggy eyebrows at his mate. But the young man was gazing thoughtfully at the water-worn boulders in the old river bed.

"As soon as I understood what they were at, I went cold all over with excitement. I tried to think it wasn't true, for fear I might be in a dream, and the waking-up would be a too bitter disappointment. I bent over closer, and a little heap of mullock fell with a splash into the water. I jumped up in awful fear, because if any of those insects had been killed I believed I would have cried. I began to see what a good thing I had on. Running from the tunnel to the creek, I fetches up two buckets of water and empties them into the pool, because I wanted the little toilers to have as much play as possible, an' besides there might be more eggs lyin' about waitin' to be hatched. By dinner time I'd carried so much water I had to board the tunnel mouth up a foot to hold the water back.

Just before knock-off time I had another look at the insects. Sure as life, they'd built up a seam of tin half-an-inch thick and two feet long. They worked exactly like coral insects, only instead of useless coral they was buildin' up good black stream tin. I felt so happy I stood there in the water and laughed, trying to pick out the gangers and wonderin' which gang was working hardest.

I tried to count them, but they was swimmin' backwards and forwards so fast it was impossible. I got two hundred and sixty-five three times, when I noticed the little fellers who did the carrying was in difficulties. They were makin' desperate efforts to reach with their little feelers a strip of bright red sand that ran about half-an-inch above the surface of the water. An idea seized me, an' I got the pick an' knocks some of the red sand into the water, bein' careful not to hurt a single insect.

Sure enough they dives straight down after it, breakin' it up and each man carrying his load to the experts at the 'face.' The boss workers bucks in to make up for lost time, poundin' the sand into grains of tin and jammin' them in the 'face.'

"I knew I'd dropped to the secret then, an' had to hum a song to stop myself from going crazy with delight. I had the insects that made the tin, and I'd found out the stuff to feed 'em with. There was plenty of the sand in the tunnel – you know that red drift that takes hell's own timbering to keep from leaking through the roof?"

The young miner nodded.

"Well," went on the old man, "that was the stuff the insects were keen on, an' you can bet I gouged out a few barrow-loads quick an' lively, and tipped them in the water close to the carters, so as they wouldn't have far to swim to reach it, an' so lose time.

"I hardly slept a wink that night. The thought of my wonderful discovery fair unnerved me. To have a rich tin mine is a fortune, but to have the things that make the tin, have them turn out pure stream tin every day — well the idea was so lovely that I daren't think about it for fear something would snap, and down would come the whole lot like a bundle of bushman's hallucinations."

"Twice I got up and walked through the scrub to the tunnel, getting deadly afraid someone might find out about the insects an' steal 'em away. I lay awake for hours calculating how long it would take those two hundred and sixty-five insects to build up a bag of tin. Each time the calculation worked out at a bag of tin a week, and at first I was quite satisfied, for that meant over six quid a week!

"However, I goes to the mine next mornin' an' gets two pleasant shocks. First I see by the amount of tin they'd made that they had worked all night without a stop, I'd calculated on them workin' their eight hours, an' then knockin' off for a spell an' a sleep, like me, you see, but what made me gasp was the sight of a neat little cluster of brown eggs, glued on the side of a quartz boulder sticking in the wash dirt. I was clean dazzled. Them eggs had a very great meanin' for me. My calculations of the night before went up with a bound."

"The heap of red sand I'd left for 'em overnight was nearly all used up, so I got a sweat up knocking out a heap more so as they wouldn't be waiting for building material. I tried to count the eggs, but they were too close together and too small. I guessed there must be an egg a man, or else the females laid eggs a-piece, an' then gone straight on with their good work. I felt very satisfied with my little gang, and pulled out the pipe to have a smoke while waiting for the eggs to hatch. And sure enough, just about dinner time out come the little things, kicking and swimming, crazy to be alive and doin' somethin'."

The old digger paused, and reached for the tobacco tin again. Smoke-oh was up long ago, but he knew if he could keep his mate sufficiently interested, the young fellow would belt in at the wash dirt and knock out enough to pay for the double smoke-oh.

"I think in them old gone days," he went on slowly, "everything moved on much faster than they does now. When all this tin an' gold an' wolfram that's in the earth is got, more will have to be made. The wopper Power that made us is only takin' a bit of a rest, Sunday like, or perhaps after overtime, while waitin'

for us to use the supply up. Then there'll be a hell of a bust up in the world, an' Nature's machinery will set things in motion an' everything will move along a million times faster than it does now, an' makes a fresh supply for another world. And in the bust up man won't be nowhere. He'll be too surprised to think even. Anyway he won't have time. Then in another million of years a fresh class of superior bein's will find another Hercules or Pompeii or whatever you call 'em, and will wonder how we built the Sphinx, if the old cove ain't busted up this time. Anyway, we're only insects.

That night I lay awake and calculated again, though me brain was so excited I could see nothing but a mountain of tin for a long time, with great long-legged animals pounding up red sand and shovellin' it on the mountain, where it rolled down the side pure stream tin. However, I calculated at last that the first lot had made about fifteen pounds weight of tin for an eight hours' shift, then each mornin' there was a fresh gang on, an' the mornin' after that there'd be two more gangs and so on. And as the first gang worked the whole twenty-four fours, I calculated a result for the week that made my head dizzy. I daren't go beyond a week for I felt that my brain in its excited state wouldn't stand it.

Well, each mornin' there was a fresh batch of eggs, an' soon I had all my time cut out feedin' the red sand to the insects, that was increasin' like a gathering army. Things got that way at last I was nearly killed with overwork. I seemed to be doin' nothin' but feedin' the insects with sand and takin' the tin away from them, and calculatin' – always calculatin'. I got poor as a mad crow, what with no sleep and excitement, an' thought I was goin' to be laid up with brain-fever. I got very careful, an' pitched me camp close to the tunnel, so I'd know if any inquisitive busy-bodies came about during the night.

That first week I bagged half a ton of tin, but before the next week the output increased so alarmingly I had to pay men to bag the tin outside the tunnel, as it took me all my time trucking it away from the insects.

In a couple of months I'd sold over five thousand pounds worth of tin that my little army of tin manufacturers had made. But the quicker the money rolled in the greedier I got. I used to lay awake at nights wonderin' and wonderin' if I could put somethin' in the water to make 'em work faster, or make 'em lay two eggs instead of one. Only I remembered in time the school-kid yarn of the goose that killed the golden eggs, I believe I would have done something mad.

At last my head got so dazed with thinking and overwork I could hardly stand up. An' I blame the thinkin' part for what happened. For three nights I hadn't slept a wink, and on the fourth I walks a couple of miles over to the

Nigger Creek pub, and buys a bottle of rum. A few nips would make the sleep better, I thought. I had a couple of drinks at the pub, and felt better for it.

I walked back to the camp, and had a good strong nip, an' then a couple more. It made me feel a good bit better, an' steadied me head. But just as I was turnin' into bunk the devil stops me and I thinks, 'How about them poor little insects workin' all night in the cold water makin' tin for me. Why not go and have a look at 'em an' drink them good luck?

Me bein' a bit sick in the head, like, the rum musta got there sooner than usual. Anyway like a damn fool I gets the bottle and a light, steps over the boarding at the tunnel mouth put there to keep the water back, and walks away down the tunnel. The insects was workin' away like mad; hundreds and hundreds of 'em, workin' so hard it made the surface of the water look like a fairy fountain with the bubbles they kicked up. The water was all crow-black in the tunnel, but where the candle light shone across it seemed to me the bubbles were dancing little lights of liquid gold. I leans across the wall and nearly cries with pure joy, I was so touched at them insects' goodness for me.

Pourin' out half a tumbler of rum, I held it above my head and made a speech of thanks to them insects. But they took no notice, only kept on workin'. I drank the rum then, and held the bottle over my head and laughed.

I pours out more rum then, and shivered, 'cause in the speechifying I had stumbled up to my knees in the water, and it was cold. My hand trembled with the bottle, and I cursed because I knew it had got to my brain. I jammed the spider with the candle in in the wall, but somehow things didn't seem to go straight, and the candle stuck there, burnin' upside down, an' flickerin' in the slight draught. Things seem to have got that way I didn't know what I was doin'. I got fearful frightened.

Everythin' seemed upside down. I looked up and saw the roof an' thought it was the bottom of the tunnel. It was two foot above my head, an' swore it was the floor an' it was slowly sinkin' away from me. In deadly terror I put up my arm to touch it, thinkin' it was my leg. I could just touch the roof, an' stood there holdin' on for all I was worth, thinkin' the floor was sinkin' away from me an' the roof was stretchin' slowly apart, an' I daren't let go.

I stretched up so much I felt like a kid's catapult, an' then them insects suddenly sprang into gigantic lobsters that came at me with a roar, their great saw teeth nippers stretched out to cut me through where I was stretched most. I kicked and prayed and tried to pull the roof down on the whole world, but it held taut, an' then they sprang and with two nips sawed me clean in two.

The roof flew to eternity with half me clingin' on to it while the tunnel bottom dropped clean down through hell, and then splash!

I was kickin' and shriekin' in the water, an' in the scrimmage the candle had gone out. The ice cold water wakes me up a lot, an' when I get my scattered senses I starts off for the tunnel mouth, gropin' at the unseeable walls with my shiverin' hands. With clattering teeth, I stumbled along when suddenly I staggered up against the boarding fixed in the mouth of the tunnel to keep the water back. Cursing, I grasped hold of it to steady myself, when the whole thing collapsed, sending me sprawling with the water rushing over me. In a second I seemed to come to come back from a trip to hell, and the dreadful horror I felt at what I'd done was terrible. As the water was rushing away it was takin' the insects with it, an' soon there wouldn't be a single insect left in the tunnel. I lay down flat and screamed an' shouted for help, tryin' to keep the water back with my body, an' just managin' to save a little.

All the camps around were woke up by my yells, and in a couple of minutes half-a-dozen men were tearing through the scrub towards the tunnel. Long Bill Stewart and Mick Moore reached me first, and as soon as Bill saw me he said, 'Why it's old Joe lyin' there in the water! He's got em' agen.' They both laid hold of me and tried to pull me up, but I clawed to the ground and yelled at them to let me alone, to block up the tunnel and save the insects.

"The horrors have got him bad, this time" said Bill."Catch hold of him, Mick, and we'll carry him to his bunk."

Then Bill gets hold of me legs, and Mick me arms, and together they carries me away, while in despair I saw the last few buckets of water run away. When I saw that everything was up, I let 'em do what they liked, which was to take me straight into Herberton hospital, where I was laid up for three months with brain fever.

I was nearly done for, I can tell you. When I came out they told me I was all the time cryin' out to block me insects. I sold the Black Swan afterwards to a company who rushed at the chance of buyin' it. I said as how I felt too broke up to work any more. Needless to say, the Black Swan produced no more tin. They worked it for twelve months and never got half a ton."

1 February 1919
I.L. Idriess

THE TUNNEL

Harman had one last look at the rich seam of tin in the tunnel face. If he came through the war all right this was to buy him and the girl their home. A noticeboard pinioned to the wash dirt told any inquisitive person that the show belonged to George Harman, miner's right No.16845, and that the said Harman had exemption until such time as he returned from the war.

Harman walked to the tunnel-mouth. Overhead was a bunch of boulders wedged together and stayed by four props. Harman had mined these props by placing in each a charge of dynamite The end of the fuse connecting each charge was concealed under the truckline which ran through the timbers. The fuse end was tipped with a dynamite cap. Should a man wheel a truckload of dirt from the face, the weight of the loaded truck would fire the cap, and in a few seconds the props would be blown to pieces, and down would come tons of rocks, which wouldn't be good for the man underneath.

Two years later Harman lay dying in a hospital in Cairo, and Harman's thoughts were bitter. He would not have cared for death had it not been for the girl. He struggled gamely, but there was no chance.

As he waited for the end the Sister handed him a home-letter and stood by for the smile. But no smile came. The letter was simply and curtly to the effect that the girl had changed her mind, and by the time he got her note she would be married to Harry Long, an old acquaintance of both of them.

All the vindictiveness of Harman's nature burned up. He wanted more than ever to live now, so that he might get his fingers on the throat of the man who had stolen more than life from him. As he turned in his bed, the stretcher-bearers were putting a new patient in beside him.

The new-comer's pain-stricken face turned towards Harman and instantly broke into a smile. "What ho, Harman." he said; "what cheer?" It was the jilt's brother. On the edge of death Harman croaked out, "Is Lucy married Yet?" "Why, no," answered the brother. "Haven't you heard? Long went in to work that tunnel of yours when the price of tin went up. The roof must have got pretty rotten because it fell in on top of him. It took them a week to dig away the rocks, and what they found of Long wasn't worth looking for."

A slow smile broke over Harman's white face. The Sister wondered what it was that made such a bad-tempered man die so peacefully.

17 April 1919
Gouger

THE DEBIL MOON

All aglimmer with pearly light lay the little bêche-de-mer lugger, hemmed in by the darkness of grim Cape Melville on the north and the granite hills of Red Point to the south. From the boat's bows to the shore ran a broad path of silvery light. And Chungoorgy knew that even the debil moon had concentrated her light on the boat to show him the evil that was happening there.

Close by, the camp-fire coals shone dully, and around it in a sprawling circle, just as the fiery rum had overcome them, lay the bucks and gins and piccaninnies of the tribe. Not the youngest gins. They were out in the boat. A deep guttural snore drew Chungoogy's fierce eyes to the dying fire. It was Chulbil, king of the tribe, his grizzled head pillowed on the roots of a ti-tree – Chulbil who had sold his youngest daughter to Yoko the Jap, for rum and red cloth. During the buying Chungoorgy had fiercely reminded Chulbil that Mundaree had been promised him, and this was the wedding night. Chulbil had replied that before the moon came again Yoko would have sailed away. Then Mundaree would return – and what mattered a few nights' waiting?

Chungoorgy's strong teeth gritted as he looked again towards the boat. He had drunk none of the Jap's rum. He had sat in his empty gunyah while the rest of the tribe had drunk themselves to sleep., and he had thought, and thought. Instinctively his hand reached out towards his bundle of spears, and he handled one perfectly-balanced weapon lovingly. It was a war spear, two feet of its point barbed with razor sharp bones of the stingaree. let one of those barbs break off in an enemy, and lucky was he who escaped the poison!

But he was thinking, thinking. Jap men were small, but very strong. Besides, there were two of them on this boat, as on nearly all the others. And even if he killed both of them the news would be spread among the other Japs of the fishing fleets by the boat's crew. For the crew did not belong to his tribe. And Japs never forget.

Chungoorgy recalled the look on Yoko's face while he pleaded for Mundaree as Chulbil pushed her into the waiting dinghy. Just like a snake Yoko was. The steely eyes saw all. The ears heard all. The cold face showed nothing. The hard mouth said nothing.

Abruptly Chungoorgy broke off one of the brittle bones of his spear. he handled it awhile fingering the sharp point, thinking hard. Picking up a hard stone, he commenced to carefully thin the barb down. Half an hour's work, and it was only the thickness of a thin splinter. Then he rose and walked noiselessly

to a clear patch among the ti-trees where the moonlight shimmered on the white bark. Here he could see to complete his work well. Straight down on him stared the great full moon. Hard, cold, merciless, like the white man.

Turning swiftly, Chungoorgy looked out towards the bay. The lugger was no longer in the moon's rays. Long black shadows from Cape Melville's cliffs were reaching out around it. Soon the moon would sink to sleep and the spirits of darkness would own the earth. Chungoorgy's eyes gleamed. The debil moon was on his side.

The bone barb was now only the thickness of a fine needle. But the point! No needle was ever so sharp, no needle-point ever so tapering. Lest he should snap it, he put aside the file-stone and completed the wearing down with a soft shell. But before the work was done he saw that he must hurry. The moon was dipping down, slowly, as if reluctant to go until she had given him all her aid for his task.

Walking to the gunyah, he took his war spear and crept west from the camp. Startled swamp-wallabies hopped off in alarm, making a great crackling among the dry pandanus leaves. But Chungoorgy's footsteps were as silent as the evil birds that he knew gazed at him as he passed under the trees. Spirits all of them. But he was not afraid. Had not the greatest of all evil spirits, the debil moon, smiled at him?

He stopped at a small sand-mound cleared of all grass. There he shivered a moment, glanced quickly round, looked once at the fast disappearing moon, then commenced hastily scraping away the sand with his hands. Soon he had a hole deep enough. Grasping his spear, he plunged it down through the sand, and drew it back. A dreadful smell poisoned the night air. Quickly he covered in the hole, and holding the spear well before him, ran back towards the camp. He must reach it before the debil moon closed her eyes in sleep, else surely Wooriwa's spirit would be on him. She had been buried in the sand mound ten days before. Breathless, he reached the camp-fire and listened. No ghostly wail broke on his ears, not even the screech of a night-bird spirit.

Suddenly all was dark. The moon had sunk in sleep.

Chungoogry blew on the live coals until they glowed . In this light he carefully, very carefully, smeared the point of his needle-bone with the black ooze on the point of his spear. Slowly he twisted the bone in among his thick matted hair, point upper-most. Then, walking to the beach, he waded out, and commenced swimming steadily, head well above water. He made hardly a ripple, let alone a sound.

A quarter mile from shore his eyes could make out a blot that was the lugger, still some hundreds of yards away. He kept well from the boat, meaning to circle back and climb up by the stern. In the stern of the lugger is always the little cabin where lie the captain and the mate. The crew would be well for'ard, asleep. They would have had some rum too, but not too much.

Carefully, with head just above water, Chungoorgy neared the stern. Plainly he heard snores coming from the crew of boys for'ard, and once the whimper of a gin. But his searching eyes saw no living thing. He drew himself up by the railing at the stern, and slowly pulled himself flat on the deck – so slowly that the drips of water from his body did not make the tiniest splash. Directly in front of him was the open panelling of the little cabin, and he thought again of the debil moon as he saw that Yoko had left a hurricane-lamp dimly burning. On his belly he wormed his way another foot along the deck, and peered down into the cabin. At the Japanese mate, sleeping on one bunk, he scarcely glanced. But at the sight of Yoko, with one brown arm flung across Mungaree, he snarled, and his spear arm rose instinctively. The spear was not there, though, nor could he have used it in the small space between the cabin roof and deck. Yoko was too old a hand to leave that opening.

For a time Chungoorgy gazed at the stairs of the companion-way that led down into the cabin. He had no desire to put his foot on a false step and land sprawling into the cabin, with Yoko and his mate on top of him. In the centre of the cabin roof was a small timber support. Reaching in, he could just get a firm hold. Very carefully he pulled himself into the cabin, drawing his knees well up to his chin as he swung over the companion-way. Slowly his feet dropped to the cabin floor. He could just stand upright.

As he bent over Yoko all his wild passions swept upon him. He peered around the cabin for a tomahawk, something with which he could cut and slash. But the only weapon was the peeping holster of Yoko's revolver under his pillow.

Then his hand went to his hair, and brought out the bone needle. He became calm again, and grinned at the thought of revenge more terrible than tomahawk or knife.

A quarter inch from Yoko's thigh he held the bone needle, point down; and then he let it fall. It quivered in the bare flesh before it dropped and rolled on to the blanket. Picking the needle up, Chungoorgy held it to the hurricane-lamp. The delicate point had been snapped off.

Replacing the needle in his hair he caught hold of the overhead support, and slowly lifted his feet up through the open companion-way. Carefully and with

great labour, he pushed his body backwards, until finally he again lay flat on the open deck. In the black darkness he slid over the stern, and struck out silently for the invisible shore.

Yoko woke in the agony of blood poisoning. He died without suspicion of what had happened to him.

4 December, 1919
Gouger

THE TIN SCRATCHERS

About eighty miles down the coast from Cooktown (Q.), on the summit of a great, lonely, scrub-covered mountain, perched among almost inaccessible ranges, there is a small camp of tin-scratchers. When I landed among them ten years ago there were twelve men and a white woman married to a nigger. There was another black man on the field commonly known as "the Coon." I remember the excitement when the first-mentioned black man and his missus got out per the monthly packer a gramophone. It was the Coon's hobby to while away part of each lonely night by sitting at his humpy-door and blowing away on an old tin-whistle some tune which was evidently a studied insult to the other nigger a little lower down in the scrub. The night after the packer's visit the Coon had hardly got his whistle to work when the silence of the mountain night was rent by "Coon, coon, coon, Ah wish mah color would fade," rendered by a shrieking gramophone. From that night on the tin-scratchers swear the Coon began to turn grey.

Once a week the mail reaches this lonely place – that is, if the mailman has been able to cross the turbulent rivers that lie in the way. Then is discussed the question of moment to the little settlement – the price of tin. It has climbed up a unit or slid down a point. The great affairs of the far-away, dim world are of little concern. What matters it so long as tin is worth enough to bring in tucker with a minimum of labor?

I was far away for a few years, and when I again visited the field the same men were there, altered only in that they had grown older and more distrustful of their neighbors. "Someone" had been "ratting" the sluice races of their tin. Men sat up all night on their claims, hidden among the dense vines, the crooning creek voices in their ears, a Winchester across their knees, and grim, bitter thoughts for company.

Christmas, like most other Christmases, had been a hot time for the jungle camp. The packer had arrived well laden with the annual order of whisky and rum. The two black men had been the first to renew their old feud. Well soaked in spirits, they had stalked each other among the trees, sniping at sight, one with a rifle, the other with a double-barrelled gun. The gun had won in the long run – with a flying shot when the enemy leapt to cover behind a fallen log. Then the whites waded in to settle long-smouldering grievances; and the aboriginals about the camps, seizing the chance while the white men were otherwise engaged, stole their fill of rum and in their turn joined in the furious mix-up which raged until Christmas was long past.

While heads were still sore I was back at the field again. The first humpy-door I knocked at was opened slowly, and a man whom I had known well gazed suspiciously at me, without returning my "What ho, Jim – how's things going?" Grey bristles were thick in his beard, and his hair was longer than I'd ever known it before. Abruptly he said:

"You called in at them new blokes before you came here. Why didn't you come here first?"

"I just bade them the time of day as I passed, Jim," I answered him. "Why, what's wrong with them?"

"A man's got to be careful in this place now," he muttered surlily. "Things ain't peaceful like they was when you were here last. Come in if you want to."

He retired into the humpy, and after a slight hesitation I followed. I asked him about the old hands and got angry answers. It appears some of them were continually "shaking" his tin. When he waited for them on his claim at night they would steal the "sweet buks" out of his garden, which was a heinous crime.

"But I'll get 'em yet," he said. "You see this!" And he moved a piece of board from a slab. It showed a two-inch auger-hole. He looked at me cunningly. "Loophole," he said. "I've got 'em in every third slab. At night I run a lawyer-vine around the humpy, about a foot from the ground. Opposite each loophole, I've tied a tin to the lawyer-vine. I've practiced every night fer a month, an' now I know which loophole to run to by the sound of the tin. You see, I picked tins what each had a different sound. Let one of these ---------s trip agen that tin an I'll fill him fuller of lead than a cheese is of weevils. I've got two rifles an' a shot-gun, an' a revolver loaded ready up to the muzzle. See? Good idea, ain't it?"

I admitted gracefully that his genius would have been priceless in the great war.

He had turned to his loophole again. Suddenly he faced me.

"Who's that talkin' to the new blokes now?"

"Oh, I suppose that's my mate."

"Is he a good shot?"

"One of the best that ever enlisted."

He grunted, and turned again to the loophole.

I sneaked out of the humpy and joined my cobber and explained matters to him. "Look here, Dick," I wound up, "all these fossils are touched. The scrub has got 'em. If we did strike a good claim we might settle down here. And in ten years' time I'd be sitting up all night waiting for you with a gun. And you're a lot better shot than me. No, I don't like it. This scrub gets on a man's nerves. Let's clear out."

Dick laughed. "Can't say I've fallen in love with any of the whiskers around here myself," he said. "We'll get."

We got.

22 January 1920
Gouger

THE BLACK MAN'S JUSTICE

Very still was the night. Very quiet. There was only the whimper of the wavelets climbing on the beach. Suddenly came the musical tinkling of a horse-bell, very clear, very distinct, from the grassy ridges. The camp-dogs instantly lifted their heads, nosed the still air, and settled for sleep again, not making a whimper.

Murranga, king of his tribe, crouched in the darkness of his gunyah, staring through the open entrance-way into the darkness of the night. The white man had come that afternoon, looking for gold, as all white men do. It was the same white man who had kicked him, Murrunga, on his last half-frightened visit to Cooktown for the big corroboree. And now the white man was camped alone on Murrunga's own tribal grounds.

Quite unconsciously Murrunga's throwing hand edged out towards the bundle of spears beside him. His eyes distended, their whites matched the gleam of ivory as his thick upper-lip dropped.

But Murrunga knew something of the white men. He feared the police. Had not his tribe already suffered, and only for spearing a lonely stockman and a few cattle?

Slowly the black man relaxed, his heavy forehead became corrugated in thought.

Perfect was the day, with the warm sunshine that puts the joy of life in man and bird and beast. Around the smouldering fires lay the broken shells of mussel and crab, relics of the morning meal. Old Naruma was already squatted by the slow fire busy with his spear-making now poising the quivering weapon to test its balance, now heating the tip, now cooling it, very careful in this hardening process that the point is not too brittle; now poising again for balance, lavishing as much care over the weapon as civilised man does over his most perfect instruments.

The gins were laughing and joking over their dilly-bag making, the piccaninnies playing in the grass with their reed spears, the men squatting in the sunshine, when suddenly every dog in the camp was up and barking furiously. The gins gave one hurried look, and instantly they and the piccaninnies disappeared among the bushes. The black men, sullen-faced, watched the white man as he kicked his way through the snarling dogs.

"Good day, which feller king?"

"Me king," grunted Murrunga.

The white man handed him a stick of nigger-twist tobacco and threw a stick to the other men. Numerous relics of pipes, burnt-out pieces of wood that might have been pipes years ago, made their appearance from the waist-cloths.

"Me look about longa gold," said the white man. "Any you boy know him feller gold?"

Murrunga held a firestick to his pipe and puffed thoughtfully. "Me know," he said at length.

"Yes! What feller you know about gold?"

"Me know where there plenty feller gold."

"Where?"

Murrunga pointed a steady hand to a group of islands about 15 miles from the coast. One showed up very distinctly, but the others were mostly mangrove-grown mudbanks under water at high tide.

The white man gazed across the sea.

"That is the Howick Group," he said. "I would have to go back to Cooktown and get a boat to go there."

"Me got canoe."

"Yes, of course. What feller gold you see?"

"Gold longa white stone."

The white man took a small quartz specimen from his pocket and handed it to Murrunga. The black man scratched at the tiny yellow specks with his broad fingernail. "That feller gold," he said.

"Right," said the white man. "You savvy gold. You take me longa island, show me gold. Me give you plenty tucker, plenty flour, plenty tea, plenty sugar. S'pose you show me gold all right, me buy you longa Cooktown plenty shirt, plenty knife, plenty tomahawk."

The black man looked up cunningly. "You buy me plenty feller red calico?" he asked.

"Yes. Plenty calico longa whole tribe. What time you take me across?"

"Longa night-time."

"Night-time? Why not day-time?"

"Tide he no good longa day."

"Tide all asame longa night-time!"

"More better tide long night!" answered Murrunga stubbornly.

"Oh, all right. Have it your own way. But what about debil-debil? You no more fright longa him longa night-time?"

"Debil-debil he no more come near white man?" asked Murrunga.

"No. Him too much fright. Him keep away."

The black man grinned. "Me no more fright longa white man."

"Oh. I see. You're a shrewd old bird. Well, you send him two feller boy longa

my camp. I send him up tucker longa you. You get him canoe ready. Suppose him gold good feller, I go back longa Cooktown, buy him big feller boat, load him up plenty tucker belonga you."

The white man turned from the group and made back towards his camp, followed by the joyous grins of the blacks as the snarling curs snapped at his heels. Instantly from the nearby bushes appeared the gins, racing to the men for a share in the white man's tobacco.

Calm as a broad river was the sea, merging on all side into the blackness of the night. Only the deep, steady breathing of Murrunga, the methodical dip of the paddle, the hiss of the breaking water at the canoe's bow, the brilliant phosphorescence and the glow of the white man's pipe, told of human life on the vast still stretch of waters.

Murrunga had been paddling for hours, and his heavier breathing now told of stronger exertion against the out going tide. Presently the white man spoke.

"What say you have 'im spell – wait here longa daylight? Plenty feller time."

"More better keep go," grunted Murrunga. "Close up longa island now."

"H'm. S'posem you run canoe up longa coral reef. What happens then?"

"Finish. Plenty feller shark."

"Well, why the blazes don't you wait till daylight, and go in on the full tide?"

"More better go along now," said Murrunga. "Bye-em-bye daylight, big feller wind come along."

"Oh, all right. You're paddling the damned canoe, not me."

The white man lapsed into silence, and stared into the darkness ahead. Well he knew that if there was a reef ahead the canoe would be on it before he could see the coral. And he knew a little about the sharks that swarm the coral reefs. Suddenly an indistinct black blur loomed up in front. He called out to Murrunga. "Mangroves," came back the answer. "Close up now."

The white man felt much relieved. Soon the canoe grated on a tiny beach, half-coral, half-sand. The two men dragged the canoe well up on the beach. The tide was already on the turn. In the east the sky was greying, and the white man looked curiously about him. But nothing could be seen but the dark water and the darker mass of the mangroves ahead that merged into the blackness of the sky. The white man squatted on his haunches on the wet sand and lit his pipe.

Murrunga grunted, and taking the two days' supply of provisions from the canoe, walked towards the mangroves.

"Here, hold hard. You don't get me going into that hole while it's dark. You're in a devil of a hurry for a nigger. You sit down until daylight."

"Daylight too late," the black man said. "Tide he come in quick feller. Bye-em-bye we cross big feller creek. Water he little feller now. Tide he soon make him big feller. No can swim- too many shark."

The white man stood up. "Go ahead," he growled. "I suppose you know best. only don't walk too quickly. I don't want to sink into a blasted mudhole." And Murrunga turned into the mangroves, wading up a creek knee-deep in water.

For a quarter of a mile the creek with its fairly firm coral sand-bottom, was good travelling, but presently the open waterway gave out where the million fantastic mangrove roots had grown across the creek. Thereafter the only walking was on the roots themselves, which, cracking under the white man's weight, continually landed him knee-deep in slimy mud. The daylight became stronger, but it only showed the countless mangroves all around, the dense foliage overhead, the tangle of roots and the mud and water underfoot.

Murrunga, twisting between the trees with his load, lightly stepping from root to root, never made one slip, never trod on an undergrown root that his experienced eye told him would not bear his weight. His teeth showing viciously, the most joyous feeling of his life surged through him as the white man slipped and fell, and slipped again, cursing vehemently behind him. Already the mangrove roots were gurgling, the swift king-tide was surging through them.

"I say, when do we get onto the high ground? That damned island you pointed out didn't seem to be as thick with mangroves as this. Where the blazes are the hills?"

"Soon feller now. Not far."

"By Caesar, it had better not be far. Look at the way this tide is coming in. A nice sort of place to be cornered in this would be. Blast you, go ahead! Surely you could have found a better place to land in than this, you black swab!"

A root cracked under the white man and down he went into mud and water above his belt. Cursing furiously, he dragged himself up onto the roots again. His oaths abruptly ceased. Lying on the mud, covered by the now swirling water, lay Murrunga's load of provisions. But the man himself was gone. Could he have been engulfed by the soft mud? But no, the water was quite clear. The white man called. He strained his eyes ahead through the interlacing trees. He shouted. But Murrunga was gone.

Hopping, jumping, twisting, the black man was hurrying back to the beach, his mouth open in a noiseless laugh, his leg-muscles quivering as he urged them at their greatest speed over the slippery, treacherous roots. Very soon he came to the creek, and found the tidal waters rushing up it at a depth that necessitated a

strong swim. As he had expected, down the creek came floating his canoe, lifted off the beach by the tide. Desperately working his paddle, he drove the canoe a mile out to sea; then using his paddle only to hold the canoe against the tide, he sat and gazed at the water-washed mangroves with the light of expectation in his staring eyes.

Two miles to the northward the hills of Howick Island rose rock-bound and solid from the sea. But the mangrove-grown mudbank that Murrunga gazed at is under water at king tide, only the branches of the tallest trees showing. And presently the primitive man's keen eyes saw a breaking branch and a white man struggling for foothold on the slender top. As shots rang out Murrunga bent low to the paddle in sudden fear. But remembering instantly that the bullets were not for him, he ceased, and laughed, and watched the last of the treetops disappear.

5 May 1921
Gouger

THE DEATH BIRD

Straight towards the long low point the woman steered the swift cutter. The sou'easter, dying out in company with the rays of a vanished sun, would have barely strength enough to drive the craft around the point and into the cove beyond.

The lines on the woman's face hardened. It had been a long chase, a bitter chase. From island to mainland. Then hide-and-seek among the Barrier islands. Now back to the mainland again. It was the natives on Flinders Island who had finally put Reynolds away. And now the woman knew that just out of sight the little cove sheltered him and his lugger, and – the other woman.

Like a soft, enveloping shroud, night fell and blotted the nearing point from view. But the woman kept straight on, her strong brown hand on the tiller-handle holding the slowing cutter perilously inshore . There would be barely enough breeze to clear the point.

With the certainty of the reckoning that was now drawing so close, the brain that shone through the bright blue-grey eyes of the woman was in a fever of bitter reproach. Through how many long years of toil had she been this man's mate, standing staunchly by him through good times and bad, never complaining of the fate that held her apart from white companionship for months, living among the blacks on the lonely island where he had established his fishing-station! She thought again of the first two years of terror, when she, a young girl, had to walk among the black men with firm step and unwavering voice, directing them with the authority of the master over their task of curing the vile smelling bêche-de-mer; of the joy at her heart as she heard the long drawn-out call of the lookout boy that signalled the lugger coming in with a fresh load of fish or shell, of the icy chill that a few days after numbed her whole body as she watched the lugger's sails disappear over the cruel sea, knowing that he would not be back for weeks, perhaps months, perhaps never.

But she had hardened. She had to. The black man saw to that. She had been driven to meet cunning with a quicker cunning; had to meet treachery and crush it before its destroying flame could leap into life. Disobedience and laziness she had to punish ruthlessly, but in such a way as never to have to pit her physical strength against that of the native men. *That* would have meant her end – suddenly. A man could use his strong fist and firearms. But she, a girl, had used her own quick wits, had pitted black man against black man, and had won through. And she had got more work out of the natives than any one man in the Barrier seas.

Then the Russo-Jap war had come and Reynolds had seized his chance. In a few years the solitary lugger had increased to a fleet of fishing boats, shell and bêche-de-mer had gone up, cyclones disastrous to the fishing fleets had left their own fleet untouched; and now they had made their fortune. It had been their dream all these fighting years – their fortune! Then they were to travel the world together, and the years to come were to be spent in realising all the anticipated joys of the world, for which they had slaved away their youth. Three months more and they would have started in quest of their earthly paradise. And now – he had stolen away with a brown-haired girl from Thursday Island.

Despite herself, the woman's hard lips trembled. What was in a man that, after all those battling years of staunch comradeship, he must leave her to run away with a weakling girl because she was pink-faced and soft and pretty?

With the last of the breeze the cutter drifted around the point. Low-voiced the woman ordered the native crew to down sails softly. The anchor was run out, the woman seeing the greased chain slipped from the winch inch by inch. She ordered the boys to get their supper quietly and without a light. Eating nothing herself, she stood gazing at the wall of blackness before her that marked the coastal range coming down to the sea. High up in silhouette against the sky were the mountain-peaks, and higher still a few stars were feebly pitting their light against fast-moving black clouds. Subconsciously, the woman's sea-mind thought; "There'll be a breeze off the land before morning."

Suddenly merry laughter echoed across the quiet waters of the little cove. The woman's strained position relaxed. She gave a queer sigh of intense satisfaction. The laughter was from the boys on Reynolds's lugger. She recognised the voices distinctly. But no light came from the boat. "She has so muddled his head that he shows no light aboard, yet allows his boys to put the whole show away," thought the woman bitterly. She sat on the companionway steps to wait.

The boys sat in a group by the bows gazing longingly across the water towards where the merry voices of their island comrades came from out of the darkness. They would have like to send a welcoming hail to the lugger and exchanged the usual news and jests. But fear of the white woman master was too great. Quick-witted, they had sensed exactly the tragedy that hung over the two tiny boats, and in low-voiced whispers gave each his opinion as to its probable outcome.

Gradually the laughing voices across the waters quietened. The boys brought their blankets up from below, and sprawling about the deck were soon fast asleep. The woman waited for two hours longer, then stood up. Taking the

revolver from the holster at her belt, she revolved the cylinder rapidly, listening with trained ear to the click of the oiled mechanism. Satisfied, she walked noiselessly across the deck, and with her bare foot prodded one of the blanket-covered forms.

The black man's eyes opened instantly. He gazed up questioningly at the woman-master bending above him.

"Toby," she whispered, "put dinghy overboard. You row me longa lugger. Quiet feller."

Quickly the dinghy was slipped overboard, the lapping of the rapidly-rising tide against the cutter's sides drowning the slight splash.

The woman sat in the stern, the boy took the oars and pulled swiftly in the direction of the lugger. Soon the black outline of the craft loomed right ahead. The woman leaned towards the blackboy. "Finish pulling," she whispered. "Let him tide take him dinghy longa lugger. You steer him longa stern."

Half a minute more and they'd glided beneath the lugger's stern. Reaching out her arms, the woman kept the dinghy from bumping, while the blackboy reached out until he could get a grip on the rail. The woman signed to him to hold on. She stood, her hand clenched hard against the lugger's damp planking, listening. From the decking up above came an occasional loud snore, but from the master's cabin, against which she was leaning, there was no sound.

Grasping the rail above her, with a lithe spring she was crouching on the lugger's deck, gazing straight down the black companionway of the little cabin.. With heart beating wildly she listened, her eyes staring into the darkness below. But not a sound came from the cabin. Could it be possible they had heard her coming? Did they have a surprise waiting for her below?

Then the pent-up fury of the woman burst all bounds. She jumped down the steps, both hands to her belt. The next second the tiny cabin was flooded with light from her torch, while she stood pointing the cocked revolver at two empty bunks.

She stood for many seconds, a wild-eyed panting eve of vengeance, her keyed-up brain refusing to believe that what she had expected to see was not really there.

Then the reaction came. First she noticed that the blankets from the bunks were missing, the familiar hurricane-lamp was gone. Involuntarily, her eyes turned sharply to Reynolds's bunk. Nailed to the planking above it was an old, old photograph, its face now turned to the cabin wall.

Uncontrollable hot tears sprang to the woman's eyes. It was her bridal

photograph. How plainly she remembered Reynolds proudly nailing it to his bunkhead on their first voyage together!

The woman sprang up the companionway, half ran across the deck, and savagely kicked the first blanket-covered form that lay in her way. Instantly she knelt down, and held her hand across the mouth of the startled native.

"Hssh! Tommy," she whispered. "Where boss?"

"He go longa shore," instantly answered the frightened boy. "He camp longa beach, longa tent, all-same picnic. He got new feller missus now, young feller"—

The woman's hands closed on the black man's throat with the strength of deadly hate. As she glared down into the rolling eyes and open mouth of the terrified man, she slowly realised that she could choke his life out with ease, and he would not move a muscle to prevent her. But it was superstitious fear that held him paralysed; this sudden apparition of the white-woman mistress from the island hundreds of miles away could only be accounted for by witchcraft.

Slowly her fingers loosened. "Tommy," she hissed, "You lie still. S'posem you call out longa boss, me come back killem you!"

She stood up, stepped noiselessly across the deck, and down into the waiting dinghy.

The blackboy pushed off from the lugger's side. "Pull longa shore," whispered the woman.

On the lugger's deck, the blackboy Tommy did not move until the welcome sun, rising strongly over the mountain tops, drove away the spirits that come with the night.

As the dinghy grounded on the beach, the woman stepped out. "You stop longa dinghy," she whispered.

The boy said nothing but his eyes spoke eloquently of fear of being left alone in the darkness.

The woman walked a few yards along the beach, and then stood still, staring into the blackness. On both sides of the small beach the hills had thrown tumbled masses of rocks down into the sea. Straight ahead the sand ceased abruptly against the wall of a dense North Queensland scrub. The woman walked cautiously on, her feet fumbling among the knotted jungle vines that had strayed out from the edge of the scrub..

Suddenly she stopped, ears strained, heart throbbing violently. But it was only the rustle of a jungle snake among the fallen leaves.

As her eyes searched the gloom she gradually made out the outline of something white against the mass of black. It was a tent. All the fierce resolve of

a set purpose came back on the woman with a rush. Hand to belt, she stepped quickly forward, her cat-like movements making not the slightest sound on the stillness of the night.

With one foot poised in the air, she stood stock still, the blood rushing from her heart under the icy chill of deadly fear. An agonising scream pierced the still air, died down, was renewed again, shriller and crueller, to end suddenly in a series of throttling gasps.

It was a woman getting her throat cut!

From the water's edge came the noise of a dinghy being hurriedly and clumsily pushed into deep water. The woman turned, and as if a fiend were behind her rushed towards the beach.

In the tent at the edge of the scrub Reynolds was doing his best to pacify a very frightened girl. As he gently freed himself from the clinging arms that came near to smothering him, he kept repeating, "It's all right, girly; it's a bird, only a bird."

"But it sounded like – like" – she gasped.

"Yes I know. Just like a woman. But it's not; it's only a bird. A cross between a night-hawk and an owl. I've only heard the darn things in these scrubs along the Cape York Peninsula coast. The natives call it the death bird. They're scared of it, and won't camp in the same spot twice where they have known the bird to call out. They reckon someone in the tribe is going to die sudden every time the darn thing screeches. Rot! Now you know all about it."

With the strong dawn-breeze behind her the woman headed the fleeing cutter straight for Thursday Island. The hiss of the spume behind her, the shriek of the gathering wind in the cordage, kept her overwrought brain a-seethe with distorted thought of the night before. But a great exultation possessed the woman over all. She had only to report to the authorities at Thursday Island, and Reynolds swinging for his murder would complete her vengeance to the bitter drop.

That same evening she abruptly thrust the cutter on to a different course and headed for the home island. She had decided to have her man back. And the hold she would have on him would keep him to her side although Cleopatra herself should beckon him away.

1 December 1921
Gouger

CHARLIE PUTS A COLLAR ON

Charlie was whistling. Therefore he was happy. There was nothing in that though. For the Pearl Queen lay still as a mouse in the quiet waterway, with nothing to remind us of the sickening months of roll, roll, roll she had just given us. All around lay the mosquito craft of the fishing fleet, all breeds of craft, from the gull-like slippery schooner to the tiny five ton cutter. And all breeds of men owned them: white men, Jap men, colored men. And frowning above us Thursday Island, with its little town, its garrison, its reservoir and its mixture of all the peoples of the earth.

Busy dinghies, echoing from the laughter of the blackboy rowers, plied swiftly to the jetties, loaded with bags full of the dried sea-slug, and bags full of the opalescent glories of the pearl shell.

And the warm sun shone kindly. And Charlie kept on whistling. I put it down to the fat cheque we had drawn. We had had a good season. And bêche-de-mer was "up."

But as the shades of late afternoon closed over the somewhat naughty little island, I missed Charlie's whistling and slipped below. Charlie was in his cabin. I crawled sideways into my tiny bunk. I had to. When a man is trying to fit on a high collar within the tiny limits of a lugger's cabin there is no space for a mouse to move, let alone another man.

Charlie was not used to high collars, and our looking glass has a wavering crack right across it, with several young ones running sideways from it. A heavy sea was responsible. A man has to study that glass for weeks before he can shave in it. In the right-hand top corner about two square inches of the mirror is whole. If you stand on tiptoe, turn your head partly sideways, you can shave all right – in patches. But you want to be careful.

Charlie was trying to put on his collar. He is not a very tall man, but had overcome this difficulty by standing on two pillows. Mine was the top pillow.

I suppose my talking silence unnerved him a bit. He was evidently ashamed of himself. Not of the language he was using, but when a man who has been used to wearing a soft shirt all his life is caught red-handed juggling with a high collar he is certain to feel embarrassed. Besides the starb'rd edge of the collar *would* jamb in his jugular.

"For Gord's sake," he said at last, "don't talk so much. The townspeople will think we've got an overworked gramophone aboard."

I filled my pipe. That is a delicate operation in a bunk where a man has barely room to breathe.

"What are you shipping the choker for?" I asked sociably.

"Fun," replied Charlie bitterly.

I did not answer. This may have unnerved him. At any rate, he tore the collar from his neck and tossed it through the open companionway. It hit the water with a hearty smack.

Charlie turned his back on me. He carefully selected another collar from a brown-paper parcel on his bunk. He stood on the pillows again. I noticed he'd torn a five inch strip from the back of his shirt. Charlie noticed it too, after he had been poking his fist through the hole in a groping way for five frantic minutes. No wonder he couldn't find the back stud. It had gone sailing out to sea with the collar. Maybe by this time a dandy fish had swallowed it.

"Why didn't you tell me there was a hole in me shirt?" he growled. "Lying there like a stuffed sea-cow with th' faceache."

"You didn't ask me," I replied.

But Charlie was really angry. He peeled off the shirt and seized another one from the brown-paper parcel. In his hurry he put it on back to front. But he didn't notice this – not until he tried to stuff the tail end down where the other part ought to go. Then he tore the shirt off. He had no idea that it would tear so easily.

Charlie seized another shirt. I began to think he'd bought all Thursday Island. But he was much more careful with this one. I suppose it was the last hope.

He drew it down over his head, then his chest, carefully. Charlie's chest shows very plainly what his ancestors were. I noticed that the forest was trembling violently. Some men are emotional.

But he got the shirt on. He stood on the pillows again. He felt around for the back stud. A sort of blank spread over his face. He sprang off the pillows, and seized both shirts on the cabin floor. But they were innocent of a stud. He searched the floor anxiously. Then he dropped on his knees and stuck his head under the bunk.

"What are you looking for?" I asked.

"Stud!" he said, in a suppressed kind of voice. "Have you seen that back collar-stud of mine?"

"Not unless it's the one that was on the collar you heaved overboard."

Charlie sprang up suddenly. It is not good to spring up suddenly in our cabin. He glared down at me for a full minute, holding his head with one hand and his breath with the other.

"Have you got any spare studs? I forgot to buy a supply," he said quietly.

"Never use 'em," I replied cheerfully.

Charlie made a dash for the companionway. From the bows I heard him yell "Pretty Polly, ahoy!"

"Ahoy!" came faintly from the Malay skipper of Pretty Polly.

"Have you got a stud aboard, Tarquay?" yelled Charlie. "Send us aboard a collar stud!"

"A whata?" came faintly.

"Stud! *Stud!* STUD!" screamed Charlie. "A damn" –

"Aw righta," bellowed Tarquay. "I send him."

Charlie paced the deck for the best part of 10 minutes. I could tell he was pressed for time, his footfalls were getting shorter and quicker. Finally came the click of rowlocks. I strolled on deck. A boy from the Pretty Polly had just rowed alongside. He reached down into the dinghy; then, gripping the lugger's rail, he handed up to the eager Charlie an iron stud, one of those bolts we use for clenching parted timbers.

Charlie gave a short, sharp howl and flew down the companionway. I leaned against the mast and smoked. Old sol had gone to bunk, starry lights were twinkling in the little town, many laughing voices floated musically across the water. It was one of those evenings when a man feels his soul is at peace. He really doesn't know what his soul is, but he feels that it is at peace, anyway.

Charlie came on deck at last. He had his collar on and a tie. Also a coat and a new hat. He did not look at me.

"Get the dinghy, Toby," he snarled.

Toby is our head boy. The mission educated him. Toby just gazed at Charlie, or rather Charlie's collar, with his big mouth half-open. Then his mouth widened. But he didn't laugh. He didn't have time. Charlie took a sudden step forward. Toby took six sudden steps backward. Then he sprang for the stern and hauled up the dinghy. He got in and seized the oars; his eyes never left the collar. Charlie got in. They pushed off for the shore.

"You're late for tea," I called casually. Charlie didn't answer. Perhaps his collar was hurting him. I noticed it had a list to his port ear.

9 February 1922
Gouger

BROWN'S DOG

Bill Brown travelled with a dog. A spotted dog. It was never satisfactorily settled on the field whether Brown owned the dog or "the dawg" owned Brown. I think the dawg won on points. Certainly, to see him trotting patronisingly ahead of Brown up the little township road, leading the way to work, and later the way back to dinner, was to get the impression that the dawg owned the whole township.

The dawg had a woolly head loaded with a perverted intellect, big brown eyes, clean teeth, about eighteen inches of bright red tongue and fleas. It grew its chest well out and its tail well up. That tail told a tale of the plump body never having tasted the toe of a boot. It was an altogether uncivilised dog.

Brown would follow obediently behind, his worshipping eyes never off the dawg. He was a nuggetty, black-moustached, rather dull man, but well liked among the opal gougers all the same.

One peculiarity of the dawg was its partiality for the pub. The joyhouse dispensed anything from plain beer to unbeatable horrors; it simply depended on the thirst of the drinker and the size of his cheque. These refreshments were served at the Old Town, three miles down the road. When the mongrel was missing an anxious Brown would make straight for the boarding-house. There, "Have you seen me dawg," he would ask hopefully of the cook.

The cook had no time for Brown, and would merely say he hadn't. Then Brown would trudge the three miles to the pub, and later on the dawg would come trotting back leading Brown.

Apart from bones there was no visible reason why the pub should have a fascination for the dawg. In his previous life he may have been a beer-chewer. Or a publican. Especially did he like the pub when a big opal-buyer had visited the field. For days the big bar would be crowded with thirsty men assimilating their cheques. At such times the dawg's eyes would literally shine their approval. He could never keep still, trotting up and down the long bar-floor among the tramping feet of the roysterers, joining in the chorus of boisterous songs with lively barking. He refereed fights and later accompanied the star artists to the pump and helped them sluice off the surplus hair and skin. He would sit on his haunches and stare open-mouthed at this operation, his big brown eyes saying plain as daylight, "Bully, boys!" Finally, no fight was complete without Brown's dawg. I have known promising fights delayed for hours simply to allow Brown's dawg to show up.

When a man had engulfed that quantity of beer which made it necessary for him to sleep it off wherever he hit the ground, the dawg always seemed to get disgusted. He would walk superciliously up to the snoring imbiber, sniff his breath reflectively, then express disdain. It was a standing joke on the field that no man had ever been properly sizzled who had not been counted out by Brown's dawg.

Strange to say, Brown drank very little himself. This failing of Brown's the dawg took very much to heart. He would look shame-faced when Brown turned the pub corner. Leading the way into the bar with drooped tail (the only time his tail *did* droop), he would point his nose invitingly at the bar, and then gaze at Brown with reproachful eyes. Brown had to drink three beers and sham very drunk before the dawg would take him proudly home.

One day the crowd being half-lit up and consequently very happy and full of strength and brains, conceived the brilliant idea of making Brown's dawg drunk. They invited him to down a long beer, which he straightway did in most approved fashion, asking plainly for another, which was immediately forthcoming. He asked for a repetition, which was delightedly put before him. The dawg then hiccuped and then walked lop-sidedly towards the bar. The laughing crowd lifted him on the bar-counter and played it low down on him. they gave him another beer dosed with whisky. One low-principled coot wished to drop his cheap cigar-ash into the pot, but the crowd counted him out. They wanted, they said emphatically, to give the dawg a fair spin.

The dawg shortly after tried a jazz on his hind legs up and down the bar-counter to a roaring song from the delighted crowd, who kept him from falling off by the simple expedient of pushing him back. The dawg then stood on his nose and tried to wag his tail while barking, but gravitation drew him irresistibly downward, where he fell into an open hogshead of sour beer at the back of the counter. Here he would have been drowned if the publican had not pulled him out by his feebly-wagging tail.

When Brown's dawg came to he tried to go home. A quarter of a mile up the road, feeling very sick, he reached Mrs. Smith's house. Mrs. Smith came down off her doorstep, and nodded her head comprehendingly. She gathered him up in capable big arms and laid him in the shade on a bag beside the fowlhouse. Then she went to the well and very soon had poured four buckets of icy-cold water over his head and back. He whined gratefully with closed eyes; but his head was all lead and he couldn't lift it.

At this time Brown came striding along the road. Mrs. Smith called: "Are you looking for your dog, Mr Brown? Here he is."

Brown came over and gazed down at the dawg in astonishment. Then fear spread quickly over his quiet face. "For Gawd's sake don't say he's sick," he pleaded in a low voice. "He won't die will he?"

"Of course he won't," said the woman practically; "he's only drunk."

"What?" Brown gazed up at the woman in a way that accused *her* of being drunk.

"They made him drunk at the pub," she said sharply.

Brown stood up and gazed amazedly down the road towards the pub. Then a look of cold fury stole over his face. He spat twice emphatically on his hands, rubbed them and rolling up the sleeves of his flannel, set off towards the pub in a walk that was almost a run.

"Don't be a fool," Mrs. Smith called after him. "There's 40 men down there. They're all drunk. They'll mob you."

Brown kept on, and after a moment Mrs. Smith ran after him. She caught him up and grasped his arm determinedly, gradually slowing him up. "Look here," she said as they walked along, "those men only did it for a joke. It was a dirty joke I know, but drunken men don't know any better. They didn't mean any harm, really. If you go down there they'll want you to join in the laugh with them. When you start fighting, they'll all turn on you. You won't have a chance. See them to-morrow or the day after – or whenever they're sober."

Gradually she stopped Brown, and soon after, still talking, piloted him into the kitchen. Brown, though brooding and sulky was soon getting outside some bread and butter and well-made tea with milk in it.

Brown's dawg joined the prohibition ranks. He never after went to the pub, and would walk a long way around to avoid even an empty bottle. Mrs. Smith's always pulled him up.

Brown liked the dawg going to Mrs. Smith's because he could go there looking for him.

Mrs. Smith was a widow woman whose fortune was a plain face, five children and a big heart.

Brown in his slow way began to do a lot of thinking. He lived in a hut with fleas in it. Mrs. Smith lived in a nice clean house with a garden. He baked his own poor dampers. Mrs. Smith baked bonzer yeast bread. Mrs. Smith's juicy roast beef was always done to a turn. A man could go three plates easy, especially with baked spuds. His own salt junk was always stringy and tough. Besides, the dawg had made a home there.

One day Brown proposed.

"You know, I've got a good opal-claim, Mrs. Smith?" Brown one day said feelingly.

"Yes," said Mrs. Smith encouragingly.

"An' you've got a good home," went on Brown quickly, "an' I've got a cow of a one. An' you're a good sort of woman, an' I'm not a bad sort of a bloke. Besides, the dawg's made his home here." Brown paused bashfully. "Wot if you take me in too?" he added.

"Meaning?" asked Mrs. Smith softly.

"We get married," whispered Brown.

Mrs. Smith gazed at the man reflectively. "I don't mind admitting I was thinking that way myself," she said quietly.

Brown reached out suddenly and caught Mrs. Smith's strong hand, with a burst of confidence.

"Struth!" he laughed delightedly, "I felt like I was asking for the whole Roming Empire with Buckley's chance of getting it. Say"-----

"Matilda," prompted Mrs. Smith softly.

24 July 1924
Gouger

THE AUGUD OF MOA

The girl dreamed upon the mission-house verandah. The evening, the island and its associations all breathed of romance. Wistfully she wondered why none of this elixir of life had come to her. She was the teacher of native children on Moa, and was proud of being enlisted as a lay missionary.

From the rear rooms came the drone of contented voices, as the missionary and his wife taught their pretty white children. What a striking contrast to the lively black piccaninnies that daily filled the schoolhouse at St. Paul's!

There was one other white man on the island, a school-teacher, too, but he lived miles away, across the big hills in the village of Poid. And problematical winds and trackless hills kept him there. And anyway, why should he visit uninteresting folks when all around him were fascinating people?

The girl sighed. The man as usual was privileged; he was not afraid to roam into the recesses of the island, to explore the sacred Zogo-grounds and spy for the great augud, which was once necklaced with human skulls. She had even caught whispers that, in secret, occasional rites were practiced yet. From behind the schoolhouse windows scholars speaking in awed whispers had pointed out old Oroki as he stalked through the village, on a visit from Poid. The girl had studied with interest the fierce face of this last of the Zogo-*le*, who strove to keep alight the fires of a people's superstition, and had inherited from the dead centuries some queer knowledge that the whites had been unable to fathom. For ages his people had drunk the blood of their enemies, and lived within the worship of their augud. They had even stolen white women. But that was before the missionary came.

Now the moon bathed Moa, with its ghostly granite hills and its valleys of silence, and its villages beneath the palms by the sea. And the lagoon all silver with thunder upon its coral ramparts, and the grandeur of Moa peak highest in all Torres Strait, and a Brisbane girl united with the silence on the verandah of St Paul's!

Within the lagoon lay three pretty vessels at a distance apart, almost as if distrustful of one another. A black cutter, manned by Torres island boys, searching for trochus. A low built, speedy Jap lugger combing our seas for pearl-shell. The third a grey ketch, with a white captain and woolly-headed Papuan crew. All had come howling in under reefed sail, seeking sanctuary from an angry storm. None had landed, for missionary people and nomads of the sea are not always the best of friends.

The girl wondered at the white man. He would be gone in the first break in the weather. Quite disinterestedly she wished he would bring her some adventure. To have come 2000 miles to work in an island of romance, and yet not to be allowed one peep within the veil, was heartbreaking.

On impulse she stole off the verandah and made for the beach. The household was asleep. The village was asleep. The moon was clouding herself to sleep. The ketch was invisible.

She dodged the village. It would not look well for a lone white girl to be seen at this hour; and, besides, she was a bit afraid to walk among the huts of colored men at midnight. She intercepted sufficient glances by day.

Thrilled and not dreaming of consequences, she stepped along, delightfully startled at every cloud flung shadow. To her feet came murmuring ripples of the sea, while landward gloomed tree-masses, and distantly the blackness of hills. The air was sweet and she caught whispers of mysterious things.

At the beach end, where starlight splashed upon rocks, there was a paddock of darkness---the mouth of a mangrove creek. She halted at the thought of mud and a possible alligator. Anyway, she would not penetrate that tangled maze. With a backward glance and a smile all to herself, she nestled upon the beach.

The grey ketch was invisible, but the star-kissed lagoon was beautiful. A collar of foam boiled far out upon the reef.

She straightened, her heart beating alertly. Distinctly came the click-clack of rowlocks. A dinghy coming from the ketch! But what for? Native women?

She hurried into the shadows and stood irresolute. If this man was coming ashore for women, then he was breaking the most rigid law of the mission. And she was a lay missionary! Her duty was plain. But would she be game to reproach him? Duty eased her conscience for spying. And besides, this tasted delightfully of adventure. She slipped into deeper shadows, and her heart livened to the rhythm of nearing oars.

The dinghy emerged from the night and disappeared into the creek. The girl heard a bump as they hit the mangroves, guessed they were fastening the dinghy; then a curse as the white man's boot slipped on a root. Almost immediately they stood close by her, four men. She crouched low, hot with the instinct of the primitive thing ready to run.

Occasionally this type of white sea-wanderer had called in at the mission. Not a bad-looking chap, brown-skinned, alert-eyed with the initiative that marks those who successfully carve out a living in the ever-changing environment of the coral seas. She admired the enormous mops of hair on the Papuan boys, who,

naked but for a lava-lava, were grinning as at a huge joke. The Torres Islander between them was not grinning. He was terrified. The girl's sympathy went to him, for in the tall, well-built body, the crinkly hair, the keen face she recognised a man of Poid.

The white man contemptuously fastened a slip-knot around the islander's neck, lashing the corded end to a Papuan's wrist, then commanded "Hurry! Quick feller!" The man shivered, glanced back over the lagoon, and stepped noiselessly into the bush. The others followed and vanished.

With a start the girl tip-toed after them and caught their shadows latticed amongst the branches. Her feet itched to race back to the beach.

The men had no thought of being followed. They wound amongst the bushes, never glancing back, and vanished down a coal-black gully. The girl, hurrying after, tripped and slid and tumbled. She crouched, too frightened to move. By a chance of Providence she caught them up again.

They slithered across the undulating country that boomerangs in to the hills; amongst timbers stunted and tall; dodging twisted branches that moaned with the wind; then over rustling grass to vanish within a cloak thrown by the black shadow of the hills. Then followed a dodging of fantastic, black-grey shapes, boulders very forbidding in the misty light. A scramble up a jungly ravine, then the first hills rising abrupt like a crescent barrier and a girl fearful lest she miss these men, for without their companionship she sensed a more fearful loneliness.

As they climbed she hastened among the rocks, with dress torn and limbs scratched and mouth opening in energetic gasps. If they had glanced behind they might have caught the glint of two frightened eyes in the starlight. They scrambled over the hills and clambered down into the pit of a valley, on the far side of which rose higher and blacker hills; and, overshadowing all, the peak of Moa.

The Islander halted. He threw himself at the white man's feet, he kissed his master's knees, he whined like an animal. The master nodded to the Papuans. They threw the Islander and gurgling their delight nearly throttled him. They gouged his eyes, and he screamed amongst the snapping twigs. The girl's heart froze. She was physically incapable of interfering, and---what of herself? She realised her utter defenselessness. These brutes now torturing a strong man--- what would they delight to do to her, a girl, and a *white* girl! Was there anything they could *not* do? She shuddered at the possibility of further adventure.

The Islander sobbed. They kicked him to his feet and pathetically he scrambled on. The girl looked around beseechingly. But only twisted shadows

and the stars answered her prayer. She crept on, the sobs of the man of Poid keeping her on their track.

She was close behind the men as they crossed the valley. She did not know that the natives whispered of it as the Valley of Despair.
Stumbling up the peak of Moa, they pushed into a jungle, and in the inky blackness the girl's hand could once have touched the rear man. Luckily for her, the Papuans were too intent on the islander to notice anything else. Within the jungle, he sank to the tree roots. The Papuans manhandled him joyously until he crawled again.

They came to a boulder, the size of a house and so black that you could not tell that it was rock until your outstretched hand touched it.

On his belly the islander crawled under the bushes, working a path along the side of the rock. Behind him crept a Papuan, his teeth snapping at the islander's heels, while his comrade gurgled laughter at every sharp intake of the breath of the Poid man. The white man came last.

The shrubbery ended. Crawling, the girl's hands told her she was on sand.

A relieved oath from the darkness ahead and the sudden flash of a torch! The girl's bewildered eyes caught cleft walls with tangled vegetation.

The white man sprang erect, expectancy on his face. Luckily, none looked behind, although the black men were plainly in a hurry to get back. The white man was all eagerness to push forward and snarled at the now frightened Papuans. With bowed head the islander did not open his eyes.

"Go on, quick feller!" snapped the white man. The girl caught the gleam of an automatic.

The cave walls widened rapidly; the roof rose into invisibility. A desperate courage warmed the girl. They walked like phantoms in the silence.

Suddenly a roaring "Hooray!" crashed from wall to wall. The white man stood amazed. The blacks dropped terrified. The girl clutched her heart to smother the stab of fear.

"Get up! Quick feller!" he roared; and the roar echoed back and silenced them all.

They slouched forward and the girl noted that the white man threw his torchlight on the floor and kept behind the boys and so made escape impossible. Presently he flashed the torch upwards..

The Papuans grovelled, but the man from Poid crouched as if he knew he was doomed.

The girl gasped, her eyes widening with understanding; her heart thumping with exultation.

For before them sat the great augud of Moa, the idol worshipped for a thousand years! Upon its dais of coral blocks and sacred shells it squatted, a monstrous figure of a man, massive in plates of tortoise-shell. Its flaring eyes were mother of pearl; its teeth nautilus-shell.

The torch flashed around and the girl stared, with spine creeping. Pyramids of skulls were built around the augud---painted skulls of men and women and children; hundreds of them, in pyramids, paying a death-like homage.

The girl's brain raced triumphantly as she remembered the legends of these people, as far as they had entrusted the missionary with their confidence. Here was their tortoise-shell augud, just as the old ex-cannibals had described; here the sacred shells, the skulls of their enemies and victims; here the black Zogo-stone once anointed with human oil; here other weird things she could not place. Then the torch flashed upon her and she shrank in the full terror of discovery.

"Well?" he asked. But she stood fearfully silent.

"Slip your tongue!" he demanded. "What are you doing here?"

"What are you?" she whispered.

"Minding my own business. And you?"

"Minding mine."

"In what way, Miss Spy?"

"I'm watching unauthorised persons upon the island!" she snapped.

"Well, what are you going to do about it?" he grinned.

She stared, puzzled.

"We'll have a straight out understanding," he said, "and lively, because I'm in a hurry. You're the little busybody at St. Paul's. Well, I'm taking this augud, because every plate is of marvelous quality, and tortoise-shell is rocketting just now. So that's it!"

He turned and booted the Papuans

"But you can't take it," said the girl.

"Why not?" he asked.

"Because it belongs to the people of Moa. It is their god. They have venerated it for centuries."

He smiled queerly. "Well, I'm blessed! And that from a missionary! Here I come to destroy the idol of the heathen, as the Bible commands. And *you*, a missionary, a prophet, speak against the book. And just remember girl with the scared face and pretty hair, that years ago the missionaries invaded these islands, and with hammer and fire destroyed the idols of these people, and did all in their power to annihilate the old heathen beliefs. Only on a few odd islands

did the Zogo-*le* manage to secrete their tools of an idolatrous trade." He smiled mockingly.

"Shame on you for a Christian! You who would prevent me from completing the good work!"

He kicked the man from Poid. "Get up!" he commanded savagely.

The girl stepped forward. Somehow she felt a little surer of herself.

"Stop that!" she said resolutely. "You have tortured that poor man enough. Let him alone."

"What? Him too?" said the man in astonishment. "How you, a missionary, do decide against all that is right! Why, this man is Judas Iscariot. He has betrayed his very god. He sold him for a bottle of rum . This way." he smiled. "Judas here is one of my signed-on boys, from Poid. A month back, out on the Barrier, he boasted that he was the succeeding priest to Oroki, the next of the Zogo-*le* to guard the god and keep alive the old beliefs, in the hope that one day the people might come against the white man. I laughed at his tale and in a boastful moment he said he could sell me the augud itself for a bottle of rum. I closed with the offer and Judas became beastly drunk. Look at him now. Get to work!" he snapped at the Papuans.

The girl sprang to the augud, facing the man, with her arms protectingly outspread on the dais. The great figure above her glared out into the darkness.

"You will *not* destroy it," she cried. "It belongs to a people and it is priceless. Wait until Mr. Morrisy says what is to be done with it. He may sell it to a museum."

"That's just what he *won't* do," said the man. "Besides, it is not his to sell. Do you, a missionary, want to thieve a people's property for a museum!"

"You must wait until Mr. Morrisy says what is to be done with it," she replied defiantly.

He regarded her amusedly. "Now I am going to get rid of you," he smiled--- "kindly and nicely but effectually."

"How?" she whispered.

"By making love to you."

She drew a startled breath and stood erect.

"You wouldn't dare," she said.

"I'll soon show you," he grinned. "Now, listen. Judas is incapable of carrying away any of this shell, so I have told him to guide you back. Go!"

The girl remained.

He stepped forward, and she shrank back against the augud. His hand caressed her hair. She flung his arm aside. "Go!" he said.

"You wouldn't dare," she whispered, and felt that the very augud could hear her heart-beats.

He flung his arms around her and kissed her upon the lips and cheek and hair, strong and fiercely. Then he whispered hoarsely: "Go! It is the third and last time I ask."

She sped into the blackness. He followed slowly, flashing the torch before her. At the cave entrance she turned and signalled him back. He stood watching her heels as they wriggled below the bushes.

But she was not yet finished with the night. For as she clawed her way from out the bushes her hands touched the falling body of Judas, with Oroki's arrow through his heart.

27 October 1927
Ion L. Idriess

MY SWAMP MAN

I found him in a Papuan swamp just in from the Dutch boarder. Strange trees grew within that swamp, Countless palms amongst them, and cable vines like mammoth snakes loop down from knotted branches. Massed reeds grew from the black water, and on the sodden islands there are tufts of wild sugarcane-like grass that tries to reach the tree branches. In occasional patches, diluted sunlight reaches the purple flowers floating on the water; but the whole swamp is gloomy and very quiet, so quiet that a barefooted man makes no more noise than a shadow.

He is a little fellow, and what shade of black he is you cannot tell, because his body is caked with mud as armor against mosquitoes. His head is partly shaved (with a jagged shell for razor), leaving two long tufts, bound with clay and reeds, jutting up 18 inches above his head. He is very proud of his toilet and its accessories, being two alligators' teeth thrust through the septum of his nose. He wears no other clothes.

His face is small and a mass of wrinkles that look like deep cuts. His mouth is very wide, and as he screws his face you get a momentary gleam of formidable teeth. His eyes are not very deep set, possibly because he seldom sees the sun, but he shows the whites frequently, as when he pauses to listen. At such times he is like a wild animal that is uncertain of its safety.

Reassured, the swamp-man gazes around in perplexity, his eyes continually alighting on two tree-trunks. Reason seems to be struggling within him every time his glance strays to those logs. Finally he picks one up, in a hesitating way. He is surprisingly strong for his size and handles the log with far more dexterity than many a sixteen-stone white man could.

He slides it into the water so that no possible enemy could hear the splash. The log sinks. The swamp-man stands in the silence, too undeveloped to know even that he is disappointed. He turns sluggishly and stares at the other log. Physical inclinations urge him not to waste labor over it, but something stronger forces him to the log. He lifts it, and it squelches from its damp bed, a phosphorescent fungus on its underside and a gigantic blue worm wriggling back into the mould.

The swamp embryo pushes the prospective liner off. It floats! A wonderful change comes over his face. The eyes dilate, the mouth opens, the deep cuts unwrinkle; he is trying to smile and it looks as though it hurts.

The swamp-man has something really great on hand now. He wades out with

the log. He straddles it; it sinks nearly under, but it bears his weight. Gripping with monkey-like fingers to retain his balance, his feet kick out in a swimming motion. As if a thing of life, the log dreamily forges ahead. A most wonderful smile cracks up the face of the man. He gurgles in sheer delight. Maybe this is the first time in his life that he has laughed. Certainly he has never smiled before to such amazing pleasure. he kicks out, he nearly cries in delight as he sees that with movements of his body and limbs he can propel and guide his craft to an island fifty yards further out amongst the reeds. He carries on, he actually makes the black water ripple; he is risking death but what cares he in the heat of this great discovery! He can go back to his tribesmen now and boast that he can get across the water without swimming, and with safety from alligators!

The navigator reaches the island safely. He carries his log with him, crooning over it, for it is far, far more precious than a baby or anything else in the world.

I smile, because I can see him in gurgling ecstasy watching his fellow-tribesmen disappointedly throwing logs into the water only to sink. But some will float, and that will be the beginning of the tribe's first dug-out!

There are similar swamps throughout Papua where the swamp-men are in different stages; some still swim, some have discovered the straddling log, a few have evolved the dug-out. The next step after the log is two logs lashed together with lawyer-cane or swamp-grass. This prevents capsizing, is far easier to propel and is of much greater safety in these waters where an ugly black snout is likely to rise up from underneath at any moment.

But I like my swamp-man best, because I saw him; I saw the birth of his great idea, its pangs and its successful delivery to help man on his long, long way. And I saw greater joy granted to a human being than many fathers experience at the birth of their first-born; I caught a hellish dose of malaria doing it, but it was worth all of that.

Papua, gloomy land, fascinating land, it is still a cradle of the human race. Men are there who as yet have hardly evolved to their first stone-scraping tool, and there are other men who build houses fifty feet in height and two hundred feet long; and men who have not yet found out that a pointed stick thrust into hot ashes becomes hard and its spear-point not nearly so liable to break. And men are there who build non-capsizable canoes fifty feet long and five feet deep, and rig them and mast them and sail them with sails they have thought of themselves, plaited from leaves of the cocoa-palm—craft that can sail faster than a modern lugger.

I wonder how many tens of thousands of years it took those men to evolve

past the straddling log. It took untold centuries, because for centuries now different Papuan tribes have been making canoes for export to the Torres islanders, canoes that have sailed all over the Coral sea.

Several tribes along the mouth of the mighty Fly River supplied this trade; the island of Kiwai housed men who have been hereditary makers of canoes, as are the Sumi tribesmen. The price of these canoes used to be so many skulls, depending on the size of the vessel. The missionary has reduced the price to armlet shells, which are rarer than heads nowadays, but less trouble in their procuring.

And the natives are still evolving--- quickly now that civilisation has rudely butted in. The Torres Strait islanders have mostly discarded the mat sails and now use "white man" canvas. Many of their men have sailed in and can perfectly manage a white-man vessel. And now many of the canoe-makers use the white man's wonder-tool, the tomahawk, instead of the stone implement and the shell scraper.

But my swamp-man may never know of these great things. He will probably live his life out as the hero of a great discovery; and the swamp moss may mould his bones before the white man's influence penetrates his silent home.

22 February 1928
Ion L. Idriess

BARE FANG

Night. And stars large in the sky. And darkness upon earth. But not all things are asleep. For this is Arnhem's Land, and untamed. No land in the world is wilder, and it is absorbingly interesting, for its living things are as God made them in the Beginning. Wild men dwell there, and the teeth of their shaggy women gnaw greedily at human bones. Their claw-like hands will strangle a baby should it be one of twins. And the mother will howl hideously in her grief if the other should die of snake-bite.

Wild animals thrive there, caged only by the coast. Inland are lagoons whose waters shun daylight beneath overshadowing foliage. Further in are hills, fantastic many of them when setting sun or rising moon paints their battlemented crags. There are plains, too, waving with cane-grass and pandanus-palm swamps. If you battle your way through that grass you will suddenly gasp at a crash like the fall of a door, and the grass will tremble before you, and you will stare at two enormous horns that from tip to tip measure your own length, and two small eyes, possibly red-rimmed, curiosity in them, and a doubt whether to charge or plod warily away. As you slip back into the gently enfolding grass the buffalo will snort disdainfully and carry on with his business.

As for the rest, volumes would not describe the men, the animals, the birds and plants and fishes that luxuriate there. It is a wonderful land, a fascinating and perilous land. Already its fringes are dotted with the bones of men who have answered its siren call.

Bare-fang, the dingo, has no illusions. A champion of his tribe he realises that he is but a creature of a moment. Feared by many, fearing few, he senses that some day the wild will get him and just carry on as before, none missing him, none caring. So he lives determinedly for the day, in order that he may see another day.

This Bare-fang is a sinewy bundle of untiring muscle and snappish temper. His coat is gingery and his pads are made of silence. The claws of his feet are wickedly sharp and strong, as needs they must be to dig out the prey which burrows deep in the hard earth. His nose is pointed, a highly sensitive organ; it is his wireless, for the currents of the air speak to him in smell. His eyes are miracles of keenness. But such coldly cruel eyes; there is no laughter in them, and they change color with the day and the night and his feelings. He is moved by swift cunning and unerring instinct. His flank is not gaunt, for in this country there is abundance of game.

As day dawned he lifted his head and with the twitch of his nostril-bristles

his eyes shaded dreamily. For he saw miles of country, grasslands with sunlit trees, water-ways and scent of lilies, ironstone ridges and flowering gums. He smelled all these things; the swiftly travelling air currents carried to his nostrils impressions of the scenes they had just passed over

As he raised his head slowly to the wind, animal life was made known to him. He sensed the wallaby, though it was over a mile away. It was feeding just out from the edge of a scrub in tall bladly grass upon forest country. The heavy scent of the scrub, with its fungus and orchid growths, came through the air and the sunshine and sweetness of the forest.

Bare-fang set out after that wallaby. He did not trouble to trot. He was well fed, and had taste for more tender game. He would not have troubled the wallaby at all except for the lust that ever nagged at him to kill.

Suddenly he bounded upwards and backwards, his hair erect and fangs bared in anger. His eyes had been green. Now they blazed. A snake lay motionless. Its beady eyes glittered. Its snub nose was ugly and expressionless. Its perfectly scaled length, a thing of satanic beauty, glistened among the grass.

Bare-fang sprang off at a fast trot. He would be vicious for the rest of the day. Snakes always affected him in that way. They bit so unexpectedly, sometimes from the unseen. They could poison in a second, and it was a foolish risk to kill them.

He disappeared in a patch of scrub. In the gloom his eyes again shone green and expectant. He licked his chops. He was utterly noiseless, a red shadow. The wallaby out on the open forest raised a pretty head above the grass. It sniffed the air, a gentle questioning in its soft brown eyes. But Bare-fang had entered the scrub against the air currents. He could smell the wallaby; it could not smell him. Its blue-grey head dropped down to feed.

The end was swift. A swish with the bound of a red body. A sound like the snap of a steel trap. A thrashing wallaby, its entrails slit out, a snarling dingo gnawing its vitals. In three minutes Bare-fang was sitting up licking his chops with a satisfied air. He had gulped down only the titbits. He disdained the rest.

Slightly appeased now that he had worked off his rage against the snake upon something less deadly, he reclined beside his kill and dozed. Bees hummed. A blue fly settled on the wallaby. Another fly appeared, up in the vast sky. It volplaned in slow, graceful circles. Its bulk rapidly grew. It landed with a thud on a tree overhead. A brown eagle-hawk, with cold eyes. A crow squawked interrogatively from the forest edge.

In late afternoon Bare-fang arose and shook himself. Crows fluttered aside. He snapped his teeth. A swarm of flies buzzed from the torn wallaby. He glided

away through the grass. He would take himself to drink. The jackals of the bush flopped back to the feast.

Bare-fang walked leisurely towards the croon of water. Its distance mattered little. When he arrived the noise was a musical crash. He stood out on a rock, gazing as if he were lord of creation. water swirled past his feet, rugged peaks loomed high above, with a patch of sky above all. Mighty things. He was but an atom, but he had powers none of these things possessed, and in an arrogant way he regarded all big inanimate things as made for him.

Back from her drink hurried a brown dingo bitch. She showed her teeth as she passed. He stood looking at her interestedly. Satisfaction stirred within him as he reflected that a day would dawn when she would come cringing to him. He lay down comfortably within a boulder's shade. He could doze, and at the same time note everything that came to drink from this frothing pool. A white cockatoo, crest rampant, screeched harshly at him from a tree on the opposite bank.

Night; and the stars and the peaceful silence, sweet to the senses of man. But it was camouflage, for the night was moving with life.

Two blazing balls that were the eyes of Bare-fang flashed and were gone, leaving the watchful silence. A slithering, very gentle, like the kiss of a baby-wind on leaves, a frantic flutter, one little screech, and silence again. A snake eats noiselessly when once it has killed. A faint crackling among the cotton-pods as an unseen animal passed. From under dried pandanus leaves peeped a wee face. Such a dainty face, tiny grey nose twitching as if it could smell all the universe. A little marsupial mouse was coming out to have a look at the world, and he expected the night to hold its breath. His beautiful eyes were little beads, swimming beads of ruby. He peered sharply all around. Particularly he peered towards the stars, maybe criticising their twinkling. You would have laughed at his wee ears; he held them so importantly. Bravely he hopped from the sheltering leaves. It was a ludicrous hop, but he thought his powers of locomotion wonderful. In pride of life, he hopped three times; and then, suddenly remembering that maybe he was shaking the earth, he tried to move without noise and commotion---this mite whose padded toes were hardly the size of a little bird's claws.

A twin comet bolted down from the sky. Of molten bronze it was but with a cruel glare. The marsupial mouse tweaked pitifully as the talons gripped him. The owl was gone in a second and a last faint tweak farewelled the earth.

All the great bush cried with noises for those who had the ears to hear. Ruthless slaughter was being waged all over hundreds of miles of country, while

countless things that lived by day crouched within the earth and in trees and among rocks, dozing through this war for existence.

Bare-fang sped on, every nerve a live-wire. He loved the night. It was his cloak. Day things are so much more helpless by night.

Through scrub and jungle and forest he hurried to his favorite hunting ground. For miles the smell of water was in his face, and the muskiness of water-growing plants. Enclosing all a rim of hills, vague and shadowy and mighty like a far-flung crater of the moon. And darkness in acre-wide patches, with the shimmer of cold water in between. The centre of the swamp crater, silvery water, lay very still. The shadows were islands of rushes, except the moving shadows, which were cloaks from the clouds.

Noisy life crackled all over this lonely swamp---unseen wildfowl of many species, ducks and swans and geese. countless croaking and clucking, cooing and honking. The eyes of Bare-fang flamed among the reeds. He loved this feathered life of the night; countless things, all alive, yet each one vulnerable to him!

A distant chorus came whirling on. It shrilled like an express train rushing overhead. It hardly dimmed, as, unseen, away out in the swamp-centre a flock of whistling ducks doused into the water. Bare-fang licked his chops.

He worked the swamp edge. There was no need to wet his feet. Plenty of ducks nested in dry places. He worked noiselessly, his ever-twitching nose parting the reeds, his body gliding through. His nose told him where the luxuries lay. One looked up to glimpse his flaming eyes. He sprang, and strong forepaws flattened the spreading wings. Others he caught and ravened the tender flesh to his heart's delight among the reeds.

Satiated, he desisted at last, but only because he had whiffed the taint of smoke. He retired snarling with bristles erect.

Heavy bellied, he walked up a gentle rise, sat back on his haunches and gazed almost pathetically at the stars. Then he widened his jaws and howled, his eyes a dull green as if clouded by tears. The dismal howl rang over range upon range, floating along valleys to be echoed into other valleys by rocky crags. Yet Bare-fang did not know what he was howling for. He was not in love, he did not wish for companionship, he was not calling the pack. He did not know what he wanted, and he was miserably happy while he cried it to the skies.

Under a distant ridge many men listened. Wild men sitting around fires that were little more than wisps of smoke. For fire is a betrayer. Tall men they were, heavy muscled, with weals across their chests and backs that were the scars of warriorhood. Their hair stood erect like sticks plastered with sun-dried

clay. Their eyes gleamed fierce as a dingo's, and their ears appeared to be ever listening. They were quite naked, as were their women, and did not feel any inconvenience from the rough ground on which they sat. Of the women, as wild as the men, some had babes at the breast, some teased their lousy hair, some spoke the language of the eyes into the fiercely desirous eyes of the young men. Ten-foot spears, evilly barbed, were ready to the hands of every warrior.

As the mournful wail died into silence an animal-like man grunted gutturally. "Bare-fang calls to the Spirit of Life."

"He knows not when he answers," grunted another.

Barely a mile distant, on the opposite side of the ridge, two others listened. White men, the first who had set foot there. So far only the bush knew, and she smiles at adventurers, but her love is cruel.

"It's enough to freeze the blood in a man's veins," one whispered.

"Um," grunted the other, "it's like the bottled hopes of a thousand years drifting to Hell."

They listened long after the echoes had quavered away. No other sound came. Their own prick-eared horses, listening uneasily, wore no tell-tale bells.

"Do you think it is the Dingo-men?" whispered the first.

"Impossible to be sure. But I doubt whether any human voice could so perfectly imitate such a devilish sound."

They were dicing with Fate, these two pioneers. Arnhem's Land holds minerals. Some even whisper diamonds! Fortune beckons. These two were just chancing a hand on the outskirts. They could expect to be clubbed into eternity should the odds go against them.

Bare-fang shook himself to a red dawn. He liked this day, as he liked all days. It was certain to be filled with adventurous interest for him. Each day he lived, he gained in experience and cunning, and the knowledge helped him to thrust further back the last day of all. He set about his business and something called him to the sea.

Far away, down a bushy valley, three hundred wild humans were happily trudging in hunting array deeper into Arnhem's Land. Behind them, swiftly travelling in the opposite direction, were two white men.

Bare-fang broke into a tireless trot, just for the joy of motion. He pulled up where his feet touched the ground, nose outstretched a joyful gleam in his eyes. His delicate nostrils sniffed at a small black hole in a dead sapling. Rising with his forepaws against the sapling, he eagerly chewed long splinters from the wood. His teeth cut with the ring of a saw. Inside the wood was a little hollow. Bare-

fang inserted his red tongue and licked ecstatically. A swarm of little native bees hummed against his eyes. He licked them in with the honey. Such bees have but little sting. He cleaned out the nest and stood licking his chops in delight. He had tasted of the nectar of the gods.

He trotted on until mid-day, not feeling hunger, travelling over wonderful country, this lord of the wild; and then he loped down a river bank. He had been there before, often. Now instinct told him the tide was fallen, and for a few hours the fresh water would overwhelm the brackish.

Half-way down the bank he eyed the water. Innocent looking water, heavily shaded by mangrove-trees. Bare-fang searched earnestly; then there was a snarl of malevolent joy in the curl of his lip. He walked straight to the edge, all intentness. Immediately that his tongue rippled the surface, something stirred beneath the tree surface to his right. It was submerged, and quite invisible but to the most warily trained sight. It was of huge bulk and loathsome. And its jaws were rowed with great teeth.

With stealthy crawl it got to within striking distance. As it lunged forward, Bare-fang bounded up and backwards, landing half-way up the bank, every hair on end, eyes gleaming, lips upstretched, snarling a hellish hate. The alligator was motionless. But Bare-fang sprang as the lithe bulk swirled and the tail flailed the bank. Knowing himself beaten, the lizard glided back into deep water. But for long Bare-fang stood snarling, one paw raised, a picture of fiendish triumph

Towards sundown he reached the sand-hills lining the coast. Why he wanted to gaze at the sea he did not know. Regularly all through life he had made this trip apparently to look out over the immensity of waters.

In depressions there grew long, sweet grasses. Bare-fang noted the snake-like heads of plain turkeys. He licked his chops suddenly realising he was hungry. He marked the feeding grounds. He would enjoy supper there. Plain turkeys are fat and tender.

At sundown he was trotting up and over rolling little hills of pure white sand. Under the soft light of evening they gleamed like snow. For miles along this strip of coast there grows a small pine-tree, with a skin-like bark the color of blood. Bare-fangs coat matched the color as the setting sun pinked the edges of the sea.

Far away out there lazed a sail.

11 April 1928
Ion L. Idriess

THE LITTLE DEBIL CLICK-CLICK

Jim Halley developed the Kodak fever, which is why the supply cutter brought him a camera. With the amateur's enthusiasm he snapped the tribal bucks, their gins and piccaninnies and even their pet mongrels. Just practice, he assured his disgusted mates, before setting after big game. Buffalo was his big game. The camp lived by buffalo. By day they shot it for its splendid hide, by night they yarned of uncertain-tempered "solitary" beasts, of mobs and herds, of hairbreadth escapes from wounded bulls, of famous buffalo horses, of rifles and Colts and sawn-off shotguns, of all the thrills of the buffalo-shooter's life. they had got the animal right into their system, too, by eating its meat all the year round.

Now Jim sported a Kodak and Bill felt sort of jealous. Anyone would think the damn thing was a woman's baby. Of nights he must listen to interminable talk about negatives and films and spools and exposures; and instead of being filled with sweet bush air the house must reek with chemicals.

So Bill smoked glumly while his mate played with the new toy. There was, nevertheless, always an appreciative audience; whenever the camera was being fondled, the hut door was packed with saucer-eyed niggers watching the debil-debil thing with the fierce little eye that blinked and made "click-click" talk and produced little men and women and hills and water and alligators and white man's canoes and yarramans. It certainly was witchcraft, and entrancing witchcraft, this mysterious little debil-debil. So they reasoned in the after quiet of the gunyahs, talking in whispers lest the thing back in the white man's hut should hear and be offended and work them harm.

The cunning Yundah thought long. To think out of its accustomed paths was hard labor for his stone-age brain, but he was secretly ambitious to win the prized job of Dimboolooloo, the witchdoctor and painful reasoning assured him it was not fighting strength alone that had gained Dimboolooloo his authority. Now if he, Yundah, only possessed this little black debil with the quick evil eye and the "click-click" talk, what magic he would be able to make, what old scores he would pay back! It was wrinkled too, like an old warrior's face.

Thinking over it, Yundah felt certain that it talked to the black man's understanding. It clicked just like the baby ducklings talking to their mother in the reedy lagoons. If only he possessed it, it would whisper to him many things. He would then oust Dimboolooloo and win the tribe's favor. He might luckily kill Dimboolooloo with black magic. And then the delicacies in food and the pick of the young women!

So Yundah spied and listened, his low brow corrugated with the effort of trying to understand the words of Jim, who talked so knowingly to the little debil---Jim who was such a dangerous shot with the thunder-stick.

One evening, intent on his photographic efforts, Jim's hand mechanically searched the table for his pipe. His fingers closed on a familiar object and lifted it to his mouth. He misunderstood the grinning natives and puffed for quite a while before he recognised Bill's pipe. "Fair exchange is no robbery," he said jocularly, and keeping Bill's pipe he pushed his own across to his mate.

Now Yundah noted all this closely, and was amazed. He knew only too well the result if for instance, he had taken the white man's pipe and offered his own instead. And yet, simply by speaking a few magical words, that similar action had now been accepted without a word of anger. And white men were absurdly particular about their pipes.

Yundah resolved to quietly question Yaloo, the white men's know-all horseboy, as to the meaning of these magic words. But Yaloo could not help him. So Yundah simply watched.

Early morning and the finish of a hearty breakfast. Saddling of snorting horses, strapping on of ammunition belts, laughter and jokes from the excited natives, ostentatious fingering of knife blades by the proud "skinner" boys. Puffs of smoke tickling the air from freshly-lit pipes as the white men rode away, followed by the abos., all eager for the hunt. The sun bright, the air tingly as they ambled towards the grassy plains and palm-girt swamps.

After the first brisk half-mile, Yundah sneaked behind a grass-tuft until the hunters disappeared and then hastened back towards the camp.

Now Yaloo, the horse-boy, had been left in charge of the white men's buildings, and he resented the unauthorised approach of Yundah. But he grinned amiably, nevertheless, for Yundah, striding ahead of his three wives, was greased and ochred with fighting bars of red and yellow. He carried barbed spears, and there was that in his eye that told Yaloo that Yundah meant business.

Winyah, Yundah's oldest, ugliest and most talkative gin, strode unburdened behind her lord. Then came Mewa, the favored youngest, heavily loaded with dilly-bags of camp things, and behind her again Munawa, a famous smeller-out of yams, not quite so young, but also top-heavy with travelling gear.

Now Yundah's brain had assured him that of all his possessions, Winyah was the one he could most easily spare.

So Yaloo greeted Yundah blandly and meekly followed him into the hut. One glance around and Yundah scowled towards Jim Halley's bunk. Winyah shinned

aboard and stretched herself out as if she owned the place. Then Yundah bound the aged spouse down with thongs of buffalo hide, spread-eagling her shanks securely to the bedposts. After which, having eagerly seized Jim's precious little "click-click" debil-debil, he stole quickly out.

Yaloo watched the hurrying figures as they disappeared towards the hills, then stood uneasily by the boss's bunk, scratching his clay-daubed head as he frowned down upon the perfectly nude lady. He slunk away; then as an afterthought, he returned and threw a horse-rug over her. Quietly closing the hut door, he left thoughtfully for the native camp.

Eventide brought the hallooing hunters home, the pack-horses loaded with hides and the natives staggering under meat. Jim and Bill stamped cheerfully into the hut and hung their beloved rifles in the rack.

The whistle faded from Halley's lips as he spied the horse-rug. He was a fastidious man and especially disliked any smell of horse sweat upon his clean blankets. Angrily, he jerked the rug off--- and stared, petrified.

Winyah glared up at him. At least one orb did; the other had been damaged in a bygone correction from Yundah's nullah. Bill glanced around at the talking silence, and caught his breath. Jim moaned; then his mouth opened like a tip-cart and he roared "Get! Get! Get!! Oh my heavens! You stinking lump of goanna grease! On my bed! My *bed!!* Get, I tell you---get! Yaloo, where's that hound Yaloo?"

Jim rushed through the crowded doorway but Yaloo was missing. He tore back and grabbed Winyah. A vindictive cackling spat up at him.

"She's tied," sniggered Bill; "you'll pull your bunk to pieces. Be gentle with the lady."

Jim howled and waved his arms; then, snatching a knife from a skinner boy, he slashed the buffalo thongs, scruffed the lady, and ran her out of the door.

The watchful Yaloo discreetly withdrew.

Halley returned to find Bill paralysed with laughter and the natives in shrieking ecstasy; but a sudden silence hit them as Halley let fly with the nullah. With a pained expression, Halley examined his once clean blankets. Sprawled on for hours by a goanna-greased body, sweating under a horse-blanket, they smelled like a---there's nothing else they *could* smell like.

Next evening the natives triumphantly dragged Yaloo to the hut. Expecting to see him flayed alive, they waited eagerly. With greyish face yaloo made his explanation:

"Yundah say, 'Makem change, no stealem.' All-same swap him pipe, no steal

him pipe. Yundah give him one feller gin longa Jimmy, changem debil-debil click-click. Makem change, no stealem."

In the stillness Bill's open mouth collapsed and he roared. The natives screamed in sympathy, then fled as Halley raged amongst them

1 August 1928
Ion L. Idriess

Ion's beloved mother, Julia.
Her grave at Broken Hill Cemetry.
Both photographs courtesy of the Williams' Family Collection.

Gouger
of
The Bulletin

Answers to Correspondents

In this fourth section of the book, I have included replies from the 'Answers to Correspondents' column about pieces Ion had submitted for approval/review. That column deserves a book in itself for the replies given to its many would-be authors/poets. Some were hilarious, some were encouraging and some were scathingly brutal! Nothing like today's attitude of not deliberately insulting/offending anyone because of political correctness. However, many people (including Idriess) eagerly looked forward to reading the replies as an essential part of their total enjoyment of the magazine. It justifiably had a fan base of its own.

Included in the articles I have found only one close to the one Idriess often quoted as one of his many knockbacks; – namely, "stick to your pick and shovel, they're the one that suits your style", (or a similar version). The closest to this I found was from 'F.T.G. Qld': 21-4-10; "Sorry to say 'advice' isn't good enough. Hang on to the shovel and keep the pen for the leisure hour." This may have been him or he might have remembered reading it in the "old days" and absorbed it. The others are listed consecutively as they were submitted from 1909 to 1912.

ANSWERS TO CORRESPONDENTS

23-09-'09 I.I.:   Keep your people in ignorance that you've become a poet. Will help in the good work by burying your doggerel about "The Row Out There".

21-04-'10 F.T.G. Qld:
"Sorry to say 'advice' isn't good enough. Hang on to the shovel and keep the pen for the leisure hour".

27-07-'11 J.L.I.:   "The king resembles most of his tribe – he has nothing interesting to say."

5-05-'10 I.L.I.(Waverley): "
It has a little humour; but that type of story needs a skilful pen."

21-09-'11 J.L.I.:   "Good attempt. Rather long and rough".

26-10-'11 J.L.I.:   "Theories has some points, but it is no porcupine. Do you think you could stick a few more quills in and make it bristle a bit?"

23-11-'11 J.L.I.   "Treatment is fairly good, but there is hardly enough in it for us."

25-01-'12 J.L.I.   "Unable to use them."

ION L. IDRIESS
1889–1979

Ion Idriess was a famous Australian author who attended Primary School in Tamworth 1897–1899.

Between 1927 and 1968, he wrote more than fifty books relating to Australian History, Culture and Natural Science.

This plaque is to recognise the
One Hundredth Anniversary of his attendance.

One of Australia's most popular authors
took out his Miner's Right in
October 1909 at Lightning Ridge
and began his writing career by sending
paras to publications often using
the pen name Gouger

ION "JACK" LLEWELLYN IDRIESS
1889 – 1979

This plaque commemorates 100 years
since Idriess mined opal on Lunatic Hill
during the heyday of the 3-Mile

Commemorative plaques at Tamworth and Lightning Ridge, both
courtesy of W & M Schofield.

Gouger
of
The Bulletin

Special Note

Included here are some other pseudonyms which may or may not belong to Idriess. Because of obvious (perceived) discrepancies in some dates and locations, his ownership of some/all of them is accordingly, open to question. Some have tenuous links to Idriess, (subject matter, location, similarity of terminology etc.), but beyond this I have no proof. In an early 1970's interview, he himself admitted that he had about 20 different names and added that lots of other contributors were the same.

13 June 1918

"Half-Moon": On a North Queensland station a bhingi stockman was dared by some of the station hands to imitate the cattle-dog which was heeling some colts in a stockyard. Without a moment's thought binghi crawled through the rails and approached a colt on hands and knees. In the fraction of a second the bite was made and the young 'un galoped to the other end of the yard leaving the nig. laughing on his belly and untouched. The heeler had dodged the flying boot by an inch or so. This is straight dinkum although I see every stockman from Normanton to Bourke incredulous.

27 June 1918

"Half-Moon": While camped on the east coast of the Gulf recently I saw the home-coming of some "spell-boys", as the Bhingis holidaying after six to eight months on the Torres Strait bêche-de-mere boats are called. These Bhingi boys arrived at the home camp well-groomed and with a plentiful supply of flour and other eatables, tobacco, mirrors and trinkets. Gargantua was absolutely outclassed by what followed. The whole camp looked at itself in the mirrors with a "before taking" air, and then proceeded to gorge, smoke and corroboree until there was nothing left to eat drink or burn. A sort of hibernation period followed after which Bhingi and wife went forth to get tucker in the primeval style. When spell-boys return to Thirsty Island to join up, their garments demand immediate replacing. Otherwise one daren't insult the august person of a Government officer with their smellful presence.

9 May 1918

" J.L.H": The queerest reason for voting "NO" came to light in Palestine. One youngster wouldn't listen to reason. "No Hope'" he affirmed; " They'll only send the old man out, and he'll be always traillin' round after me and jawin' about one thing and another."

5 September 1918

"Half-Moon": Thursday Island pearlers have about a score of luggers out for shell and, so far, they have managed to freight the catches – splendid shell too-- to U.S.A. But the chances of ship space are decreasing every day, and Sam wants the goods f.o.b. before he unleashes the dollars. Trochus shell, because of the shortage of m.o.p. on the market, is now nearly £50 per ton and rising.

5 September 1918

"Half-Moon": Thursday Island pearlers have about a score of luggers out for shell and, so far, they have managed to freight the catches —splendid shell too-- to U.S.A. But the chances of ship space are decreasing every day, and Sam wants the goods f.o.b. before he unleashes the dollars. Trochus shell, because of the shortage of m.o.p. on the market, is now nearly £50 per ton and rising.

October 1918

"Half-Moon": While vagabonding about the Torres Strait Archipeligo I met an old Danish diver who showed me some mementoes of the various sunken wrecks he had worked at. Amongst the collection was a bright golden curl. "See that?" he said: "It cost me a gruesome experience. Down at the wreck of a passenger ship on the Bananaland coast I went along one of the alleyways and opened a cabin door. In the cabin was the body of a woman with a little girl's body clasped in her arms .What prompted me to cut this curl from the child's head I don't know; but as I moved back the way I had come, the bodies caught in the swirl, followed me until I was able to close a door behind me. I've seen a good deal, but that fairly blew me out for a day."

24 October 1918

"HALF-MOON": The European captain of a bêche –de-mer lugger working north of Cooktown, was fishing in a dinghy, when a big "king" was hooked. After some trouble it was got into the boat but managed, during the process, to secure a bulldog grip on the captain's leg. The bite was worth 10 stitches later. Haven't heard of the kingfish doing the cannibal act before.

6 March 1919

"HALF-MOON": The Thirsty Island cemetery holds the graves of many Japanese divers who paid the penalty for diving in search of deep shell. This season, after four years' interval, the pearlers are giving the deep-water grounds another turn. Nippon knows the risk of a pressure at from 70lb. to over 90lb.per square inch, but being a fatalist, and shell being plentiful in 30 or 40 fathoms, he doesn't let himself brood over his chances. All the same, he exercises the utmost care with his gear and in selecting his crew.

20 March 1919

"Half-Moon": While anchored inside the mouth of the Small River (Cape York Peninsula) recently, I saw an aboriginal crone bitten by a death-adder. The gall bladder of the slain worm was promptly extracted by the bucks (the bite was scarified meanwhile) and the contents rubbed into the wounds. Immediately after treatment Mary resumed her interest in my tobacco pouch. If, in such cases, the attacking reptile escapes, which isn't often, Dr. Binghi has a reserve and effective herbal remedy.

1 May 1919

"Speargrass": According to the papers, the Easter excursion trains from Sydney were stopped by a bungle. Apart from those who fleece the tourist while he waits, the country was not violently agitated by the bungle. At present the back-country denizen entertains a grim feeling of satisfaction that the city, which generally takes care to get everything good that is going, has at last got something that makes the country appear a very desirable place by comparison. Years and years of careful and conscientious centralisation, with the country drained to fill the city with good things, have not made the bush resident too friendly towards the octopus, and there is a certain amount of unholy joy in the knowledge that the place that has extracted tribute from everything that he had to sell or to buy is now paying the price of its bloating.

17 July 1919

"Boomerang": has a large idea:–
There are outlets still where public money might be very profitably employed at no risk whatever, and with great advantage to the State . All Australia has to do is play trumps and make a Govt. monopoly of the wholesale import trade; also monopolise the wholesale trade in our own manufactures. In this way, Australian manufacturers can get a sure preference over imported goods, which is necessary for the purpose of keeping our money within the Commonwealth. Government can in supplying the retailers get a reasonable commission. The process should be gradual in order to gain experience before plunging in up to the neck. Make a monopoly, say, of the hardware import trade for a start. Properly managed it would be a golden egg as good as the Commonwealth Bank, or more so. The profits might be applied to paying off our war loans first, and then after that, the State loans. In time we would kill the import goose, but would continue to get the golden eggs through the commission on

9 December 1920
"Boomerang":   I don't think the Japs were responsible for introducing faked dogs' teeth for use in the currency of Northern New Guinea. In '09 it seemed to me that the country must at one time been over-run by billions of wild dogs. The farther inland we went, the more dogs'-teeth necklaces did the villagers parade. All the old men and women possessed at least one necklace apiece, and each was composed of about 100 dogs' teeth. I had the curiosity to examine one of these valuable relics. Then I found that the teeth possessed no nerve ducts, but were solid; in a word they were frauds. The next German settlement cleared up the mystery. In the plantation store were piles of boxes containing these porcelain fakes. And they were days when the Japs weren't allowed to do much trading in these parts.

14 April 1921
"Boomerang":   They still quote old Jack, a typical Cornishman, who years ago, was a shift-boss on the Broken Hill Proprietary. Once he had some men grafting below him on construction work. "How many of 'ee down the-ah?" bawled Jack from up above. "Three!" cried one of the men. "Three!" he roared back. "Too many altogether. Half of 'ee come up here!"

12 October 1922
"Boomerang":   "Old Sofala!" The name brings up memories of the boom days of roaring pubs, gambling hells, slant-eyed Chows and roughs of all nationalities. Now a few pensioners are the sole supporters of the town's two crumbling pubs. In its wildest days there were 29 pubs and 26 stores, nine of these latter run by Chinese. There Larry Foley first earned a reputation by outing three hefty lads in quick succession. He was backed by Steve Swain, uncle of Emily Soldene. Bill Day, who later went bushranging, put up a new record for a side wager of £10 by carrying an anvil weighing 3cwt. 9lb. three-quarters of a mile. R.D. Meagher's father was the sergeant in charge of gold escorts. Wally Hickenbotham, veteran trainer, claimed it as his birthplace. Fitzgerald Bros., of circus fame, were also born on the Turon. James Rutherford (Cobb and Co.) made a fortune there with his coaches. There were so many thousands of Chinese in the place that a celestial circus played the same turns every night for six months to packed houses. And to-day it is as silent, as lonely and almost as poor as the grave.

26 October 1922

"Boomerang": Has any Abo. gone to the trouble of measuring kangaroo jumps, miscalled "hops"? When the animals are going leisurely to feed and water, they average from 3ft to 6ft. But the manager of a station told me he saw an old man leap over an 8$^{1/2}$ ft stack, and upon measuring from where he sprang to where he landed, it taped 37 ft.! I didn't query it--- he was bigger than I.

31 July 1924

"Darnley": Sergeant Blank, in charge of the police station in a South Australian township, had caught red-handed a couple of residents shooting ducks out of season. The birds – he secured one pair only – were confiscated, and the sergeant hung them up for safe-keeping on his back verandah while he went along to the clerk of courts to lay an information and dig out the storekeeper-justices. The case was fixed for 2 o'clock and Blank, arriving home for lunch, walked out to see that the evidence was all right. A string of embellished comments brought out Mrs. Sergeant Blank "Those ducks?" she inquired. "Oh, they're on cooking – why, I thought you'd had them given you!" As Blank couldn't very well explain in court that the evidence had been eaten, he had to skip round hurriedly and withdraw the information; but in future "Exhibit A" is going to be clearly branded and located in a safe place.

11 September 1924

"Half-Moon": Beef at Thirsty Island is from 60 to 100 per cent dearer than it is anywhere else in Queensland. Tired of importuning the Prices Commissioner, people are taking to dugong and turtle, in addition to fish. The flesh of the two former is very palatable, and requires less energy in chewing than the butcher's joints.

23 October 1924

"Darnley": If equine combatants are included, one bomb dropped in Palestine had a particularly grim record. During the offensive in November and December 1917, our brigade was holding the line in front of El Burg, in the Judean hills, and the horses were sent back to Ludd. One bright night a Hun 'plane, flying very low, paid the horse-lines a visit and dropped a "pill" between the horse and bivvy lines. Result: 60 horses killed and wounded, mostly killed, and 25 casualties amongst the troops.

12 February 1925

"SPEARGRASS":   We were camped beside a desert well on the edge of Centralia; my mate was bending towards the billy when a spear hissed from the darkness and buried itself in the sand behind him. We both rushed into the night, firing and shouting, but the natives had vanished. By daylight we examined the spear and experienced the same pleasant thrill a prospector gets when he finds colors in the dish. The barbs, instead of being jagged quartzite, bound to the haft with tree gum and 'roo sinew, were fragments of opal showing red and orange fire. We collected some tobacco and a few presents, mounted and rode on the nigs' tracks. The reading was easy, for the broad brown book was sand-strewn, and the writers had dotted the pages with footprints. Five miles away we came on some 50 bucks, gins and piccaninnies squatting about and grinding up nardoo. The yelps of their mongrels gave them the alarm, and the whole mob were soon streaking towards a rough sandstone gully as if a thousand devils were behind them. Yelling in all the dialects we knew that we were friends, and waving aloft sticks of tobacco as guarantees, we galloped after them, but they had soon disappeared among the tumbled rocks lining the gully's edge. All except one young gin who, by the greatest of good luck, and thanks to my highly skilled old prad, I managed to head off. She ran screaming beside the horse as we galloped parallel with the gully's side. Just as I thought she was going to break between the animal's legs into the gully, my mate wheeled up alongside, and, reaching down a long arm, clawed his fingers into the mop of dried clay, ochre and goanna fat that ornament the damsel's hair. Her yells redoubled, despite all our coaxing. We showed her the spear, and she yelled more. We showed her the tobacco and a pocket-knife and an old shirt of my mate's and pledged ourselves by all the energetic sign words we knew to endow her with all these things and more if she'd only show us where the barbs came from. Thereat she stopped screaming spasmodically and became one unbroken scream. My mate lost his temper and threatened her with a hiding. I didn't think she could scream any louder, but she did. We let her go at last. She went! Just a chocolate-colored streak of legs that disappeared in an instant among the boulders. We never found the opal field.

19 March 1925

"SPEARGRASS":   Saw a big mahogany chopped down in N.Q., and embedded six inches within the wood was an old-time tomahawk, handle intact. Some long-forgotten pioneer whose body is dust must have buried the blade deep in the tree and forgotten it or the tree's whereabouts, and the bark and growing

wood reached about the encumbrance and simply "swallowed" it. I've often known horseshoes hung on limbs to be engulfed in this way. A little more difficult of explanation are the tiny frogs that are occasionally found encased deep within living wood. In such cases no crack is open for air or tucker, and how the frog got there, and why the tree does not completely close in the tiny chamber that fits the living mummy's body, I have never heard explained.

4 June 1925

"Life Line": Like "Albatross" (B. 21/5/1925), I sometimes wonder if there is anything in palmistry. On the way to the Big Scrap our padre held a séance on the boat-deck one afternoon. "I don't see any fighting in your hand", he told one youngster; the same boy contracted rheumatic-fever as we lay in Lemnos Harbor a week before the Landing, and was sent back to Australia. "I see sickness and wounds, honors and promotions", he told another. This Digger had pneumonia, was wounded three times, and returned to Australia hung all over with decorations. Two others were told by the Reverend – in fact, Very Reverend – seer that their future was not clearly revealed; later he confided to me that neither would last very long, and both were killed in the first week at Anzac. But I still wonder if there really is anything in palmistry, for I myself was told of wealth in store for me, and "Time is slipping underneath my feet".

25 June 1925

"Half-Moon": The Papuans about the Fly River delta have the largest flutes in the world. They get a bamboo as long and big as possible and cut out longitudinal strips in alternate positions between each notch. This is set up facing the wind, and weird Aeolian music is thus produced. When a number of these flutes are going together in a strong wind, the moaning of a thousand lost souls would be a mere whisper by comparison.

17 September 1925

"Half-Moon": A monument to commemorate the landing of Captain Cook on Possession Island (Torres Strait) is being built there. Previously a cairn on a bold promontory on the north-eastern corner of the island served the purpose , and the site was an ideal one within view of all vessels using the Inner Route. Those associated in the erection of the new monument - the Geographical and Historical Societies and the Queensland Government – are allowing it to be placed on another site quite unsuitable as regards either visibility or prominence.

The reason given is that it is too much trouble to carry the material any further. So thoroughly in keeping with the spirit of the great navigator.

10 December 1925

"BOOMERANG": The abo.'s version of the Creation (B. 22/10/25) resembles in broad outline our own Biblical story. His belief, however, regarding the origin of animals, fish and birds is inverted. These creatures had originally been abos., and immortal, but for their misdeeds they had been changed into the lower forms. For instance, the porcupine had been guilty of such misdeeds that his whole tribe rose against him and buried their spears in his flesh. He was then driven out, condemned ever afterwards to creep on all fours, with the deeply-embedded spears or quills in his body, a warning to others.

7 January 1926

"DARNLEY": Torres Strait mothers are loading their infants with novelette names, though sometimes it is the Government official who suggests something classy like Algernon or Marmaduke. One name beat me recently. "Glass! Glass!" I said to the mother. "Where you find that one? All same bottle, eh?" "No!" replied the parent scornfully; "he no all same bottle – he proper white-man name; teacher he put that one." And she hauled out a piece of paper on which had been written – "Clarice".

21 January 1926

"DARNLEY": On the east side of the Murray Island there is a stone called Dopem. Dopem was once a woman, and this is her sad story. On the opposite side of the island there lived a company of Kris-Kris (locust) girls; also a number of Ti-Neur (sunbird) girls. One day, before going out fishing on the reef, they made a kop-maori to cook some ager (a native tuber). After they had gone off, leaving the food to roast in its earthen oven, Dopem happened to stroll along, and, seeing the mound, became inquisitive. Glancing round to see that no one was about, she uncovered the layer of sand and removed the best of the contents. When the girls returned hungry after their excursion, they hurried to the kop-maori, to find that only the poorest part of the food remained. They cooked their fish, but did not touch what was left of the ager. Next day they made another kop-maori, and went off fishing as before. When they returned it was to find once more that their cupboard was bare. Then they decided to leave one girl to watch, telling her that she must conceal herself in the bush and let

them know what happened. Dopem came again, and the watcher saw her carry away all the carefully-prepared cooked food. When the sentry's companions returned she told them the story. 'Very well," said they, "to-morrow only a few of us will go to the reef, the others must stop here." Those who were left made their preparation, sharpening up their double-pointed spears and getting out the stone gabba-gabba clubs. Dopem was seen walking along the beach, and, coming to the place where the kop-maori had been made, she began to remove the sand. There was a sudden whizz of spears and out rushed the angry girls brandishing their clubs. Falling upon the raider, they killed her, and then rolled the body into the sea. But instead of going right out, it floated into the next bay. The avengers hurled it out again, but it drifted round to the beach at an adjoining village. The girls pushed it forth again, till, slowly travelling round, it came at length to Karog, the former home of Dopem, where it turned into the stone you now see. The girls, satisfied, left the body and went into the bush, and at a creek, Lakob, they placed a mound of stones and called it Lag (the mosquito). That is the place where *zogo* is made for the mosquito; it will be shown you by old Passi any time you like to visit Murray Island.

17 June 1926

"Coralier": Nature has lavished the best of her artistic soul upon the coral reefs. The colors of the rainbow have been wedded to wonderful creations. You admire some coral grass and become aware of a black eye, sinister and unwavering, watching you from among the anemone fronds. Uncertain of the thing, you probe with a bamboo and are amazed to see a tiny fish dart off into a coral cavern. On his side was painted the eye you saw. Binghi swears that this bluff is to scare off any hungry enemy. Black Brother naturalist also says that when the young fish grow canny at maturity they lose the protective eye. You touch a big anemone and it blows out water, then shrinks to a piece of seeming coral. Touch a bladder of sponge dressed in scarlet and it rolls away wrapped within itself. Prod a thing of purple spikes embedded in a ball of green and it inflates to five times its size, then slowly shrinks to a small colorless marble.

24 March 1927

"Cudgeree": The tree frogs in the Queensland palm-swamp spend the night carrying on a kind of Morse-code conversation by ringing the combinations of one, two and three harsh croaks. Occasionally four croaks are heard in succession. One night last winter a hobo blew into a telephone-construction

camp with a bottle of rum, and after having shouted all round he drew attention to the sing-song the frogs were having, and awakened the sporting instincts of the gang by offering odds on one particular frog. They bit, and by the time the rum had run out the hobo had won seven pounds by backing this particular croaker to croak as he predicted. Then he left for his camp, which he said was a bit down the road. The cook's profanity woke the camp next morning. Seeking the cause, he pointed out that the frog that had cleaned them out must have been sitting on the fence quite 200 yards away from the edge of the palms, and he reckoned that the hobo had a mate up there who did all the croaking. The camp learned later on that every railway gang for 30 miles up the line had been cleaned out by this cute swaggie.

2 May 1928

"Boomerang": A tradition still lingers that a valuable cache left by bushranger Ben Hall in the Weddin Ranges (N.S.W.) was unearthed by two Yankees, who were better posted than anyone else about its exact location. They claimed to be prospectors and made their way to a point 25 miles from Grenfell, where they commenced excavations. The direction was westerly, and the place was known to be close to where the bushrangers were wont to divide their spoils. The farmer from whom the two adventurers borrowed certain tools, etc., was still resident in the district in 1920, and he informed me that the pair mostly worked on moonlit nights, and were six weeks in the vicinity. Weeks after they had gone he accidentally came upon their excavations about five miles from his farm, and found the distinct imprint of two oil barrels or drums – just what the old bushrangers used to bury gold in. He was convinced that the two Yanks discovered Ben's cache.

1 August 1928

"Boomerang": The most wonderful exhibition of boomerang throwing I ever saw was given by a young abo in Central Queensland. He kept five 'rangs alive in the air for as many minutes – two little practicing weapons intermingled with three hunting ones. And before anyone could interfere, the flash buck broke the forelegs of a sick camp dog about 30 yards away. He concluded by throwing four 'rangs with two throws, using both hands, so that they returned almost simultaneously.

8 August 1928

"Boomerang": Very profitable to their owners were the sapi-sapi mints of the old days of the Trobriand Group, Papua. Sapi-sapi was manufactured red shell money, made from the inner layer of a bivalve found chiefly along the rugged shores of Rossel Island in the Louisiade Archipelago. A suger-bag of the raw shell brought £25, and made into money its value increased fourfold to tenfold according to the keenness of the trafficker. The mint was generally run by an old sea-fossil called the breaker, who saw that the shells were broken into the prescribed sizes – an operation that required expert knowledge so that none of the valued inner red layer was wasted. Grinding and polishing was done by dusky Juliets, who broke the monotony by swift flirtations with glad eyed Romeos. Always they chewed betel. The sapi was worked into earrings – 26 discs in each – price 10s. All the Papuans' earnings went into the bagi (cash-box).

3 April 1929

"Boomerang": As the train got underway from Cooparoo (on the Brisbane – Cleveland line) a porter yelled "express to Wynnum" (about eight miles distant), and an old chap who was booked for an intermediate station began to curse the railway service, from the Commissioner downwards, with all the earnestness of which he was capable. He had a fine flow of language, and he kept his commination service up for most of the journey, in spite of friendly fellow-passengers assuring him he would get a slow train back from Wynnum very soon after arrival there. Sure enough, when we reached Wynnum a train for the return journey was just starting; the old fellow rushed across the platform and managed to scramble in as it was moving. Simultaneously a porter yelled "express to Cooparoo". I am still wondering to what heights of profanity the ancient rose on the return journey.

1 May 1929

"Half-Moon": In a prosperous Queensland farming community mainly composed of people of German extraction, I noticed a remarkable number of children with impediments in their speech. Some youngsters of 10 to 12 years of age spoke as imperfectly as average four year olds. The affliction puzzled me till a medical friend summed it up in one word – in-breeding. The inhabitants it seemed, seldom went outside their encircling hills for mating purposes, and almost all were nearly related.

1 May 1929

"HALF-MOON": Steamers of half a century back were built of tough material. I was on board a Thursday Island pearling-lugger recently when a Japanese diver descended near Quetta Rock (Torres Strait). On his return he reported that portion of the skeleton of the ill-fated Quetta was still visible, although it is nearly 40 years since, torn from stem to stern by the uncharted Pinnacle rock, she sank in four minutes. I remember being told by a European diver who inspected the sunken vessel immediately after the disaster, that the engine-room telegraph on the bridge showed "Full speed ahead". She was under before the navigators realized what had happened.

1 May 1929

"HALF-MOON": In the humid months scorpions are plentiful in tropical Queensland. A black variety is particularly venomous. Certain abo. tribes on Cape York Peninsula vaccinate themselves against the effects of its venom. They scratch their skins with the sharp hard tail of the insect and squeeze into the scratch the contents of the venom, also situated in the tail. Thereafter the sting of any scorpion is no worse than a pinprick. The vaccine is effective for at least a year.

13 November 1929

"MISANTHROP": The Mandated Territory must be the world's happiest hunting ground for the anthropologist. Every month sees a new worker in the field. Dr. Fortune, who as Dr. Margaret Mead wrote learnedly of Samoa and the Samoans, has been studying the Admiralty Islanders with her husband. Hortense Powdermaker is learning the ways of the New Islanders and Beatrice Blackwood is cataloguing the complexes of the black brothers of the Mandated Solomons. There are some he-scientists at work as well. Gregory Bateson, with a dictaphone, has been in the Bainings, New Britain, learning the talk-talk of the natives, and is now living with the Kanakas in a native village up the Sepik River, on the New Guinea mainland. Pitt-Rivers has just published a book about the natives of the North-Western Islands, where recently he spent some time studying the depopulation problem. An American party, which contained everything from an ichthyologist to a cinema operator, went up the Sepik also a few months ago. Incidentally, the Government maintains its own ethnological expert, Pearson Chinnery, who spends odd months in out-of-the-way villages dealing with the more practical side of the science; and some of the missionaries, such as Father Kirschbaum, of Marienberg, are world-famous authorities on primitive races.

4 December 1929

"Sapi Sapi": Something new in Australian coin issues will be the cupro-nickel currency about to be issued in Mandated New Guinea. The coins will be of penny and halfpenny values, pierced in the centre after the fashion of the Egyptian nickel coins with which the A.I.F. was so familiar. They are primarily for native use. The hole in the middle will enable the pocketless darky to bank his currency on a string, as he did with his own shell money.

26 February 1930

"Coralier": A recent dust-up between the police and half-castes of Thursday Island was a chapter of a long and gory serial. Constable Stephens, who was put in hospital, not for the first time, by the piebald fighters, carries on his body many souvenirs of such encounters. Two years ago I saw him in hospital covered in awful wounds inflicted by the teeth of "Tiger", a half-caste whose performances do not belie his name. In one particularly terrible bite the double row of teeth had met. A human bite is credited with being extremely poisonous, and the doctor thought Stephens ran a grave risk of blood poisoning, but he pulled through. The 'castes at T.I. are a nasty crowd in a mob if put out, especially if they hold a few drinks, and the little roads and lanes of T.I., pitch dark at night, afford plenty of cover, especially among the rambling dens of Chinatown and the patchwork maze of "Yokohama".

26 March 1930

"Platypus": The incredible blood hunger of sharks was brought home to me in Torres Strait. With a shipment of remounts for India we ran aground on reef off Thursday Island. There was nothing for it but to wait for high tide. Four of the horses had kicked the bucket, and after much trouble we got them on deck from whence we heaved them over the side into the three or four feet of water between the ship and the shore. Within a few minutes sharks gathered in dozens. The water became a swirl of swift, darting bodies that hurled themselves at the carcases to whip away with lightning speed carrying great lumps of torn flesh. In less than five minutes the horses had disappeared. Even then their friends were not satisfied. They turned on several of their own kind and tore them to pieces amid a bloody froth of tossing water.

23 July 1930

"TO": It takes a lot to defeat the N.Q. digger. One old bird who scratches tin in the Herberton lost his set of false teeth, and made himself another, washing tin oxide from the alluvial and smelting it to supply the metal in the form he wanted. And the tin fangs paid him better than he knew. Whenever he got short of funds he put them in with the publican, who proudly exhibits them to all and sundry – Premier Moore examined them when he visited Herberton.

23 July 1930

"Stanmore": The Chinese cook aboard the Shanghai-bound steamer had expired two days previous to reaching the Chinese coast, and his countrymen had prepared the body for burial. Pat O'Regan, the first mate, chancing to stroll up as they were in the act of closing the lid of the box, noticed three shillings inside. Pat went to the purser, who had been in China for many years, and asked him if he could explain it. "That's their custom", said the purser. "They believe that before they can enter heaven they must cross three bridges, and at each bridge they are required to produce a decent-sized silver coin". "Well", commented Pat as he turned away, "Oi know one Chink that wont get across if he can't show a season ticket".

30 July 1930

"Platypus": In the '93 flood a house belonging to a man called Lye was completely submerged for some days in a hollow near Sandy Gallop in the Ipswich (Q.) district. Lately Lye's sons decided to cut down his bedstead so that the old man – he's now 91 – could get into it more easily. When the saw got to work on the first post out rushed a quantity of muddy water and the other three legs each yielded a quantity of water and slush. Apparently this water seeped into the hollow posts when the flood waters covered home and furniture 37 years ago.

6 May 1931

"Tum Tum": The people of the Tai-asai-pu of central Malaita (Solomon Islands) make music for religious purposes. Their orchestras are composed of never less than 20 men, and the instruments are reed flutes after the pattern of the pipes shown in the pictures of Pan. From 12 to 20 reeds are used in a flute, and these range from 3in. to 24in. long, blown, not by the mouth, but with the nose. The music, though weird in the extreme, is delightful to listen to, especially in the pitch blackness of a native village at night and from a distance of say, 50 or 60 paces. The Tai-asai-pu, from which the tribe takes its name, is the god who governs all calamity, and his ear is supposed to be tickled by this brand of music. If he gets it in sufficiently large doses he sees that nothing untoward happens to the tribe, so it is quite common for the band to perform for 48 hours continuously. The bandsmen are almost nude, such things as calicoes, shirts or pants being strictly taboo, though no objection is raised to shell ear-ornaments, armbands or beads. Boys below the age of puberty are not admitted to the band for fear of offending the old gentleman's sensitive ear with notes of discord, in which case he would surely cause the mothers and sisters of the offending parties to become sterile.

www.ingramcontent.com/pod-product-compliance
Lightning Source LLC
Chambersburg PA
CBHW020752160426
43192CB00006B/318